Exploring Leadership

'*Exploring Leadership* is both a very timely and highly relevant book. It has long been recognized that the nature of effective leadership owes much to context. But, recent history points to an acceleration in the shift of the contextual backdrop. International events of late demonstrate vividly the way in which the coalescence of the voices of the many on social media have supplanted the traditional power of individual leaders and their oratory which used to be the norm. As the authors emphasize, the related insights build only slowly over time and the delicate balance in the blend of individual and shared influences shifts as context changes. So, we now live in an age-where a diversity of leadership styles is an absolute requirement to address the ambiguity inherent in our complex world: an eclectic approach to leadership is indeed today's requirement. Hence, the theme of "rerouting" rather than "uprooting" leadership studies is absolutely relevant as we face the challenges of the future, and this book makes the case with both conviction and fluency'.

Sir Brian Burridge, Vice President, Strategic Marketing, Finmeccanica UK, and Former Air Chief Marshall, Royal Air Force, UK.

'"Another" book on the "panacea" that is leadership? Importantly, both these issues are dealt with quickly and seriously in a very timely book. Given the focus on leaders and leadership in recent years, both with respect to the general view that our leaders are responsible for our difficulties and the vast amounts devoted to developing leaders, we need a critically balanced view that helps assess where we are and what questions need to be considered to take us forward. And that is what we get here'.

Jeff Gold, Professor of Organisation Learning, Leeds Metropolitan University, UK.

'There are thousands of books on leadership but I wouldn't recommend many of them. I would recommend this one. It's a gem: contemporary, critical, well-written and provocative. What more would you want?'

Keith Grint, Professor of Public Leadership, Warwick Business School, UK

'This multi-authored volume provides an engaging exploration of leadership from a variety of perspectives, but still manages to speak with a clear and compelling voice. The authors explain a wide range of issues and ideas in a lively manner that will involve readers in the uncovering of assumptions and the making of connections across contexts and disciplines. *Exploring Leadership* will encourage and inform reflection and debate among those who study, research, and participate in the dynamics of leadership on the personal, organizational, social, and even global level'.

Eric Guthey, Associate Professor of Intercultural Communication and Management, Copenhagen Business School, Denmark.

'Among the opening lines from this provocative book, coined by a gifted team of writers from the Centre for Leadership Studies (CLS), are the rhetorical: Not "another" book on leadership! My follow-up to this statement has to be noted for the record: But this is not your "typical" book on leadership! It is a journey through a leadership landscape that is like no other; so be prepared to hold onto your seats. *Exploring Leadership* is just that; an exploration into new territory in leadership studies, focusing less on classic individualistic approaches, in favour of alternative contemporary emphases on leadership's critical, relational, interpretive, and subjective nature. In this journey, readers will stop off for a refreshing critique of such emerging popular accounts as authentic, emotionally intelligent, competency, strategic, positive, and virtual models of leadership. They will also visit enlightening reviews of heretofore overlooked matters, such as work toxicity, nomadism, communityship, and anarcho-syndicalism. This volume needs to be read by all students of leadership, young and old. But I caution those expecting to be brought closer to a chimerical universal theory of leadership, be prepared for disappointment. Conversely, for those fearing that the account's demystification will result in a leadership nihilism, I say, fear not. The authors have committed to "re-routing" us to leadership studies that in their processes are deeper and more nuanced – mapping the reality that confronts us – and in their outcomes, in the authors' words, more "equitable, effective, and engaging"'.

Joe Raelin, Asa S. Knowles Chair of Practice-Oriented Education, Northeastern University, USA.

'There is no doubt that that this book will do what the authors themselves suggest, "to help readers navigate the complex and confusing terrain" that is leadership. Navigating this landscape is not an easy one given the popularity and plethora of material written on the subject. However, this experienced team of authors are all well known in their field and are well placed to offer an authoritative and considered "reality check" on the substance and importance of leadership in contemporary society'.

Richard Thorpe, Professor of Management Development and Pro Dean (Research), Leeds University Business School, UK.

'Offering important critical perspectives on the meaning and purpose of leadership, this book reframes leadership for the twenty-first century, and comes from a group of authors who have already made a significant contribution to the field. A vital book for all leadership scholars and students who seek to question the leadership assumptions that dominate mainstream leadership texts'.

Sharon Turnbull, Visiting Professor, University of Gloucestershire, UK, and Former Director of Centre for Applied Leadership Research at the Leadership Trust, UK.

Exploring Leadership

Individual, Organizational, and Societal Perspectives

Richard Bolden

Beverley Hawkins

Jonathan Gosling

Scott Taylor

OXFORD
UNIVERSITY PRESS

OXFORD
UNIVERSITY PRESS

Great Clarendon Street, Oxford OX2 6DP

Oxford University Press is a department of the University of Oxford.
It furthers the University's objective of excellence in research, scholarship,
and education by publishing worldwide in

Oxford New York

Auckland Cape Town Dar es Salaam Hong Kong Karachi
Kuala Lumpur Madrid Melbourne Mexico City Nairobi
New Delhi Shanghai Taipei Toronto

With offices in

Argentina Austria Brazil Chile Czech Republic France Greece
Guatemala Hungary Italy Japan Poland Portugal Singapore
South Korea Switzerland Thailand Turkey Ukraine Vietnam

Oxford is a registered trade mark of Oxford University Press
in the UK and in certain other countries

Published in the United States
by Oxford University Press Inc., New York

© Richard Bolden, Beverley Hawkins, Jonathan Gosling, and Scott Taylor 2011

The moral rights of the authors have been asserted
Database right Oxford University Press (maker)

First published 2011

British Library Cataloguing in Publication Data

Data available

Library of Congress Cataloging in Publication Data

Data available

Typeset by SPI Publisher Services, Pondicherry, India
Printed in Great Britain
on acid-free paper by
MPG Books Group, Bodmin and King's Lynn

ISBN 978–0–19–954765–4(Hbk.)
ISBN 978–0–19–954766–1(Pbk.)

3 5 7 9 10 8 6 4

To our students, whose questions have prompted so much thought.

⬜ TABLE OF CONTENTS

☐ LIST OF FIGURES AND BOXES

Figures

Boxes

☐ AUTHOR BIOGRAPHIES

Dr Richard Bolden is a Senior Lecturer at the Centre for Leadership Studies (CLS), University of Exeter Business School. His research interests include distributed/shared leadership, leadership in higher education, cross-cultural leadership, and the relationship between leadership development and performance management. Teaching responsibilities include the Exeter MBA, CPD award, BA in Management and Leadership, and MA in Leadership Studies. Prior to joining CLS he was a research psychologist at the Institute for Work Psychology, University of Sheffield. He has an extensive publication history, including numerous journal articles, book chapters, conference papers, and research reports.

Dr Beverley Hawkins has been a lecturer at the Centre for leadership Studies at the University of Exeter Business School since January 2009. She has published work on recruitment and selection practices, leadership and corporate culture, resistance to leadership and teamworking practices. Currently, Beverley is involved in a number of research projects, all of which share a processual, collaborative, performative take on organizational and leadership practice. Her PhD, completed at Keele University in 2009, focused on self-managed teamworking practices and the negotiation of corporate culture schemes amongst a group of recruitment consultants. She has a special interest in ethnographic research.

Professor Jonathan Gosling is Director for the Centre for Leadership Studies, University of Exeter Business School. He trained as an anthropologist before working for several years as a mediator in neighbourhood conflicts in London. After taking a mid-career MBA, he moved into management education at Lancaster University, where he directed the MBA and other executive programmes, and co-founded, with Henry Mintzberg, a new approach to management education: the International Masters in Practising Management. In 2003, Jonathan joined the University of Exeter as Director of the Centre for Leadership Studies and Professor of Leadership Studies. He has published articles in numerous key management and leadership journals, and several books, including: *Nelson's Way: Leadership Lessons from the Great Commander* (2005, Brealey); *Leadership: The Key Concepts* (2007, Routledge); and *John Adair: Fundamentals of Leadership* (2007, Palgrave Macmillan). Jonathan advises companies, international agencies, and government departments on their leadership-related issues.

Dr Scott Taylor has worked as a senior lecturer in the Centre for Leadership Studies at University of Exeter Business School since 2008. Before this, he lectured and researched at Manchester Metropolitan, Open, Birmingham, and Essex universities, where he was involved in under- and postgraduate education. Scott's interest in leading and being led centres on practical and theoretical overlaps with religious and spiritual beliefs. He is currently writing about the development of 'spiritual leadership' from two perspectives: first, as a set of managerial practices that assume US society is exceptional, and second, as a means of representing standard products as more meaningful to employees or consumers.

☐ ACKNOWLEDGEMENTS

The creation of a book such as this is inevitably a collective process, building on the influences and insights of numerous people besides the authors. Over the years we have each been fortunate enough to work alongside some incredibly gifted and generous colleagues who have contributed significantly in terms of informing our thinking, assisting our teaching and research, and motivating us to continue with our enquiries into the nature and purpose of leadership. In particular we would like to acknowledge the contribution of our past and present colleagues at the Centre for Leadership Studies, at the University of Exeter, including Inmaculada Adarves-Yorno, Jackie Bagnall, Peter Case, Patricia Gaya-Wicks, Alan Hooper, Donna Ladkin, Antonio Marturano, Anne O'Brien, Georgy Petrov, Annie Pye, Ian Sutherland; and Martin Wood. We would also like to thank our administrative colleagues, in particular, Tricia Doherty, Sue Murch; and Maggie Bishop, without whose support we would undoubtedly have struggled to find the time to complete this project. We also thank members of the CLS Professional Network, our colleagues within the field of leadership, management and organizational studies more widely, and our students with whom we have engaged in debate, and who have tested our thinking and frequently demonstrated the limitations of our understanding. Finally, we would each like to make some personal acknowledgements. Richard would like to thank Angela, Eddie and Martha for their support, understanding and occasional distractions; and his father, Keith, for sparking his interest in leadership in the first place. Beverley would like to thank her family for their wisdom, friendship and love. Jonathan would like to thank Paul Regan, Chair of Citizens UK, whose example has been a benchmark for 30 years. And Scott would like to thank his parents Karen and Duncan, for leading him to value reading, learning and critical reflection so highly.

1 Introduction: Exploring Leadership

This book sets out to explore some perennial debates within the field of Leadership Studies that are of significance to everyone charged with studying, developing, and providing leadership within groups, organizations, and communities. It has been written with the intent of exposing the common assumptions that inform the ways in which we go about recognizing, rewarding, and developing leaders and leadership, and subjecting them to a degree of scrutiny and critique.

Take, for example, the current fascination with celebrities in Western society and the extent to which this influences the kinds of leaders we look for in business, politics, sport, and elsewhere. The most recent national elections in the United Kingdom and the United States were fought predominantly on the basis of personality rather than policies, and popular business programmes such as *The Apprentice* embrace the spectacle of reality TV and the cult of the 'heroic' leader. Such occurrences reveal much about the enduring allure of charisma and hint towards a search for fame, power, and reward on behalf of many of those seeking out senior leadership roles within our organizations and societies (see e.g. Guthey et al., 2009).

Are leaders born or made? Does each society get the leaders it deserves? How, and why, is leadership 'rhetoric' different from leadership in reality? These are the sorts of questions we will be exploring in this book in an attempt to shed some light on the enduring allure and very real challenges of studying, developing, and practicing leadership.

Not 'Another' Book on Leadership!

Why though, you might ask, is it necessary to have another book about leadership – what makes this one any different from those that already clutter up many a book shelf – and how come we (the authors) might have something different to say on this ubiquitous subject? This book, we feel, is different from those currently on the market in a number of important ways.

First, as illustrated above, we take a broadly *critical* perspective on leadership. Our aim, however, is not critique for the sake of it but to illustrate how the ways in which we think and talk about leadership impact upon the kinds of leadership practice that occur within our organizations and societies and, in so doing, open up possibilities for engaging with it in different ways.

Second, we take an *interdisciplinary* perspective on leadership. While the vast majority of research on leadership has been conducted in psychology departments and business schools, much can be learnt from other areas, such as sociology, philosophy, anthropology, history, literature, and politics. In this book, we draw on a range of sources and position leadership as something that has a part to play in all areas of human endeavour, not just business.

Third, we take a *multilevel* perspective in which we explore the manner in which social and cultural practices at the 'macro' level interact with the 'micro' level behaviours and practices of specific individuals. Through looking at how leadership is framed and enacted at different levels, it becomes possible to achieve a systemic understanding of how different factors impact upon one another.

And fourth, we endeavour to offer a *balanced* perspective on leadership that weighs up the pros and cons of various approaches. The burgeoning literature on leadership, and the associated industry for leadership development, may well leave one feeling somewhat bewildered about what to do, with each author and/or consultant, asserting the importance of a different set of factors.

Within this book, our aim is to help you navigate this complex and confusing terrain. We do not purport to offer definitive answers or recommendations about how you should go about your work, for each of these is very much dependent on who you are and the context in which you find yourself, rather we seek to equip you with a range of perspectives, evidence, and ideas that should help you to determine for yourself which line(s) of approach and/or enquiry are most useful in your circumstances.

In terms of our legitimacy and authority in writing this book, we draw on an extensive experience of researching and teaching Leadership Studies in a variety of contexts and for a variety of audiences. All four authors are employed as members of faculty at the Centre for Leadership Studies (CLS), University of Exeter Business School, and each of us has worked elsewhere in similar, and different, roles. In compiling this book, we draw on our experience of working with undergraduate, postgraduate, and executive students and the challenges of eliciting and conveying an understanding of this elusive and emotive subject for practitioners, policymakers, and students of leadership. We do not claim to be experts in the 'doing' of leadership (although each of us has held leadership roles) but rather thoughtful academic practitioners with both a genuine belief and healthy scepticism about the part leadership has to play within contemporary society. Within our own scholarly work, we have been inspired by the mission of our Centre 'to build knowledge, skill and confidence to deal with the challenges of leadership as it is and as it could be'

Box 1.1 CLS VALUES

- *Relevance*: as a university centre, CLS aims to develop substantial knowledge about various aspects of leadership. We therefore expect our work with leaders and organizations to provide insights and experience that are relevant to our research interests and projects.
- *Curiosity*: to help leaders to ask pertinent questions and to structure their enquiry in ways that are likely to be fruitful. In so doing, we will not shirk from challenging conventional wisdom.
- *Inconvenience*: we are interested in asking questions that might challenge accepted ways of seeing, established patterns of privilege, and assumed notions of what is good.
- *Creativity*: we expect to be engaged in work that requires us to be inventive. We are more interested in dissolutions than in solutions. We seek powerful intellectual solutes in which to dissolve pat explanations and off-the-shelf nostrums, and to act as catalysts for the emergence of new, more relevant, creative, and curious insights into leadership.
- *Closeness*: we value work that is close to the decision point, to where perceptions and preferences have an impact on choice and behaviour. Our academic programmes try to stay close to the experience of participants; our research tends towards engagement in the qualitative activities of individuals, groups, and organizations; our consultancy stays close to the needs of our clients; our networks foster connections that have an impact on leadership practice.
- *Influence*: we aim to do work that 'matters' and that will have a beneficial and enduring influence on both the practice and theory of leadership. We seek to be engaged in work with a clear impact on policy, ideas, and actions (while retaining our independence and criticality) and to concentrate our efforts where these are most likely to contribute to more humane, creative, and sustainable ways of life.

(Centre for Leadership Studies, 2010) and the CLS values as outlined in Box 1.1. In particular, we find ourselves drawn to the notion of 'inconvenience' (first suggested by a former colleague, Martin Wood) whereby we seek to challenge ourselves, and those we work with, to push the boundaries of our comfort zone and experiment with new, and perhaps unsettling, ways of engaging with what we do.

Fundamentally, however, this is a book about 'exploring leadership' and our core audience will be students on academically informed leadership programmes. This does not mean, however, that it has no relevance to the practice of leadership. On the contrary, we firmly believe that leadership theory and leadership practice go hand in hand. As Gardner and Laskin (1996: 297) suggest: 'we are more likely to secure responsible leadership in the future if we can demystify its constituent processes. In that sense, enhanced knowledge about leadership may go hand-in-hand with more morally desirable forms of leadership.' Or, as Keith Grint (2005a: 4) proposes:

Leadership, then, is not just a theoretical arena but one with critical implications for us all and the limits of leadership – what leaders can do and what followers should allow them to do – are foundational aspects of this arena. Leadership, in effect, is too important to be left to leaders.

In order to cover the ground outlined here, this book is structured into seven chapters. The introductory and concluding chapters are probably rather self-explanatory in firstly presenting the overall context and frame of the book and secondly summarizing key arguments and considering their implications for leadership theory, research, practice, and development. The intervening five chapters each take a somewhat different perspective on leadership in terms of the main focus of enquiry. Chapter 2 takes a theoretical perspective, exploring how models and views on leadership have evolved over time; Chapters 3, 4, and 5, in turn, consider leadership from an individual, organizational, and societal perspective; and Chapter 6 considers some emerging perspectives and enduring dilemmas in Leadership Studies. Together, it is hoped, these entries will encourage you, the reader, to consider both the specific practices through which leadership occurs on a day-to-day basis and the wider sociopolitical context in which these practices are constructed, communicated, and consumed.

Inevitably, decisions have been made about what to include and exclude and we in no way suggest that this is a comprehensive review of the field of Leadership Studies. Instead, we hope to give an overview of key issues that, it is hoped, will provoke the reader to engage in further reading and enquiry around this surprisingly complex and emotive subject.

To begin, in this chapter we will briefly consider the current fascination with leadership, its development as an area of study and education, and some of the key questions and concerns that will be explored throughout this book.

Leadership: The Panacea of our Times?

While the subject of leadership has been of interest to scholars and practitioners for thousands of years, it has reached a new high (or low, depending on how you look at it) over recent decades. Leadership has become perhaps the most talked about issue in business and organization – heralded as both the cause of and solution to most of the problems facing contemporary society. It is hard to turn on the television, open a newspaper, or attend an event without coming across numerous references to leaders, leadership, and leading. A search of google.co.uk in July 2010 returned 131 million pages for the word 'leadership' alone, while amazon.co.uk listed 160,253 entries in the books category and the Scopus publications database revealed 64,873 published articles.

The current focus on leadership is an international phenomenon, as is increased investment in leadership and management development. Fulmer (1997) estimated an annual corporate expenditure of $45 billion on leadership development (up from $10 billion one decade before), while Raelin (2004) put it at $50 billion. Within UK Higher Education, there are now 117 members of the Association of Business Schools (up from just two in the whole country in the mid-1960s) and in the years between 1996/7 and 2006/7 the number of students of Business and Administrative studies rose by 40 per cent (from 222,321 to 310,255) with the greatest rate of change for postgraduate students (up by 66 per cent), especially those on business and management programmes such as the Masters in Business Administration (MBA) (HESA, 2008).

Such trends are typical of the expanding global market for leadership and management development—driven, in part, by the desire of educational providers to enter into what is seen to be a lucrative market and fuelled by political and corporate assertions about the value of effective leadership and the need to address a leadership and management 'skills gap'. From an employer perspective, the primary triggers for investing in leadership and management development are considered to be the rapidly changing nature of the external environment, closely followed by business needs and Human Resource (HR) strategy, and students are increasingly regarding leadership and management-related programmes as enhancing their employability and career prospects.

Amid this flurry of activity, however, a number of concerns arise. There is no widely accepted definition of leadership, no consensus on how best to develop leadership and leaders, and remarkably little evidence of the impact of leadership or leadership development on organizational performance (see Chapter 4). Like so much within the field of Leadership Studies, the issue of leadership development and its impact remains highly contentious. While many reports propose that enhancing leadership capability is central to improved investment, productivity, delivery, and quality across public, private, and voluntary sectors, in most cases any investment remains a leap of faith.

One likely explanation for this disconnect is the fact that the theories and models upon which these practices are based still tend to be couched in a very individualistic notion of leadership whereby it is conceived of as a property of the 'leader'. While this might make life easy for those recruiting and developing leaders (you simply need to identify the right people and right skills/competencies to develop), it dissociates the practice of leadership from the organizational and social context in which it occurs. Perhaps a more useful perspective is to consider leadership as a social process – contextually situated within the relationships between people (be they 'leaders' or 'followers'). From this perspective, what is more important than the leadership qualities of a number of individuals are the underlying processes that give rise to organizational effectiveness.

If considered in this way, it is perhaps possible to understand why many leadership development activities fail to achieve the sorts of outcomes desired by those investing in them. While leadership can undoubtedly be instrumental in organizational performance, the development of a small number of individuals in isolation is unlikely to result in marked improvements to these or other outcome measures. As Raelin (2004: 131) suggests: 'most leadership training that is being conducted in corporate off-sites is ill-advised [...] because the intent of most of this training is to *put leadership into people* such that they can transform themselves and their organizations upon their return' (initial emphasis). He and other writers propose that this simply does not work and, instead, that leadership (and management) development should be aligned with the organizational culture, context, and objectives, among a wide array of other factors. To this extent, it could well be argued that much current leadership development is going to waste and that effort would be best spent on increasing the quality and precision, rather than the quantity, of provision (Burgoyne et al., 2004).

Changing Perspectives on Leadership

As a field of study, research and investment in leadership has grown almost exponentially over the past century. During this period, there have been substantial developments in leadership theory, beginning with the progression from universalistic trait and style theories to more contextually sensitive 'situational leadership' models (see Chapter 2). Despite the recognition of contextual factors (primarily characteristics of the task and followers), however, all these models remain predominantly focused on the actions of the individual 'leader', treating followers as somewhat passive recipients. The move to 'transformational leadership' (Burns, 1978; Bass, 1985) in the 1980s and 1990s went some way to recognizing the dynamic nature of the relationship between leaders and followers but through its predominant emphasis on charisma and a 'grand vision' perhaps did more to reinforce than challenge the image of the 'heroic leader'.[1]

Recent years, partially in the wake of corporate scandals such as Enron and catastrophes such as 9/11 (and more recently the global financial crisis and the need to address climate change) and accelerated through the accessibility of information and speed of communication, have seen increased calls for greater inclusion and participation in leadership and decision-making that shift the perspective from *who* is leading to *how* leadership is accomplished. This approach regards leadership as 'a social influence process through which emergent coordination (i.e. evolving social order) and change (i.e. new values, attitudes, approaches, behaviours, ideologies, etc.) are constructed and produced' (Uhl-Bien, 2006: 668) – no longer an attribute of individuals themselves but a property of the system.

One of the more influential leadership models of recent years is 'distributed leadership' (see Bolden, 2011 for a review). Informed largely within the United Kingdom by the work of the National College for School

Leadership (NCSL), and subsequently adopted by much of the education sector, distributed leadership presents an image of leadership as widely dispersed. Such a perspective suggests that leadership is an emergent property of a group or network of interacting individuals; there is an openness to the boundaries of leadership; and that varieties of expertise are distributed across the many, not the few (Bennett et al., 2003). A distributed approach to leadership, therefore, draws attention to some very different aspects of leadership than do traditional leader-centric perspectives – it 'puts leadership practice centre stage rather than the chief executive or principal' (Spillane, 2006: 25) and proposes that 'leadership practice takes shape in the interactions of people and their situation, rather than from the actions of an individual leader' (Spillane, 2004: 3).

While this approach may militate against leaders and followers being seduced by overly simplistic accounts of personal agency[2] (i.e. the belief that leadership effects arise simply from what leaders do), by highlighting a diverse and potentially limitless range of alternative factors, it makes the concept of leadership far harder to pin down. Furthermore, despite the best efforts of distributed leadership theory to dislodge the simplistic 'leader–follower' distinction, it struggles to provide an alternative vocabulary and/or to provide empirical evidence that does not focus heavily on the contribution of people in formal leadership roles. A number of key questions remain, therefore, such as why is it that some people are regarded as 'leaders' rather than others? What is it that enables certain people with limited formal authority to exert considerable influence while others remain relatively powerless despite holding a formal role? How is leadership experienced by those involved as it unfolds? And how is personal agency constrained and/or enhanced through access to, and control of, resources and other sources of power?

Studying Leadership

Leadership has been a focus of scientific enquiry for some time, yet despite this attention there have been only limited advances in methodologies for its study and a general lack of critique. As John Storey remarks:

The accumulation of weighty and extensive reports to date tends, in the main, to regurgitate a now familiar thesis – but it is a thesis which remains incomplete, insufficiently tested, inadequately debated and not properly scrutinised. (Storey, 2004: 6)

While more recent theories may highlight the processual, relational, and socially constructed nature of leadership, this remains difficult to research in a way that does not privilege the accounts and actions of formally recognized 'leaders' and retrospective analyses of past 'leadership' rather than emergent and future acts that may come to be regarded as examples of 'leadership'. The reasons for this are unsurprising to the extent that it is perhaps most expedient to go to 'leaders' when looking for evidence of 'leadership' and that we can be more time efficient when exploring past leadership rather than waiting around for it to emerge. The problem is, of course, if we keep looking in the same places we keep finding the same things and may keep missing other equally, if not more, important factors (Wood, 2005).

In their book about studying leadership, Jackson and Parry (2008: 3) propose that 'there are broadly five ways that one can go about studying leadership. You can actually attempt to lead, you can observe leadership in action, you can talk about leadership, you can read about it and you can write about it.' Given the nature of academic work, it is not surprising that the preponderance of current literature is based on the latter three of these categories – that is, talking to people about leadership (through interviews, teaching, etc.), reading about (and critiquing) previous accounts, and writing (and constructing) new accounts of leadership. While several writers now acknowledge the value of studying leadership in action (e.g. Ospina and Sorenson, 2006; Wood and Ladkin, 2008), the practicalities of doing this while continuing to carry out the other activities expected of them within universities are very hard to manage, and the rigours of peer review render reflections on one's own leadership practice problematic in terms of disseminating and generalizing findings.[3]

DOES GOOD LEADERSHIP RESEARCH HAVE TO LEAD TO BETTER LEADERSHIP PRACTICE?

James Macgregor Burns (2005), in his introduction to the inaugural issue of the journal *Leadership*, noted that while the field of Leadership Studies is becoming more international and interdisciplinary, it still tends to frame leadership as a fundamentally positive force that leads to socially beneficial outcomes. Despite the tendency to focus on 'good' or 'ethical' leadership in studies thereof, however, this is only one side of the coin. Barbara Kellerman (2004a) and Jean Lipman-Blumen (2005) propose that much can be learnt from studying 'bad' or 'toxic' leadership, not least the possibility of preventing it happening again, and authors such as Conger (1990), Maccoby (2000), and Dotlich and Cairo (2003) highlight how a degree of narcissism may be exactly what propels some people into significant leadership positions in the first place (although if left unchecked may cause them and/or their organization to derail in the long term). Thus, the line between 'good' and 'bad' leadership is a difficult one to draw and brings to light deep ethical questions about means and ends.

Another common assumption embedded within the leadership literature is the need for theory to be grounded in and to inform practice. More than many academic subjects, there is a sense that leadership research should address real-life challenges and speak directly to the concerns of practitioners. Pragmatic concerns tend to be given privilege over critique and conceptualization, and leadership education is expected to develop skills as well as knowledge.

The ethical and practical imperatives of Leadership Studies, as outlined above, lead to a tendency for theory and research to be applied in a normative fashion, whether or not this was the initial aim. The idea of 'normative leadership' (coined by Barrow, 1977) refers to approaches that endeavour to prescribe the most effective form of leadership intervention for a given situation. The label was initially applied to models such as behavioural and situational leadership, but can equally be applied to other approaches, including transformational, servant, and distributed leadership (see Chapter 2 for an explanation of these concepts). While the intent to use theory to inform practice is admirable, it may well become misleading if generalizations transcend the contexts in which the theories were developed. Furthermore, while many of these models (e.g. transformational and distributed leadership) are based upon descriptions of leadership practice (or, to be more precise, the preferences of followers and/or leaders for different styles of leadership), rarely is any serious attention given to their relative effectiveness vis-à-vis other forms of leadership (i.e. desirability is given precedence over effectiveness).[4] In consequence, a lot of advice is given to those charged with leadership on the basis of fairly flimsy or contentious evidence – as Chester Barnard (1948: 80) famously said 'leadership has been the subject of an extraordinary amount of dogmatically stated nonsense'.

A practical example of this challenge can be seen in the British National Health Service (NHS) Leadership Qualities Framework (NHS, 2002) which described a set of key characteristics, attitudes, and behaviours that leaders in the NHS should aspire to in delivering the NHS Plan (DoH, 2000). This framework was a central pillar of the NHS Modernisation Agency (now disbanded) and their strategy to 'modernize' the NHS to cope with the demands of twenty-first-century health care. The framework had a number of applications and formed the foundation for setting leadership standards in the NHS; assessing and developing high performance in leadership, individual, and organizational assessment; integrating leadership across the service and related agencies; adapting leadership to suit changing contexts; and benchmarking of leadership capacity and capability. Despite its widespread application across the health service, however, the research on which it was based was derived simply from a number of self-report interviews with Chief Executives and Directors (NHS, 2003). The extent to which the 'qualities' identified through this research represent objective criteria that can be meaningfully applied to other job roles in different parts of the organization, at different periods in time, is highly debatable, yet they are presented as a rational, evidence-based approach to leadership. A descriptive snapshot of a limited sample is hence applied prescriptively as if it were a general truth (see Bolden et al., 2006 for an extended critique of this framework).

The 'rush to the normative' (a topic of plenary debate at the *5th International Conference on Studying Leadership* at Cranfield University in December 2006) is symptomatic of leadership research in general. In an edited book arising from this conference, Turnbull James and Collins (2008: 3) propose:

> Perhaps more than any other field, leadership studies appears to be caught between studying and advising. Many studies do not restrict themselves to describing and analysing leadership phenomena, but instead draw implications from their research about who should be appointed to leadership roles, how organizations should distribute autonomy and the behaviours that should be rewarded.

Throughout our years of researching leadership we, the authors of this book, have frequently experienced this tension from funders, participants, and practicing managers calling for practical recommendations from the earliest stages of research. It is a difficult balance to retain between description and prescription; analysis and prediction, and current pressures to measure and predict the economic and social impact of research may further reinforce this trend.[5]

In order to maintain a sense of perspective it is, in our own experience, desirable to collaborate and share ideas with other scholars, practitioners, and policymakers before seeking to generalize and prescribe recommendations. The expansion of disciplinary and contextual boundaries highlighted by Burns (2005) points to leadership enquiry as a collective pursuit and, as illustrated in the earlier quote by Grint (2005a), something that is of relevance to all of us. While leadership may offer the prospect of emancipation and empowerment, it also carries the potential for alienation and control (Gemmill and Oakley, 1992), fantasy (Sveningsson and Larsson, 2006), and misdirection (Mintzberg, 2004a). Through an overdependence on particular research philosophies and methodologies, and a desire for the immediate application of findings, the same may also be true of leadership research.

Dissatisfaction with Leadership and Management Theory and Education

The perceived disconnect between the theory and practice of leadership is symptomatic of a wider trend within management and organization studies to question the relevance and practical significance of much current theory and research.

For example, in December 2007, the Academy of Management (AoM) published a special issue of their journal reflecting on the past fifty years of management research and setting an agenda for the future. In this edition, a number of leading scholars in the field added their voices to the growing concern about a field that has become overly theoretical at the expense of practical relevance. Thus Donald Hambrick, a former president of the AoM, argued: 'our insistence in the field of management that all papers contribute to theory may actually have the unintended perverse effect of stymieing the discovery of important theories' (Hambrick, 2007: 1351) and Jeffrey Pfeffer (2007) proposed that most management research fails to have an effect on actual management practice. Indeed, such is the current concern with relevance that the focus of the 2008 AoM conference in Anaheim, California was on 'The Questions we Ask' – particularly exploring how theory and research can more meaningfully inform management practice, while in the same year the British Academy of Management conference was entitled 'The Academy Goes Relevant' – focusing on how to achieve both relevance and rigour in management research.

Although increasingly high profile, calls for enhanced relevance are not new to the field. Indeed both the authors cited above had previously questioned the extent to which management research was relevant or seen to 'matter' (Hambrick, 1994, 2005; Pfeffer and Fong, 2002) and numerous others have queried the extent to which business and management education is 'fit for purpose' (e.g. Mintzberg, 2004a; Bennis and O'Toole, 2005; Raelin, 2007).

Given the level of investment now made in management and leadership education and research, however, why might this be the case? Sara Rynes in a review of the contributions to the 2007 special edition of the *Academy of Management Journal* identified three repeating themes: balance, boundaries, and legitimacy; and three underlying tensions: competing criteria for judging quality; tensions between research and other activities; and tensions between management and source disciplines such as economics, psychology, and sociology (Rynes, 2007). The field is thus presented as one that in its struggle to assert its status and credibility as a legitimate academic discipline may have overstated its reliance on particular methodologies, approaches, and assumptions. In particular, there has been a tendency to promote 'scientific rigour', grounded in the quantitative analysis of empirical research data, as the route to knowledge and understanding, as illustrated in the following quote from Bennis and O'Toole (2005: 98):

During the past several decades, many leading Business schools have quietly adopted an inappropriate – and ultimately self-defeating model of academic excellence. Instead of measuring themselves in terms of the competence of their graduates, or by how well their faculties understand important drivers of business performance, they measure themselves almost solely by the rigor of their scientific research. They have adapted a model of science that uses abstract financial and economic analysis, statistical multiple regressions, and laboratory psychology. Some of the research produced is excellent, but because so little of it is grounded in actual business practices, the focus of graduate business education has become increasingly circumscribed – and less and less relevant to practitioners.

However, while Bennis and O'Toole critique one important aspect of management education – the knowledge production process – they do not really question what counts as 'useful' or 'practical' knowledge, nor how this is learnt and applied by 'practitioners'. Their call for more 'practical' knowledge is not uncommon but carries its own assumptions about what sorts of information are required by practitioners and fuels another tendency within the field – that of focusing predominantly on the development of technical knowledge rather than 'practical wisdom' (also called 'phroensis') (Flyvbjerg, 2006; Grint, 2007). Raelin (2007: 496, 507) proposes:

The dominant empiricist epistemology governing our educational enterprises in higher education as well as in corporate training and development leads us to separate theory and practice in an aspiration to define the best conceptual models to map external reality [. . .] Unfortunately [. . .] our professionalized form of education has emphasized the technical over the interpersonal skills, the accumulation of facts over wisdom, and a focus on individual accomplishment over intersubjective appreciation.

An interesting illustration of this distinction is the observation that MBA students make more utilitarian decisions relating to ethical dilemmas in business than do experienced executives (Harris and Sutton, 1995) and the assertion that management education had a role to play in the criminal misconduct of executives in companies such as Enron, Global Crossing, and Tyco (Ghoshal, 2005), and more recently the banking crisis of 2008. In these cases, clearly the learning acquired through Business Schools is 'practical' but perhaps not in ways we would like to encourage.

In his book on Studying Organizations, Chris Grey (2009) goes further to suggest that 'there is *absolutely no evidence* that taking a management course has any effect on making people better managers' (p. 134, initial emphasis). He proposes that 'management education is deeply flawed, and will continue to be so until some fairly fundamental truths are recognized' (Ibid.: 135). Central to these, he argues, is 'the conceit of management knowledge to offer a way of exerting systematic, predictable control over organizations is just that, a conceit: flawed, incoherent in theory, unrealizable in practice' (Ibid.: 135). For Grey, management education functions as a process of acculturation or a rite of passage by which people demonstrate their commitment to managerial principles and acquire the vocabulary of 'management speak' rather than as a scientific basis for informing management practice.

Whatever your views on the utility of management education and enquiry, achieving *both* relevance *and* rigour in research is not an easy task.[6] Pettigrew

(1997) termed it the 'double hurdle' and Colville (2008) proposes that its origins may lie in processes of sensemaking and discourse that render it unlikely that academics, practitioners, and policymakers will find the same things interesting or relevant due to differing aims, objectives, and outputs (a challenge he termed the 'double dialectic').

Reframing Leadership Studies

We find ourselves, therefore, at a time when potent calls are emerging for a reframing of the field of Leadership Studies (see e.g. Grint, 2005a; Goethals and Sorenson, 2006; Sinclair, 2007).

1. *Firstly, there is a call to redress the balance accorded to individual and collective accounts of leadership, and the relative importance attributed to leaders and followers.*

In response to the limitations of 'heroic' perspectives that place the responsibilities and rewards for leadership firmly in the hands of a few senior individuals, a process-informed perspective endeavours to convey a 'post-heroic' representation whereby leadership arises from the collective efforts of a wide number of people and variables.

Wilfred Drath (2001) has likened leadership to the 'deep blue sea' – with 'leaders' as the white wave caps but the true power and force residing more broadly within the mass of water (people) from whence they came. Tolstoy in his epic novel *War and Peace* likened the political leaders of the Russian Revolution to a bow wave – always there ahead of the ship but ultimately produced and propelled by the force of movement through the water. To understand history, he argued: 'we must leave aside kings, ministers, and generals, and study the common, infinitesimally small elements by which the masses are moved' (Tolstoy cited in de Rond, 2003: 168).

Despite this, there remains a tendency for our attention to keep returning to the wave crests – to seek comfort in the presence of 'leaders'. Such dependence, however, may ultimately be detrimental both for individuals and organizations. Gemmill and Oakley (1992) accuse leadership of being 'an alienating social myth' that 'functions as a social defence whose central aim is to repress uncomfortable needs, emotions and wishes that emerge when people work together' (Ibid., reprinted in Grint, 1997: 273). In over idealizing the leader, they argue, members deskill themselves from their own critical thinking, visions, inspirations, and emotions and unconsciously maintain the status quo.

What balance, therefore, needs to be struck between individual and collective accounts of leadership, and which factors determine an appropriate approach for the situation?

2. *Following on from these concerns, come calls to reframe how we recognize, reward, and develop leaders.*

Day (2000) draws a useful distinction between 'leader' and 'leadership' development. While, he argues, leader development is about developing individuals in leadership roles, leadership development is concerned with the development of the collective leadership capacity of the organization.

In this way, each person is considered a leader, and leadership is conceptualised as an effect rather than a cause. Leadership is therefore an emergent property of effective systems design. Leadership development from this perspective consists of using social (i.e. relational) systems to help build commitments among members of a community of practice. (Ibid.: 583)

He goes on to suggest that 'leader development' can be considered primarily as an investment in the *human capital* of selected individuals, whereas 'leadership development' is an investment in *social capital*[7] via the nurturing of interpersonal networks, cooperation and collaboration within and between people and organizations. Both are important, although traditionally development programmes have focused almost exclusively on the former.

The tempering of leader-centric perspectives forces us to look elsewhere for leadership yet, in so doing, renders it less tangible and more elusive. Studies informed by feminist theory, for example, note the tendency for relational aspects of leadership to 'disappear' (Fletcher, 2002; Sinclair, 2007) or to be treated as 'invisible' (Sorenson and Hickman, 2002), thereby reinforcing masculine stereotypes and approaches. The challenge, then, is how to offer a process-informed perspective on leadership that feels concrete and real rather than abstract and ephemeral? Furthermore, how can we meaningfully capture the full array of factors that contribute towards effective leadership and attribute appropriate recognition and rewards? And how can we challenge taken-for-granted assumptions about who is involved in leadership and open up opportunities for those whose voices have previously been silenced?

3. *The points above indicate a need to review our methodologies and approaches to the study of leadership.*

Despite leadership having been a topic of study for centuries, systematic empirical research did not really commence until the 1930s and 1940s. Since its inception, Leadership Studies has remained a topic of particular interest to social psychologists and those from the behavioural sciences. While increasingly an interdisciplinary subject with contributions from many fields (see e.g. Goethals and Sorenson, 2006), the dominant research approaches remain based upon 'scientific' enquiry with a broadly objectivist epistemology and positivist ontology.[8]

Such approaches, while helpful in offering a sense of rigour, consistency, and legitimacy to the field, also limit the extent to which we can meaningfully capture the relational, ethical, and emotional dimensions that are increasingly considered essential aspects of leadership practice. In consequence, many authors are now calling for a more qualitative approach grounded in an inter-pretivist epistemology and constructivist ontology (e.g. Conger, 1998; Collinson, 2005; Grint, 2005a; Sinclair, 2007) that recognizes the contextual and discursive nature of leadership practice (e.g. Alvesson, 1996; Fairhurst, 2007).

Chapter Summary

As mentioned at the outset of this chapter, this book seeks to draw together a range of perspectives on leadership that should enable the reader to reflect more critically on their experience of leadership theory, development, and practice. In this chapter, we have argued that over recent years leadership has emerged as a significant topic of academic and practitioner debate. Despite substantial investment of money, time, and effort, however, leadership remains a highly contested concept and questions remain about the degree to which past and current theory and research contributes in a constructive way towards enhancing leadership development and practice. It is proposed that we find ourselves in a time when there are substantial calls for a reframing of Leadership Studies in terms of: (*a*) the balance accorded to individual and collective accounts of leadership; (*b*) the manner in which we recognize, reward, and develop leaders; and (*c*) the ways in which we research and develop theories of leadership practice. These ideas will be explored further in subsequent chapters.

☐ NOTES

1. The concept of 'heroic' leadership has been widely utilized to refer to those approaches that portray leadership as something done by particularly gifted, committed, brave, ambitious, or in some other way exceptional, individuals. It portrays successful leadership as the product of effective leaders. More recent theorizing tends to take a 'post-heroic' perspective in which, it is argued, leaders do not necessarily have to be extraordinarily gifted and that much of the work of leadership may be rather mundane and, at the very least, the consequence of collective endeavour.

2. The term 'agency' is used to express the degree of free choice a person has (or believes himself/herself to have) when deciding how to act within a particular context/situation.

3. Thereby meaning that the majority of literature relating to the first two categories remains the domain of relatively uncritical biographical and autobiographical accounts of what particular leaders did and/or propose that others should do. Exceptions to this are studies based on a first person ethnographic methodology (e.g. Parker, 2004; Kempster and Stewart, 2010) although these remain rare within mainstream literature on leadership.

4. Perhaps because, like leadership, 'effectiveness' is very hard to define and definitions may well be contested.

5. For example, 'impact' measures are now required for most funding applications to the UK Research Councils and are key criteria in the Research Excellence Framework being introduced to assess research quality in UK universities.

6. 'Relevance' is defined as 'the importance of the research topic and the contribution to our knowledge made by the findings from the study' (Hammersley, 1992: 78) to researchers, practitioners, or both. 'Rigour' is considered to be the 'proper' application of research methods. Criteria vary according to the type of research but typically include validity, reliability, replicability, and generalizability for quantitative methodologies, and factors such as credibility, transferability, dependability, and confirmability for qualitative methodologies (Gray, 2009).

7. Defined by Adler and Kwon (2002: 17) as 'the goodwill that is engendered by the fabric of social relations and that can be mobilised to facilitate action'.

8. Epistemology is a branch of philosophy, concerned with 'the study of criteria by which we determine what does and does not constitute warranted or valid knowledge' (Gill and Johnson, 2010: 240) – in effect how we come to know what we know. The two most commonly contrasted positions are *positivism*, which proposes that the social world can be studied objectively using similar methods to those used to investigate the natural world, and *interpretivism*, which suggests that in order to understand the social world we must engage with the subjective interpretation of social actors. Ontology is 'the study of the essence of phenomena and the nature of their existence' (Ibid.: 241) – in effect what is the nature of social reality. The two most commonly contrasted positions are *objectivism*, which suggests that social reality exists independently of social actors, and *constructivism*, which proposes that social reality is 'constructed' by social actors in context and therefore has no enduring essence.

2   Theoretical Perspectives on Leadership

Chapter 1 outlines the general context of this book. It has been written at a time when there is dissatisfaction with traditional leader-centric models of leadership yet amid the sense that more complex, process, and relational models often fail to speak to the everyday concerns of practicing managers. In developing ever more elaborate models we may have lost sight of the fact that leadership is ultimately a human endeavour that draws on and is influenced by our emotions, desires, and sense of identity. In this chapter, we summarize the main developments in leadership theory and the current concerns and developments that inform scholarly work in this field. We begin by considering the contested nature of leadership and its relationship to management. The bulk of the chapter then considers principal theoretical perspectives and concludes with a working definition of leadership.

The Contested Nature of Leadership

Although Leadership Studies is relatively new as an academic discipline, it is a topic that has been studied for thousands of years. Despite the high level of consideration, however, there remains a certain mystery as to what leadership actually is or how to define it. In a review of leadership research, Ralph Stogdill (1974: 259) concluded that there are 'almost as many definitions of leadership as there are persons who have attempted to define the concept', and eleven years later Meindl et al. (1985: 78) proposed that: 'it has become apparent that, after years of trying, we have been unable to generate an understanding of leadership that is both intellectually compelling and emotionally satisfying. The concept of leadership remains elusive and enigmatic.'

At the heart of the problem of defining and understanding leadership lie two fundamental challenges. First, like notions such as love, freedom, and happiness, leadership is a complex concept open to subjective interpretation. Everyone has their own intuitive understanding of what it is, based on a mixture of experience, learning, and acculturation, which is difficult to capture in a succinct definition. Second, the way in which leadership is defined and understood is strongly influenced by one's philosophical beliefs on human nature. There are those who view leadership as the consequence of a set of traits or characteristics possessed by 'leaders', others regard it as a process of social influence emerging from group relationships, while some question its very existence as a discrete phenomenon at all.

It is for this reason that Grint (2005a) describes leadership as an 'essentially contested concept', revealing a number of different ways of thinking about the phenomena that makes consensus highly unlikely. First, he indicates that leadership could be considered as the property of a *person*, leading us to focus on the personal attributes of the 'leader'. Second, he proposes that it could be considered as *results*, leading us to focus on the achievements of leaders. Third, it could be conceived of as a *position* (akin to management), prompting us to ask where leaders operate and what responsibilities they hold. Fourth, he proposes that leadership may be regarded as a *process*, thereby encouraging us to turn our attention to the functions and processes of leadership more broadly.

While these categories may be somewhat simplistic, they reflect something of the diversity of views expressed within leadership theory, practice, and development. Reflect, for a moment, on your own organization (or one that you know well) – to what extent is leadership regarded as the preserve of a few key individuals? How is leadership recognized and rewarded? How much are the successes and failures of 'leaders' the direct consequences of their own actions and/or a wider range of social and organizational factors?

The answers to questions such as these begin to reveal something of the nature and complexity of leadership and its interrelation to other processes. In all likelihood you will have noticed a number of different and potentially competing ways of thinking about leadership within your own organization, each of which informs and shapes what actually goes on. In considering these issues you are also likely to have touched upon some other important challenges, in particular those of 'epistemology' and 'ontology'. These are both key concepts in the field of social research and are particularly important when considering elusive notions such as leadership.

EPISTEMOLOGY AND ONTOLOGY: THE HITLER PROBLEM

Epistemology is a branch of philosophy that explores the nature of knowledge. Without doubt, one of the key epistemological questions for the study of leadership is that of ethics. Thus, for example, while some people argue that 'leaders are like the rest of us: trustworthy and deceitful, cowardly and brave, greedy and generous' (Kellerman, 2004b: 45), others propose that in order to be considered as a 'leader' a person must be acting in an ethical way (e.g. Burns, 1978; Bass, 1985). This tension has been referred to by Joanna Ciulla as the 'Hitler problem' in that:

The answer to the question 'Was Hitler a good leader?' is yes, if a leader is defined as someone who is effective or gets the job they set out to do done. The answer is no, if the leader gets the job done, but the job itself is immoral, and it is done in an immoral way. (Ciulla, 1999: 168)

Clearly, there is no definitive answer to these questions and limited chance of agreement between opposing camps. They represent fundamentally different ways of thinking about leadership and lead to the recognition and exploration of different issues.

Ontology refers to philosophical questions about the nature of being. Within Leadership Studies, a key ontological question is where leadership is considered to reside – as an attribute of leaders themselves or as an emergent property of the system(s) to which they belong? In a recent paper, Drath et al., (2008) highlighted that nearly all theories of leadership are founded on an assumption that the basic building blocks are 'leaders', 'followers', and 'common goals'. Such a way of thinking means that where these factors are present we may be able to recognize and describe what goes on as 'leadership'. Where one or more is absent, however (such as within a professional partnership where people engage as equals, or within a social community where there is no common goal to be addressed), 'leadership' is unlikely to be explicitly recognized. Drath and colleagues propose that such a representation is extremely limiting in terms of the opportunities it affords for challenging the dominance of the so-called 'leaders' and the belief that leadership is something done *by* leaders *to* followers in order to achieve some particular outcome. Instead, they propose that 'direction', 'alignment', and 'commitment' might be better things to look out for if we are searching for evidence of leadership. From this perspective, leadership is not something that resides within leaders, ready to be unleashed at the opportune moment, but is a collective endeavour that can only be made sense of within the context in which it occurs. In reference to the question of Hitler's leadership in Nazi Germany, for example, Grint (2004) argues:

A person did not need to be a Nazi to support Hitler, but the network was constructed and held in place so that the only way to achieve anything was to fall in line with Hitler's demands. The power of Hitler, though, derived from his temporary control over the hybrid of people, flags, ideas, songs, uniforms, tanks, guns, oil, and so forth; it did not derive from him alone, however charismatic he may have appeared to some.

While the points raised above may challenge us to think about leadership in different ways, however, they still assume that leadership is a discrete phenomenon to be described, studied, and/or practiced. A more radical perspective is to propose that leadership exists only in its ability to influence and shape our ways of thinking and should be considered as a discursive phenomenon (see later in this chapter). In a seminal paper, Gemmill and Oakley (1992) described leadership as 'an alienating social myth' that disempowers followers and builds dependency, and Alvesson and Sveningsson

(2003: 359) suggest that 'thinking about leadership needs to take seriously the possibility of the non-existence of leadership as a distinct phenomenon'. Such perspectives will be explored in further detail throughout this book.

Philosophical Origins of Contemporary Leadership Theory

So it is that leadership remains a hotly debated and contested concept. It is a word that is used in many different ways and senses – at times a noun, referring to the leader or leadership team, and at times as if it were a verb, referring to the process of leading (Ciulla, 2005). A clue to the confusion surrounding the notion of leadership may be found, perhaps, if we consider briefly the linguistic and philosophical origins of the term.

The roots of the English word 'leadership' can be traced back to the word 'lead', first introduced into the language around AD 800 from the old Anglo-Saxon word for 'to travel' and subsequently adapted, around 400 years later, to mean 'to guide' (Grace, 2003). The term 'leader' originated *circa* AD 1300 in recognition of the role played by politicians and statesmen but was not applied in organizations until the early nineteenth century, around the same time that the term 'leadership' began to be used to describe the activity carried out by 'leaders' (Ibid.). Thus, it seems, that historically leadership has been the preoccupation of people of Anglo-Saxon descent (Bass, 1990) and is largely 'a 20th Century concept [...] related to the democratization of Western Civilisation' (Rost, 1991: 43, cited in Grace, 2003: 4), used more recently to 'help Americans find significance in their search for the meaning of life' (Rost, 1991: 7, cited in Grace, 2003: 2).

The 2008 US Presidential Election is about as vivid an example of this issue as you are likely to find, where Barack Obama became the physical embodiment of the American Dream yet, as subsequent history has shown us, the hopes and beliefs projected onto such individuals may be unrealistic and unachievable. Leaders are both constrained and enabled by the systems in which they find themselves and their successes and failures are integrally linked to the contributions of those that precede, succeed, and surround them.

Despite the relatively recent use of the concept of leadership in relation to organizations and Western democracy, however, philosophical teachings and writings on this subject date back thousands of years. Amongst the earliest of these were the *Tao Te Ching* by the Chinese philosopher Lao Tzu (also know as Laozi) and *The Art of War* by the military general Sun Tzu in the fifth- to sixth-century BC.

For Lao Tzu, the key to good leadership was facilitating others to accomplish a task, not through coercion but via a more subtle process of interpersonal influence. He argued that:

A leader is best
When people barely know he exists
Not so good when people obey and acclaim him
Worse when they despise him
But of a good leader, who talks little,
When his work is done, his aim fulfilled,
They will say:
We did it ourselves. (Lao Tzu, cited in Manz and Sims, 1991: 35)

Sun Tzu not only echoed a similar concern for maintaining balance and harmony but also recognized that the ultimate responsibility rests with the leader, who needs to be prepared to take decisive action when required: 'the leader of armies is the arbiter of the people's fate, the man on whom it depends whether the nation shall be in peace or in peril' (Sun Tzu, 2009: 107).

While the ideas expressed within these texts have an enduring relevance and have seen a resurgence of interest in recent years,[1] Western thinking on leadership has perhaps been most strongly influenced by Greek Philosophy. The root of many of these ideas can be traced back to Socrates, although, as he wrote no books himself, they are conveyed primarily through the writings of Plato, Xenophon, and Aristophanes (see Adair, 1989). For Socrates, a key prerequisite for holding a leadership position was professional and/or technical competence and he also pointed towards an increased need, or desire, for leadership in times of crisis. Of the various forms of authority available to people – position/rank, personality, and knowledge – Socrates put precedence on the latter. This idea was particularly captured in Plato's book *The Republic* (fourth-century BC), in which he outlined the difficulties of democratic society that promotes decision-making by consensus and argued, instead, for leadership by those with the most appropriate knowledge and skills, as illustrated in the following metaphor:

The sailors are quarrelling over the control of the helm [...] They do not understand that the genuine navigator can only make himself fit to command a ship by studying the seasons of the year, sky, stars, and winds, and all that belongs to his craft; and they have no idea that, along with the science of navigation, it is possible for him to gain, by instruction or practice, the skill to keep control of the helm whether some of them like it or not. (Plato, cited in Adair, 1989: 15)

Xenophon, an experienced military general himself, concluded however that there was more to successful leadership than knowledge and experience alone. In his various books he distinguished between leaders who achieved 'willing obedience' and those who simply gained grudging compliance (Adair, 1989;

Mitchell, 2009). At the heart of this argument was a question about the nature of the leader–follower relationship and the extent to which a leader is able to inspire commitment, within which it is possible to identify the seeds of transformational leadership, as well as concerns about corporatism and the significance of rhetoric in leadership (Gosling, 2009).

Aristotle, a student of Plato, is another Greek scholar whose work has been largely cited in relation to leadership. Like his teacher, and Socrates before him, Aristotle argued the case for a ruling elite, proposing that leaders should be selected on the basis of their experience and knowledge. In considering what constitutes useful knowledge for leaders, Aristotle distinguished between a number of different forms, including *technē, epistēmē, phronēsis*[2] – described thus: 'whereas *epistēmē* concerns theoretical *know why* and *technē* denotes technical *know how, phronēsis* emphasizes practical knowledge and practical ethics' (Flyvbjerg, 2001: 56). The latter of these concepts, *phronēsis* (often referred to as 'practical wisdom'), is gaining increasing attention within leadership and management studies and regarded as an important basis for the education of managers (see e.g. Grint, 2007).

All of these early writings on leadership were heavily influenced by the political, social, cultural, and economic context of the times, but these dimensions were perhaps most clearly evident within the works of Machiavelli in sixteenth-century Italy. Although widely criticized as advocating an instrumental approach to leadership (the ends justify the means), his book *The Prince* was a thoughtful and provoking insight into the processes of leadership. Within this work, Machiavelli argued that people are basically weak, fallible, gullible, and not particularly trustworthy. His approach to leadership, therefore, proposed that others should be treated as impersonal objects and manipulated whenever necessary to achieve one's own ends. The fundamental premise was not necessarily to endorse acting immorally for the sake of it but, rather, to highlight the inefficacy of acting morally in an amoral world. Thus, for Machiavelli, 'it is much safer to be feared than loved when one of the two must be lacking' (Machiavelli, cited in Grint, 1997: 60), because fear is a more effective mechanism for the achievement of outcomes in a society with no consistent moral framework.

Ideas and ideals of leadership have been explored throughout history by writers including Shakespeare, Conrad, and Tolstoy (see Villiers and Gosling, forthcoming), and together evoke something of the emotional lived experience of leading and being led. They have become part of the cultural fabric of our societies and still today shape our expectations of leadership. Yet, we may be somewhat selective in which aspects we choose to focus on and promote. While, for example, Shakespeare spoke of many flawed leaders, such as Hamlet and Richard III, it is perhaps the heroic speeches of Henry V that remain with us (in Britain and the United States at least). To that extent, perhaps, it can be argued:

The nature of management and managers and of leaders and leadership is highly problematic: there is no agreed view on what managers or leaders should do and what they need to do it. And there never can be, since such definitions arise not from organizational or technical requirements, but from the shifting ways in which over time these functions are variously conceptualised. The manager, as much as the worker, is a product of history. (Salaman, 2004: 58)

Leadership is Sexy and Management is Boring... or are they?

One of the many ways in which people have attempted to make sense of leadership in recent years is to contrast it to management. Zaleznik (1977) arguably began the trend with his *Harvard Business Review* article '*Managers and Leaders: are they different*', in which he presented the image of the 'leader' as an artist, who uses creativity and intuition to navigate their way through chaos, while the 'manager' was presented as a problem solver dependent on rationality and control. Since then the leadership literature has been littered with bold statements contrasting the two, such as: managers 'do things right' while leaders 'do the right thing' (Bennis and Nanus, 1985: 21) and 'management works in the system; leadership works on the system' (Covey et al., 1994: 268).

Central to most of these distinctions is an orientation towards change. This concept is well represented in the work of John Kotter who concluded that 'management is about coping with complexity', while 'leadership, by contrast, is about coping with change' (Kotter, 1990: 104). He proposed that good management brings about a degree of stability and consistency to organizational processes and goals, while leadership is required for dynamic change.

In distinguishing the central role of leadership in bringing about change, Kotter (1995) identified eight activities in which a leader must engage, as follows:

1. Creating a sense of urgency.
2. Forming a guiding coalition for change.
3. Articulating a clear vision.
4. Communicating the vision.
5. Removing obstacles.
6. Planning short-term wins.
7. Producing continuous change.
8. Institutionalizing new approaches.

The distinction of leadership from management as represented by Kotter and his peers clearly encourages a shift in emphasis from the relatively inflexible, bureaucratic processes typified as 'management' to the more dynamic and strategic processes classed as 'leadership', yet even he concludes that they are both important, and to a large extent complementary, processes:

Leadership is different from management, but not for the reason most people think. Leadership isn't mystical and mysterious. It has nothing to do with having charisma or other exotic personality traits. It's not the province of a chosen few. Nor is leadership necessarily better than management or a replacement for it: rather, leadership and management are two distinctive and complementary activities. Both are necessary for success in an increasingly complex and volatile business environment. (Kotter, 1990: 103)

Despite the popular appeal of a contrast between leadership and management, there remains serious doubt as to whether such a distinction is either useful or an accurate description of practice. First, there is increasing concern about the way in which such analyses tend to denigrate management as something rather boring and uninspiring. Joseph Rost, for example, highlights the need for consistency and predictability in many aspects of management and leadership behaviour and concludes that 'down with management and up with leadership is a bad idea' (Rost, 1991: 143). John Gardner makes a similar remark in his book *On Leadership*, arguing that:

Many writers on leadership take considerable pains to distinguish between leaders and managers. In the process leaders generally end up looking like a cross between Napoleon and the Pied Piper, and managers like unimaginative clods (Gardner, 1990: 3)

This denigration of management leads to a second, and perhaps more significant, difficulty of the leader–manager distinction – far from being separate practices, they are an integral part of the same job. From detailed observations of what managers actually do, Mintzberg (1973, 1975) identified ten key roles, one of which was 'leadership', concluding that, within organizations at least, leadership is just one dimension of a multifaceted management function.

Much of the difficulty and confusion that arises from contrasting leadership and management, therefore, comes from the tendency to map them to different individuals. Thus, we talk of 'managers' and 'leaders' as if they were different, and to a large extent incompatible, people – we consider leaders as dynamic and charismatic, with the ability to inspire others, while managers are portrayed as bureaucrats who focus only on the task in hand. Such a view, however, does not coincide well with the lived experience of being a manager. People are generally recruited into 'management' rather than 'leadership' positions within organizations and are expected to complete a multitude of tasks ranging from day-to-day planning and implementation, to longer term strategic thinking. None of these are done in isolation, and throughout it is essential to work alongside other people – to motivate and inspire them, and also to know when to relinquish the lead and take a back seat. As Gosling and Mintzberg (2003: 54–5) argue:

Most of us have become so enamoured of 'leadership' that 'management' has been pushed into the background. Nobody aspires to being a good manager anymore; everybody wants to be a great leader. But the separation of management from leadership is dangerous. Just as management without leadership encourages an uninspired style, which deadens activities, leadership without management encourages a disconnected style, which promotes hubris. And we all know the destructive power of hubris in organizations.

Thus, while the distinction between management and leadership has been useful in drawing attention to the strategic and motivational qualities required during periods of change, the bipolar representation of managers and leaders as completely different people can be misleading and potentially harmful in practice. Indeed, if it is believed that leaders and managers are different people, one might well conclude that (*a*) it is necessary to change the management team regularly as circumstances change, and (*b*) it is not possible for managers to become leaders (and vice versa). Such a view is severely limiting and greatly underestimates the abilities of people in management roles. This is not to say, however, that all people will be equally adept at all aspects of leadership and management nor that there is one profile that is appropriate in all situations, but that to achieve maximum effect we should seek to recruit and develop 'leader–managers' capable of adopting the role in its most holistic form.

It is for this reason that, like Mintzberg (2004b), we will use the words 'management' and 'leadership' and 'manager' and 'leader' rather interchangeably throughout this book. This is not to imply that the two are directly equivalent, but to recognize that within organizations there is a high degree of overlap and that, in practice, the two cannot be meaningfully separated. Furthermore, it is to recognize that common distinctions between the two arise largely through how they are conceptualized rather than through how they are practiced. As will become apparent in this book, whilst representations of 'leadership' and what constitutes a 'leader' remain highly contested, notions of 'management' and 'manager' are more frequently tied to specific organizational roles. Given that a significant focus of this book is on leadership within organizations, the leader–manager divide may not be best suited to expanding our understanding of either function.

Contemporary Theories of Leadership

In this section, we review the various ways in which leadership has been analysed and represented over the past century. While many of these ideas have been subject to extensive critique, they all continue to exert some degree of influence over how leadership is recognized and developed today and, as such, are important to be aware of when exploring our assumptions and practices.

This section is structured into three parts, beginning with a series of approaches that broadly consider leadership as arising from the contribution of 'leaders'; then as the outcome of leader–follower relationships; and then as an emergent social process within organizations and groups. While these are neither absolute nor exclusive categories, they indicate three broad ways of thinking about and describing leadership. Theories have been assigned to each category on the basis of their predominant argument and chronological sequence.

It should be noted that this is not intended to be a comprehensive review of leadership theory (see e.g. Northouse, 2004; Yukl, 2006), but rather an overview of the main perspectives. It should also be noted that the vast majority of theories and research discussed here, as within leadership and management studies more generally, are Western in origin (primarily the United States and the United Kingdom) and, in many cases, heavily shaped by the contexts in which they were researched and developed.

LEADERSHIP AS A PROPERTY OF LEADERS

Despite the classical writings on leadership described earlier in this chapter the field of Leadership Studies as we now know it emerged in the early- to mid-twentieth century, predominantly out of research conducted in the United States during and after the First World War to inform the recruitment and development of military officers.

The trait approach to leadership

Initial research in this field endeavoured to distinguish the core *traits* of effective leaders in order to identify those individuals with a predisposition to take on leadership roles. It took as its starting point the 'Great man' view of leadership (Carlyle, 1866), whereby effective past leaders (usually male) were considered to have achieved their success through possession of a range of distinguishing characteristics and qualities that made them 'born to lead'.

While this approach appeared promising at first, with each new study a different set of traits was identified (see Stogdill, 1974 for a review). Further-more, the linkage of many of these factors to underlying and largely unchange-able characteristics (such as personality, physique, intelligence, etc.) rendered them of limited utility in developing leaders and/or enhancing diversity, and insufficient as predictors of future performance. Shaw (1976) and Fraser (1978), for example, found that leaders tend to score higher than average on scores of ability (intelligence, relevant knowledge, verbal facility), sociability (participation, cooperativeness, popularity), and motivation (initiative and persistence) – although clearly the presence of any or all of these does not make someone a 'leader', nor does their absence preclude that person from being a 'leader'. In effect, what this approach offers is a list of attributes that may render someone more or less likely to be *perceived as a leader* in a given context (i.e. by virtue of these traits they may appear more credible or legitimate to potential followers) and/or to *aspire to be a leader* (i.e. more likely to seek opportunities to take on a leadership role).

Leadership styles and behaviours

An alternative to the trait approach was to consider how leaders behave, rather than their underlying characteristics. Interest in this approach was popularized by the work of Douglas McGregor (1960), which proposed that management and leadership style is influenced by the persons' assumptions about human nature. He summarized two contrasting viewpoints of managers in industry. 'Theory X' managers take a fairly negative view of human nature, believing that the average person has an inherent dislike of work and will avoid it if possible. Leaders holding this view believe that coercion and control is necessary to ensure that people work, and that workers have no desire for responsibility. 'Theory Y' managers, on the other hand, believe that the expenditure of physical and mental effort in work is as natural as play or rest, and that the average human being, under proper conditions, learns not only to accept but to seek responsibility. Such leaders will endeavour to enhance their followers' capacity to exercise a high level of imagination, ingenuity, and creativity in the solution of organizational problems. It can be seen that leaders holding different assumptions will demonstrate different approaches to leadership: Theory X leaders preferring an autocratic style and Theory Y leaders preferring a participative style.

Other influential behavioural theories include Kurt Lewin's Leadership Styles (Lewin et al., 1939), the Ohio State Two-Factor Model (Fleishman, 1953; Halpin and Winer, 1957; Hemphill and Coons, 1957; Fleishman and Harris, 1962), and the Blake–Mouton Managerial Grid (Blake and Mouton, 1964). Each of these models identifies two dimensions of behaviour: a focus on 'task' (also termed 'production' or 'structure') and a focus on 'people' (also termed 'team' or 'relationships'). From this, it is possible to identify a range of leadership styles varying from highly directive (focusing mainly on task) to highly participative (focusing mainly on people). In each case it was argued that a high focus on both people and task was likely to constitute the most effective style of leadership, although it has since been recognized that leadership behaviours should be adapted to the context.[3]

Situational and contingency approaches

While behavioural theories introduced the notion of different leadership styles, they gave little guidance as to what constitutes an effective leadership approach in different situations. Indeed, most researchers today conclude that no one leadership style is right for every manager under all circumstances. Instead, situational theories were developed to indicate that the style to be used is dependent upon situational factors such the nature of followers, task, organization, and other environmental variables.

Fiedler's contingency theory of leadership (1964, 1967) distinguished between managers who are task or relationship-oriented. Research evidence indicated that task-oriented managers focus on the job-in-hand and tend to do better in situations that have good leader–member relationships, structured tasks, and either weak or strong position power. They also do well when the task is unstructured but position power is strong, and at the other end of the spectrum when the leader–member relations are moderate to poor and the task is unstructured. Such leaders tend to display a more directive leadership style. Relationship-oriented managers do better in all other situations and exhibit a more participative style of leadership.

Hersey and Blanchard (1969, 1977, 1988) had similar ideas but proposed that it is possible for a leader to adapt their style to the situation. They argued that the developmental level of subordinates has the greatest impact on which leadership style is most appropriate. Thus, as the skill and maturity level of followers increases, the leader will need to adapt their task-relationship style from directing to coaching, supporting, and delegating.

Despite the progress made by situational and contingency models of leadership in theorizing how leadership occurs in context, offering practical guidance to leaders in determining the most appropriate course of action, and giving legitimacy to the field of leadership development (moving away from the notion of leaders as 'born' to the idea that they can be developed), the approach remains problematic in many ways. The dominant tools are somewhat simplistic (although this is also part of their appeal) and fail to engage meaningfully with some of the practical challenges of leadership, such as how to master multiple leadership styles while remaining consistent; how to respond to multiple, complex, and poorly defined tasks; how to determine the needs of followers and balance leadership styles for individuals and groups; how to allow for leadership by more than one person and across multiple and changing groups; and what to do if the dominant style of the leader is ill-suited to the needs of the followers and situation when a change in leadership is not an option (Northouse, 2004). Furthermore, there is very little supporting empirical evidence for models such as that developed by Hersey and Blanchard, and a fair degree of conceptual ambiguity (see e.g. Graeff, 1983; Yukl, 2006: 224–5).

Leadership skills and functions

While the previous models focus on the traits and behaviours of leaders, a further set of approaches focused on the skills and functions of leadership – that is, what a leader (or group of leaders) needs to do and achieve.

One of the most influential such models – '*Action Centred Leadership*' – was developed by John Adair (1973), who proposed that the functions of leadership include: defining the task; planning; briefing; controlling; evaluating; motivating; organizing; and setting an example (largely echoing Fayol's functions of management (1949)). While he acknowledged that many people may contribute towards each of these functions, he argued, it is the formally designated leader who is accountable for the outcomes.

Similar to situational models, Adair proposed that the most effective approach within a given situation will be dependent on meeting both the leaders' and followers needs and aspirations. His influential 'three circles' model indicated how the leader must balance the requirements of the task, team, and individuals, varying the level of attention paid to each according to the context. Thus, for example, in time-critical situations the needs of the task should take precedence over team and individual needs; however, once the deadline has been met the leader should turn their attention back to the needs of individuals (including themself) and the team. Despite the simplicity of this model it remains highly influential, particularly within organizations such as the Royal Air Force where it continues to form the basis for much leadership development activity (Burridge, 2007).

Evidence of a skills-and-functions approach is also still highly evident in competency-based approaches to leadership that tend to combine traits, behaviours, and functions to propose a core set of competencies, qualities, and/or abilities to be exhibited by leaders in particular organizations. In a review of this literature, Perren and Burgoyne (2001) identified 1,013 individual management and leadership abilities that could be classified under eighty-three management and leadership ability sets, which, in turn, could be grouped under eight meta-categories: strategic thinking; leading direction and culture; managing resources; managing projects; managing information; managing quality; managing activities; and managing and leading people.

Although a skills-and-functions approach to leadership has become popular due to the clarity it offers for both leadership development and assessment, it can overemphasize the individualistic nature of leadership and underestimate the significance of contextual factors and personal differences, the implications of which are discussed in Chapter 4.

LEADERSHIP AS A RELATIONSHIP BETWEEN LEADERS AND FOLLOWERS

While a number of the models mentioned above take some consideration of followers, they are generally presented as somewhat passive and the emphasis is almost exclusively on what leaders need to do in order to get the most out of them. As early as the 1940s, an alternative approach was proposed by

Mary Parker Follett (2003 [1942]) who argued for recognition of leadership as a reciprocal relationship requiring an active partnership of leaders and followers, although it is only in more recent years that such a perspective has been taken seriously and scholars have endeavoured to explore the nature of the leader–follower relationship. The theories described below take a more relational perspective than those described previously in that they regard leadership as arising from the interaction between leaders and followers. Three broad groups of theories are outlined: leader–member exchange (LMX) and follower-centred perspectives; transformational and charismatic leadership, and quiet and servant leadership.

LMX and follower-centred perspectives

LMX theory describes the process(es) by which a leader establishes and maintains relationships with followers over time. In contrast to the situational models described previously in which 'followers' are treated as a rather homogenous group to which the 'leader' applies an average leadership style, LMX theory considers the extent to which differences might exist between the relationships of the 'leader' with each of their 'followers'.

Early research in this tradition (initially termed 'vertical dyad linkage' theory) explored how leaders and followers negotiate their relative roles within work groups (e.g. Dansereau et al., 1975; Graen and Cashman, 1975). From this work it was concluded that two forms of relationship ('linkage') could be identified: (*a*) *in-group*, based on individually negotiated role responsibilities and typified by mutual trust, respect, and liking; and (*b*) *out-group*, based on formally agreed employment contracts and typified by a lack of mutual trust, respect, and liking. In terms of the implications of this, it was argued that: 'whereas in-group members do extra things for the leader and the leader does the same for them, subordinates in the out-group are less compatible with the leader and usually just come to work, do their job, and go home' (Northouse, 2007: 154). Such an approach is closely allied to the Human Relations school of theory and subsequent research has indicated that high-quality relations (along the line of *in-group* linkages) are positively correlated with a number of individual and organizational outcomes, such as employee retention, performance ratings, job satisfaction, and career progression (see Graen and Uhl-Bien, 1995 for a review).

An alternative to LMX that also takes a follower-centred approach is 'implicit leadership theory' (Lord and Maher, 1991; Schyns and Meindl, 2005). From this perspective, it is argued, individuals possess a range of beliefs about what distinguishes leaders from non-leaders, and that what is important is not so much what leaders do as how they are perceived by (potential) followers. These beliefs develop in a number of ways and are strongly associated with the processes of education and acculturation. House and colleagues (2004) used this rationale as the basis for their GLOBE study of leadership across sixty-two societies, in which they identified six global leadership styles (charismatic/value based, team orientated, participative, humane orientated, autonomous, and self-protective), follower preferences for which varied according to societal culture.

A further set of theories that focus on how followers perceive leaders are those based on the 'social identity approach'. This perspective, developed from a combination of *self-categorization theory* (Turner, 1985) and *social identity theory* (Tajfel and Turner, 1979), proposes that the extent to which a leader is accepted or chosen by a group depends on the degree to which they are perceived as 'prototypical' group members (van Knippenberg and Hogg, 2003; Haslam, 2004). From this perspective, it is argued, leaders must be 'entrepreneurs of identity' in which 'leadership activity and leadership effectiveness largely revolves around the leader's ability to create identity definitions and to engage people in the process of turning those definitions into practical realities' (Reicher et al., 2005: 556). To this extent, leadership can be conceived of as an identity project in which leaders endeavour to align follower identities to a shared and meaningful sense of group membership.

Transformational and charismatic leadership

In their attempts to consider leadership in a systematic, rational, and objective manner, the models discussed in earlier this chapter tend to represent the leader as an instrumental rationalist, carefully weighing up the options and adapting their style accordingly – leadership is presented as a series of inputs and outputs that impact upon performance. In response to this rather dry and analytic representation, James MacGregor Burns (1978) put forward the notion of 'transforming' leadership. For Burns what really matters is the moral and reciprocal relationship between leaders and followers, whereby 'one or more persons engage with others in a way such that leaders and followers raise one another to higher levels of motivation and morality' (Ibid.: 20).

At the core of this approach is an emphasis both on the leader's ability to motivate and empower followers as well as on the moral dimensions of leadership – in effect, the notion of 'winning hearts as well as minds'. While Burns conceived of transforming leadership as a perspective that could be applied across a range of leadership styles and situations, subsequent work has generally focused on the notion of 'transformational leadership', as a distinct style in its own right and as particularly beneficial in times of change and uncertainty (Bass, 1985; Bass and Avolio, 1994).

In their model, Bass and Avolio (1994) identified four I's (Idealized influence, Inspirational motivation, Intellectual stimulation, and Individual consideration) that distinguished 'transformational' from a more traditional 'transactional' approach to leadership (with reward and recognition contingent on effort and position). The manner in which these forms of leadership are contrasted with one another echoes the debate about 'management' versus 'leadership' discussed earlier, with 'transactional leadership' being largely synonymous with representations of management and 'transformational leadership' as inspirational interpersonal influence. As with the management–leadership debate however, as Bass (1985) argues, transactional and transformational leadership are not opposite ends of a spectrum but two separate concepts that may well complement each another. Most leaders, it is proposed, will draw on both styles depending on the circumstances.

Alongside an interest in transformational leadership, has been an extensive focus on the role of charisma in leadership. In much the same way as transformational leadership, the concept of the 'charismatic leader' became popular in the 1980s and 1990s when charismatic influence was viewed as an antidote to the demoralizing effects of organizational restructuring, competition, and redundancies within many Western organizations at the time. The charismatic leader was seen as someone who could rebuild morale and offer a positive vision for the future (Bryman, 1992; Conger and Kanungo, 1998).

This approach, in effect, combines both notions of the transformational leader as well as earlier trait and 'great man' theories. Researchers have taken different positions, but overall four major characteristics of charismatic leaders can be identified: (a) a dominant personality, desire to influence others, and self-confidence; (b) strong role model behaviour and competence; (c) articulation of ideological goals with moral overtones; and (d) high expectation of followers and confidence that they will meet these expectations (Northouse, 2004: 171).

Despite the hype, however, confidence in this approach to leadership is rapidly declining. A number of high-profile corporate scandals, plus the tendency of charismatic leaders to desert organizations after making their changes and/or become dysfunctional or 'toxic' (Maccoby, 2000; Lipman-Blumen, 2005), have highlighted that this may not be a sustainable way to lead (see Chapter 6 for further discussion). There is a resistance to this view of the leader within many industries (particularly the public and voluntary sector) and organizations are seeking alternatives that develop quieter and more inclusive forms of leadership as described below.

Servant and quiet leadership

While the move to transformational leadership went some way to recognizing the need to engage followers in an inspiring and emotive way, through its emphasis on vision and charisma it may actually have done more to reinforce rather than challenge the image of the 'heroic' leader (Yukl, 1999). In contrast to such an image stand the ideas of 'servant' and 'quiet' leadership.

Servant leadership brings into focus the motives of leaders. The originator of this idea, Robert Greenleaf (2004: 6), proposed that:

...becoming a servant-leader begins with the natural feeling that one wants to serve...then conscious choice brings one to aspire to lead. He or she is sharply different from the person who is leader first, perhaps because of the need to assuage an unusual power drive or to acquire material possessions.

Like Burn's early conceptions of transforming leadership, the emphasis is on the moral and ethical dimensions of leadership, although this time the leader follows their path out of a desire to serve rather than out of a desire to lead. The focus on serving a greater purpose has made this approach popular within religious, community, and not-for-profit organizations but has had limited uptake within the commercial sector.

A related yet different concept is that of *quiet leadership*, which has been used to refer to the influence exerted by less visible leaders. Henry Mintzberg (1998) first utilized the notion of 'covert leadership' to refer to the subtle way in which the conductor of an orchestra can elicit certain types of performance from musicians, and built upon these ideas in his notion of 'quiet management', which he describes as follows:

Quiet management is about thoughtfulness rooted in experience. Words like wisdom, trust, dedication, and judgment apply. Leadership works because it is legitimate, meaning that it is an integral part of the organization and so has the respect of everyone there. Tomorrow is appreciated because yesterday is honoured. That makes today a pleasure [...] Indeed, the best managing of all may well be silent. That way people can say, 'We did it ourselves.' Because we did. (Mintzberg, 1999)

Within this description, Mintzberg clearly alludes to much earlier accounts of leadership, most notably that proffered by Lao Tzu in the sixth-century BC. He also draws attention to the need for a careful balance between leadership and empowerment and argues that 'too much leadership' can be just as problematic as too little (Mintzberg, 2004a).

Another author who has called for greater appreciation of the role of quiet leaders is Joseph Badaracco (2001) who has extolled the virtues of putting things off until tomorrow, picking your battles, bending the rules (rather than breaking them), and finding a compromise. These are quite different from the usual list of attributes assigned to leaders and offer greater opportunities for leadership throughout the organization, not just by people in formal positions of power.

Together these approaches place a focus on the ethics of leadership and for whose purpose it is performed. They challenge the degree to which we assume that in order to be a good leader one must be seen to be dictating what goes on, and encourage us to reflect on the motivations of people when taking on leadership roles. They also, however, pose some serious challenges for leaders in the extent to which they are seen as 'authentic' (see Chapter 3) and/or that their contribution is recognized. While leaders such as Nelson Mandela,

Mahatma Gandhi, and Martin Luther King Jr., for example, may be inspirational role models, they are a hard and daunting act to emulate; in each case were regarded as revolutionaries or even terrorists by some; and may be styles that do not transfer well to an organizational context in the present day.

LEADERSHIP AS A SOCIAL PROCESS

Together the theoretical perspectives outlined so far tend to represent leaders as somewhat exceptional individuals who, by virtue of their traits, expertise, adaptability, position, vision, charisma, and/or sense of purpose, manage to elicit a positive response from their followers. While such accounts undoubtedly enhance our understanding of leadership, they may also reinforce traditional stereotypes and say almost as much about those people making the assessment as the leaders themselves.

In his book *Great Leaders*, for example, John Adair (1989: 227) acknowledges that, while 'undoubtedly there were men and women in the past, as there are today, who exhibited extraordinary courage, firmness, or greatness of soul, in the course of some journey or enterprise. We, as humans, also have a tendency to admire and venerate them for their achievements and noble qualities.' Such a tendency, he goes on to argue, can 'even make a fairly ordinary leader into a hero simply because they need a hero to worship'.

To this extent, while heroic accounts of leadership may possibly inspire us into action, they also have the potential to be misleading, paving the way to exclude particular people from leadership roles and/or enabling others to abuse their powers. In this section we will summarize a number of more recent developments in leadership theory that shift the focus from *leaders* to *leadership* – from something done by leaders (either on their own or in relation to followers) to a shared social process to which many people contribute.

Shared and distributed leadership

Reflect for a moment on your own experience of being a leader: did you perform this role alone or in conjunction with others? Were you the only 'leader' or were there times when other people stepped forward to take the lead? Could you have achieved what you did without being part of a wider group?

From the questions above it is likely that you were part of a shared-leadership process in which it is possible to identify several leaders each contributing in their own significant way to a particular outcome. It is also likely that despite your leader role you were also a follower in relation to certain other people.

Some of the most compelling empirical accounts of leadership illustrate the manner in which responsibility for leadership is divided between two or more people. Heenan and Bennis (1999), for example, describe evidence of 'co-leadership' in a number of successful organizations where two people work alongside one another to fulfil a job that is too big for one person. Klein et al. (2006) describe how emergency care teams use 'dynamic delegation' to enable senior and junior staff to step in and out of leadership roles depending on the context.

Despite this, the idea of the individual leader still dominates popular thought. As O'Toole et al. (2003: 251) argue: 'shared leadership for most people is simply counterintuitive: leadership is obviously and manifestly an individual trait and activity'. They illustrate this point through reference to inspirational leaders such as Gandhi and Luther King, Jr., proposing that:

We don't immediately remember that, during the struggle for Indian independence, Gandhi was surrounded and supported by dozens of other great Indian leaders, including Nehru, Patel, and Jinnah, without whose joint efforts Gandhi clearly would have failed. We also forget that, far from doing it all himself, King's disciples included such impressive leaders in their own right as Jesse Jackson, Andrew Young, Julian Bond, Coretta Scott King, and Ralph Abernathy. When the facts are fully assembled even the most fabled 'solitary' leaders relied on the support of a team of other effective leaders. (Ibid.: 251)

Such a deeply embedded tendency to underestimate the contribution of more than a few key figures, it is argued, 'stems from thousands of years of cultural conditioning' (Ibid.: 251) and, as such, remains incredibly difficult to challenge even if the evidence points this way. The implications, however, are significant for how we go about studying, developing, and practicing leadership.

A 'shared' perspective considers leadership as 'a dynamic, interactive influence process among individuals in groups for which the objective is to lead one another to the achievement of group or organizational goals or both' (Pearce and Conger, 2003b: 1). At the heart of this approach lies the distinction between hierarchical and shared influence, with the former fitting most traditional views of leadership and the latter being the dimension brought by shared leadership (Pearce et al., 2008).

Shared and emergent leadership has been identified in many different areas, including business start ups (Ensley et al., 2006), self-managed work teams (Elloy, 2005), emergency care teams (Klein et al., 2006), web design teams (Brown and Gioia, 2002), and jazz music and rowing groups (Pescosolido, 2002). According to Pearce and Sims (2002, cited in Pearce et al., 2008: 623), 'shared leadership between peers accounts for more variance in team self-ratings, manager ratings, and customer ratings of change management team effectiveness than the leadership of formally designated team leaders'.

The concept of 'distributed leadership' is one particular form of shared-leadership theory that has gained some popularity and is becoming embedded in sectors such as school education (see e.g. Leithwood et al., 2006). This approach argues for a systemic perspective on leadership, whereby responsibility is dissociated from formal organizational roles, and people at all levels are given the opportunity to influence the overall direction and functioning of the organization. Gronn (2002: 7) describes it as 'emergent work-related influence'. Distributed leadership encourages a shift in focus from the traits and roles of 'leaders' to the shared activities and functions of 'leadership'.

In an early review of the literature, Bennett et al. (2003), as mentioned in Chapter 1, suggest that distributed leadership is based on three main premises: (*a*) that leadership is an emergent property of a group or network of interacting individuals; (*b*) that there is openness to the boundaries of leadership (i.e. who has a part to play both within and beyond the organization); and (*c*) that varieties of expertise are distributed across the many, not the few. Thus, distributed leadership is represented as dynamic, relational, inclusive, collaborative, and contextually situated. It requires a system-wide perspective that not only transcends organizational levels and roles but also organizational boundaries. Thus, for example, in schools one might consider the contribution of parents, pupils, the local community, employers, and public services as well as teachers and governors as the impact of good or bad school leadership extends far beyond the classroom.

Through extending the boundaries of leadership, both in terms of who has a part to play and who is affected by the outcomes, distributed leadership offers a powerful, non-individualistic lens through which to observe leadership practice. Spillane et al. (2004: 5) suggest that leadership is 'stretched over the social and situational contexts' and highlight the significant influence of material and cultural 'artefacts' (language, organizational systems, physical environment, etc.) in shaping leadership practice. More recent research in this traditional illustrates the 'hybrid' nature of leadership practice and the multiple 'configurations' that it can take (e.g. Gronn, 2008, 2009; Pearce et al., 2008; Bolden et al., 2008b).

Discursive and constitutive leadership

The final perspectives that will be explored in this chapter are those of 'discursive' (Fairhurst, 2007) and 'constitutive' (Grint, 1997) leadership (as with the other theories discussed, they will be revisited throughout the remainder of this book). Both of these approaches position themselves in contrast to psychologically informed theories (such as those discussed in previous sections) by considering leadership as a 'socially constructed' concept with no inherent essence. From this perspective, it is impossible to arrive at an objective, enduring, or generalizable account of leadership because it exists only through its capacity to shape the ways in which we think and talk about particular social processes. Such processes, it is argued, are heavily influenced by dynamics of power that may be hard to notice but nevertheless enable and/or constrain the array of behaviours, knowledge, and beliefs that are available to various actors.

Consider, for example, the case of Nazi Germany described earlier in this chapter. Undoubtedly many forms of leadership (and non-leadership) behaviour were available to the people who found themselves part of this system and there were numerous different ways in which they could make sense of their actions. Most who participated in the atrocities were not coerced to act in a particular way but nonetheless the system to which they belonged predisposed them to do things that, to those outside, were reprehensible. A similar situation occurred with US soldiers and Iraqi prisoners in Abu Ghraib and for innumerable other groups in other situations. Whether or not we believe these people were following the orders of their leaders, the system to which they belonged enabled such horrific incidents to occur.

For discursive leadership scholars the question is how leadership is accomplished and communicated through language: '*how* a text functions pragmatically, *how* leadership is brought off in some here-and-now moment of localized interaction' they ask '*what* kind of leadership are we talking about and how have the forces of history and culture shaped it? [They] reject prediction and control as key functions of theory, while never viewing description as *mere* description or prelude to the real work of theory building' (Fairhurst, 2007: 15, initial emphasis). From a discursive perspective, organizations and other social systems are never fully formed, but always in a state of 'becoming' and leadership can be considered as a form of 'organizing activity' that may influence this process (Hosking, 1988).

Similarly, a 'constitutive' approach, as proposed by Grint (1997: 5), argues that 'what the situation and the leader actually are is a consequence of various accounts and interpretations, all of which vie for domination'. According to Grint (Ibid.: 5–6), 'the critical issue for this approach, then, is not what the leader or the context is "really" like, but what are the processes by which these phenomena are constituted into successes or failures, crises or periods of calm, and so on'. What is important from this perspective are the processes by which accounts of leadership are generated, communicated, and consumed within groups and societies and the manner in which issues of power, authority, and experience influence these sensemaking processes.

A good example of this is given in Grint's analysis (2005b) of the representations of the 'War on Terror' in Iraq in the 2004 US presidential campaign. George W. Bush, he argued, presented the situation as a 'critical' problem demanding immediate and decisive action while his opponent, John Kerry, framed it as a 'wicked' problem with no immediate solution.[4] The outcome of this election, as we are aware, was decided by an American public, based on what they perceived to be the most convincing and engaging argument at the time.

Together then, these perspectives offer a very different way of thinking about leadership than those discussed earlier in this chapter and bring into question the validity of endeavouring to capture an objective and/or generalizable account of leadership. They draw attention to the need to explore the underlying sensemaking processes (Weick, 1995; Pye, 2005) by which certain things, and not others, are referred to as 'leadership' and to the potential of 'leaders' and other actors to intervene in shaping these sensemaking processes.

So, What is Leadership?

In this chapter we have outlined some of the many ways in which the concept of leadership has been theorized and described. In doing so, a number of themes emerge, including the distinction between individual and relational perspectives, leadership and management, the significance of ethics, varying conceptions of performance and success, the role of language and culture, and the importance of context. Leadership has variously been presented as a 'science', 'art', or 'craft', and conceptual clarity has proved elusive.

In a recent review of leadership definitions, Joseph Rost (2008: 98) argued that it 'may give a false impression that the majority of leadership scholars and commentators are moving away from the traditional heroic paradigm of leadership. That certainly is not true'. Instead he suggested that:

The majority of leadership authors, both scholarly and practitioner-orientated, are ensconced in the industrial paradigm of leadership, which Rost defined as 'great men and women with certain preferred traits who influence followers to do what the leaders wish in order to achieve group/organizational goals' effectively (1991: 95). Shortened up, leadership is 'good management' (p. 94). (Rost, 2008: 98)

Despite these variations, in an extensive review of leadership theory, Northouse (2004) identified four common themes in the way leadership now tends to be conceived: (*a*) it is a process; (*b*) involving influence; (*c*) that occurs in a group context; and (*d*) is directed towards goal attainment. He thus defines leadership as 'a process whereby an individual influences a group of individuals to achieve a common goal' (Ibid.: 3). Yukl (2006: 3) similarly proposes that: 'most definitions of leadership reflect the assumption that it involves a social influence process whereby intentional influence is exerted by one person over other people to guide, structure, and facilitate activities and relationships in a group or organization'.

Uhl-Bien (2006: 668), in describing relational leadership theories, offers a more collective definition where leadership is regarded as: 'a social influence process through which emergent coordination (i.e. evolving social order) and change (i.e. new values, attitudes, approaches, behaviours, ideologies, etc.) are constructed and produced'.

In selecting an appropriate working definition of leadership for this book, it is important to choose one that is capable of describing leadership as experienced in organizations and societies. There is a need, therefore, to be wary of prescriptive models (particularly those that provide normative assessments of the moral and ethical requirements of leadership) and to choose one that is sufficiently broad to allow for a variety of forms of leadership practice. To this extent, the latter definition by Uhl-Bien, while fitting Rost's category (2008) of 'post-heroic' leadership, allows the possibility for leadership by specific individuals as well as that more widely dispersed within groups and thereby forms a good basis for a working definition of leadership.

In drawing out common and significant themes between this and other definitions, leadership can be described as:

1. a process
2. of social influence,
3. to guide, structure, and/or facilitate
4. behaviours, activities, and/or relationships
5. towards the achievement of shared aims.

The notion of 'structuring' allows for both initiatives to transform or maintain social order as well as those arising from individuals, groups, and/or organizations. While it might be argued that this definition bears a close resemblance to many definitions of management, it is more open, is dissociated from formal organizational roles and hierarchies, and endeavours to offer a descriptive rather than prescriptive account of leadership.

According to this definition, the purpose of leadership is to mobilize people to work together in pursuit of some shared enterprise. As such, it offers a degree of flexibility in terms of the manner in which leadership is 'configured' (Gronn, 2009) and accomplished – allowing the possibility that it is something done by 'leaders' as well as that it may be more widely distributed and/ or socially constructed. It even fits with a discursive perspective for which a preferred definition cited by Fairhurst (2007) is as follows: 'leadership is exercised when ideas expressed in talk or action are recognized by others as capable of progressing tasks or problems which are important to them' (Robinson, 2001: 93, cited in Fairhurst, 2007: 6).

Thus, despite a wide diversity of views on leadership, it is possible to arrive at a definition that more or less spans a range of theoretical positions. More problematic, however, is the extent to which any such definition is useful in terms of helping us understand (*a*) *where* leadership resides and (*b*) *how* it is accomplished. By glossing over fundamental differences in how leadership is conceptualized, a generic definition or description may constrain rather than enable us, and restrict our capacity to open up underlying assumptions and processes for scrutiny.

This is a point made by Joanne Ciulla (2002: 340), who proposes that 'the scholars who worry about constructing the ultimate definition of leadership are asking the wrong question, but inadvertently trying to answer the right one'. To illustrate this point she cites Rost's review (1991) of leadership definitions, proposing that: 'all 221 definitions basically say the same thing – leadership is about one person getting other people to do something. Where the definitions differ is in *how* leaders motivate their followers and *who* has a say in the goals of the group or organization' (Ciulla, 2002: 340).

She goes on to propose that 'the real difference between the definitions rests on their normative assumptions. The underlying question is "how should leaders treat followers and how should followers treat leaders?"' (Ibid.: 340–1). For Ciulla it is these issues that need to be scrutinized and the answers to which offer the greatest potential for informing and enhancing leadership practice.

The ultimate question about leadership is not 'What is the definition of leadership?' The whole point of studying leadership is, 'What is good leadership?' The use of the word *good* here has two senses, morally good and technically good or effective. (Ciulla, 2002: 341)

Questions of ethics and effectiveness are implicit within much research on leadership but are rarely scrutinized in detail. They are problematic questions with no easy answers and are inextricably linked to the culture and context in which leadership is enacted. This is the messy business of Leadership Studies and seriously challenges any claims that can be made about the universality and prescriptive application of leadership models and/or approaches. Such concerns lie at the heart of this book and our endeavour to outline a number of alternative perspectives.

Chapter Summary

In this chapter we have outlined the many ways in which leadership has been represented over the years and the challenges of identifying a common definition. As can be seen, leadership is a highly contested construct with varying representations and definitions. In describing leadership, we have contrasted it with management and concluded that the two concepts are highly interdependent, such that it is not meaningful to separate them out, especially when talking about leadership within organizations.

In presenting theories of leadership, we have grouped them into three main categories: (*a*) those that regard leadership as the property of 'leaders';

(*b*) those that regard leadership as arising from the relationship between leaders and followers; and (*c*) those that regard leadership as a social process. While these are not discrete or exclusive categories, they do capture some of the range of views on what leadership is and where it resides.

Finally, this chapter concludes by considering how to define leadership. From reviewing the perspectives presented in this chapter, it is proposed that leadership is 'a process of social influence to guide, structure, and/or facilitate behaviours, activities, and/or relationships towards the achievement of shared aims'. While this definition permits some flexibility in terms of the models to which it can be applied, however, it is proposed that there may be more fundamental issues to consider, in particular, the extent to which different perspectives on leadership embed different assumptions around ethics and effectiveness. Thus, it is proposed that a definition of leadership, while in many ways desirable, may also constrain our capacity to recognize alternative and unexpected forms and to seriously reflect upon its purpose within organizations and societies.

☐ NOTES

1. *The Art of War*, for example, is widely cited in popular culture, including the movies and programmes *Wall Street*, *The Sopranos*, and a movie and video game of the same title.
2. A fourth form of knowledge identified by Aristotle was that of '*theoria*' (contemplation), although, as indicated by Case and Gosling (2009), this is seldom mentioned in contemporary accounts of management and leadership.
3. Further details on these, and other models described in this chapter, are available in many leadership and organizational behaviour textbooks, as well as online resources such as Wikipedia and businessballs.com
4. Drawing on Rittell and Webber's typology (1973) of tame and wicked problems, in which a 'tame' problem is one that is relatively contained and that has been encountered before (and hence we can apply previous knowledge, or some sort of rational process, to address) and a 'wicked' problem is one we have not previously encountered and which, to many extents, can be considered as intractable. A 'critical' problem is described as one that is time-sensitive and which demands a rapid and decisive response even if insufficient time is available for a thorough analysis of the situation.

3 Individual Perspectives on Leadership

This chapter offers a review of thinking within the field of leadership in relation to the leader as an individual. It explores the role of the leader's personality, behavioural styles, and identity, as well as looking at the leader as a (potentially) emotional, authentic, storytelling being. The overarching argument presented here is that while lists abound of traits, behaviours, and styles which we associate with 'leaders', perhaps leader*ship* itself must be considered more broadly (Grint, 2005a). Indeed, as indicated in the previous chapter, recent developments in Leadership Studies focus less on the characteristics and behaviours of leaders, and more on the emergent, interactive, and localized interactions through which we can influence others and create meaningful change.

Nonetheless, the concept of the omnipotent, 'heroic leader' remains a very powerful one, embedded in our everyday thinking about what leadership means to us. Regardless of their context or relationships with others, individuals in power are expected to 'demonstrate' leadership, to enact – and be seen to be enacting – those traits, skills, and behaviours which are thought to result in positive change. In this chapter, we lay out – and question – some of the ways in which leadership has been thought to reside within the individual, starting with the assumption that personality can determine leadership potential.

Leadership and Personality: What are Leaders LIKE?

How many times have you heard the phrase 'a born leader'? As Chapter 2 indicated, it is commonly assumed that some people are born with personality traits likely to make them better leaders. The trait theory of leadership draws on exactly this assumption. During the twentieth century, many theorists including Mann (1959), Stogdill (1974), and Kirkpatrick and Locke (1991) tried to establish a definitive list of these traits, leading to an ever-increasing number of competing frameworks for leadership, listing such a vast array of traits that it would be impossible to find them all in one single person.

Nonetheless, the idea that leaders have similar personality traits is intuitively appealing. If you ask yourself the question '*what are leaders LIKE?*', you might find yourself answering by listing some of those traits identified by this research, such as extroversion, intelligence, stability, dominance, and creativity. You might also be able to list the names of leaders you consider to possess these traits (Richard Branson? Barack Obama? Lord Alan Sugar? Tony Blair?).

It is apparent that the leaders who form part of our everyday consciousness are often those who display these 'leadership' characteristics. Yet there are plenty of other people in leadership positions, who do not display these characteristics so openly. We could point to Microsoft mogul Bill Gates or ex-Prime Minster Gordon Brown as possible examples from within this group. Perhaps these leaders are not foremost in our consciousness because they do not enact leadership in line with Western assumptions about *'what leaders are like'* (Grint, 2005a). This line of thinking would suggest that what constitutes a 'true leader' is influenced by our cultural norms and conventions – in particular, a Westernized preoccupation for the heroic. Certainly, the personality characteristics identified by Mann (1959), Stogdill (1974), and Kirkpatrick and Locke (1991) are less aligned with Eastern perspectives on leadership, which favour relationality, participation, servitude, and guidance (see e.g. Prince, 2005).

Despite the lack of any definitive list of leadership traits, and the exhaustive number of traits themselves, the concept that leaders are 'born' continues to influence organizational practice, as a way of categorizing and measuring an individual's potential. The longevity, breadth, and sheer number of studies into leadership traits suggests that personality does have a role to play in influencing who becomes a leader, and who does not (Northouse, 2004). People in organizations continue to be assessed as to their psychological personality traits in the form of psychometric testing, an increasingly common part of managerial selection processes. The leadership trait theory is an important one then, because it offers a way to 'benchmark' individuals and to predict success in leadership roles.

Psychometric tests often aim to display the extent to which an individual possesses qualities purportedly associated with successful leadership. Ladkin (2005) divides psychometric tests into two categories. First, there are *preference-based* tests which acknowledge that individuals can choose from a range of possible ways of behaving, but which seek to assess their preferred types of behaviour within this range. These tests do not suggest that there are 'right' and 'wrong' ways of behaving, simply that individuals have preferences as to the kind of behaviour that feels 'right' for them.

Two of the most well-known preference-based psychometrics are Honey and Mumford's *Learning Style Indicator* (1982) and the *Myers-Briggs Type Indicator* or MBTI (Myers and McCaulley, 1985). This latter example was based upon Jung's psychological functions (1923): sensing; intuition; thinking; and feeling. For example, as part of the MBTI, individuals are tested to find out whether they tend to show a preference for making decisions by 'thinking' or 'feeling'. While these tests appear 'scientific', they can be shown to have their roots in 'unscientific' beliefs or assumptions. For example, Case and Phillipson (2004) trace the roots of the MBTI back through Jung's four psychological functions (1923), to show how Jung's model was informed by his interest in alchemy and astrology: two disciplines which would certainly not be considered 'modern' or 'scientific' today! Drawing on Latour's argument (1993) that *we have never been modern*, Case and Phillipson use this example to demonstrate that the instruments we use to classify and measure people in organizations today might be considered 'neutral' or 'objective', but are often developed out of assumptions which date back to the premodern.

The second type of psychometric test aims to measure an individual's *underlying personality traits*. Classifying individuals in this way dates back once again many hundreds of years, to ancient Greek times, when the temperament of individuals was thought to belong to one of four 'humours': phlegmatic; sanguine; melancholic; and choleric (Zuckerman, 1998). In more recent times, Eysenck and Eysenck (1975) demonstrated that this model could be related to combinations of psychological dimensions. They developed the Eysenck Personality Questionnaire (EPQ), which seeks to measure individuals across three dimensions: extraversion (E); neuroticism (N); and psychoticism (P) (Barrett et al., 1998).

Other tests adopt a similar approach to measuring personality traits, including the 'Big Five' personality factor test which focuses on the extent to which individuals possess traits of openness, extraversion, conscientiousness, agreeableness, and neuroticism (Goldberg, 1990). Research has been conducted which suggests that this test can act as a predictor of transformational leadership potential (Judge and Bono, 2000) and career success (Seibert and Kraimer, 2001). An additional model, the 16 Personality Factor Inventory (16PF), was developed by Cattell (Cattell and Mead, 2008) in an attempt to categorize people according to sixteen core factors and their opposites, such as 'shy; uninhibited and reserved; outgoing'.

As Ladkin (2005) suggests, such tests make some important assumptions. It is assumed that personality traits can be identified, categorized, and measured accurately. Indeed, both personality factor tests and preference-based tests make the assumption that individuals are able to make a reasonably accurate judgement about their personality. Furthermore, they assume that an individual's personality remains stable and distinct regardless of the situation they are placed in. These assumptions themselves are the source of much debate in the literature on psychometrics. Debate centres not just on the assumptions embedded within the tests but also on how the tests are implemented – for example, the extent to which psychometric tests should only be administered and interpreted by experts, and the results monitored against individuals' future performance to ensure accurate results. Cooper and Baker (1995) claim that many organizations fail to adequately monitor their psychometric testing processes, such that they offer limited insights into the relationship between personality and performance.

Other critiques of psychometric tests often question the extent to which our identities are constant, or stable enough, to be adequately measured. Sociological definitions of 'self' suggest that our sense of self is much more fluid; our identities are thought to emerge as we progress through the relationships, interactions, and contexts that characterize our lives, rather than existing independently (e.g. Gergen, 1999 a, b). If this is the case, it would be meaningless to measure personality traits in an individual as if they were fixed essences, when in fact they are likely to be in a state of constant flux.

Haslam's social identity approach (2004, also discussed later in this chapter) suggests that psychometric tests which assume a stable, fixed personality might be flawed, because our identities are in part constructed through membership of social groups. Attempting to predict leadership potential by examining individual characteristics is questionable because these characteristics change over time and as a result of changing group memberships. Haslam refers to the Hawthorne Studies, a series of investigations conducted in a Western Electric factory in Chicago in the 1920s and 1930s, which tested the impact of group membership on productivity and motivation among factory workers. Groups of women employees were isolated from the rest of the workforce and were observed as they worked while experimenters changed various aspects of their workplace environment, such as lighting, heating, and the length of rest periods and working days. The researchers discovered that output, attendance, and job satisfaction were in fact more strongly influenced by the groups' relationships and establishment of in-group norms than by the changes to other aspects of the women's work. These experiments demonstrated that employees' attitudes to work, motivation, and productivity are not solely the result of their individual personalities, but are affected by group norms and regulated by other group members. Haslam's citation of Mayo (1949: 99 in Haslam 2004: 11), a key figure from the Hawthorne studies, points to the challenges of using individual assessment techniques to predict leadership potential or any other kind of behaviour at work: 'The belief that the behaviour of an individual within the factory can be predicted before employment on the basis of a laborious and minute examination of his technical and other capacities is mainly, if not wholly, mistaken'.

Despite a burgeoning literature describing alternative ways of conceptualizing leadership, and some criticism of the value of psychometric tests as a way of identifying and assessing leaders, it is clear that most organizations continue to place some emphasis on the existence of 'leadership traits' as a way of determining 'leadership potential'. Yet the trait theory has some other drawbacks. If personality traits are thought to be unlikely to change, the assumption that leaders are 'born' offers little scope for leadership development and training. This has led to a strand of thinking about leadership which focuses on the *actions and behaviours* of leaders, as opposed to the inherent personality characteristics.

Leadership Styles and Behaviours: What do Leaders DO?

Locating leadership within the leader as an individual requires us to consider not just the personality characteristics of leaders but also the appropriate behaviours and *ways of leading* demanded of leaders. When debating leadership styles and behaviours, instead of asking '*what are leaders LIKE?*', we are asking the question '*what do leaders DO?*'.

This change in focus stems from the late 1940s, following a shift in the notion of what could be achieved through research into leadership. As Parry and Bryman (2006) point out, the trait theory points out the kinds of people likely to become leaders. In comparison, the style theories aimed to identify what kind of behaviours we should look for when selecting the leaders of the future.

Chapter 2 of this book offered a description of some of the key style theories of leadership, including McGregor's Theory X/Theory Y (1960), and Blake and Mouton's managerial grid (1964). These theories suggest that leaders' actions are the result of the assumptions they make about how followers need to be led. Theory X managers, for example, assume that followers require discipline, and direction, leading to an autocratic leadership style, whereas Theory Y managers assume that followers must be facilitated and given responsibility leading to a more democratic leadership style (McGregor, 1960).

As our understanding of leadership has developed through the latter part of the twentieth century, perceptions of desirable leadership style have also evolved. As has been explored more fully in Chapter 2, charismatic and trans-formational leaders are said to be a catalyst for creating powerful social and organizational change. But how do they do this? What actions are required of them to unite followers in this way? Several attempts have been made to pin down the charismatic leadership style. Conger and Kanungo (1987), for instance, argue that charismatic leadership is characterized by a 'constellation of behavioural components' (p. 640) including:

- articulating and striving to change the status quo,
- acting as a role model for the set of values and beliefs to be shared by the group,
- willingness to incur significant personal cost to achieve a goal,
- encouraging the development of followers so that they share the desire for change.

Senge's influential work (1990) on the 'learning organization' also had new implications for how leaders DO leadership. Senge argued that organizations had to accept a non-linear, more holistic approach to change, and that this alternative approach to learning must take place at all levels and through all relationships in the organization. Senge's view was that 'the leader's task is designing the learning process' (Senge, 1990: 345). He drew, like the charismatic leadership theorists, on the importance of building a shared vision and encouraging all members of an organization to pursue its values. To accomplish this, he proposed three new leadership styles:

1. *The designer* – in which the leader shapes the 'policies, strategies and systems' (Ibid.: 342), which facilitate the functioning of the organization itself. This requires more than ad hoc alterations to existing operations. Instead, designers are expected to have an understanding of how the organization operates as a whole – starting with intangible aspects, like its values and purpose. These are the tools used by members of an organization which help them respond to the challenges they face.

2. *The steward* – in which the leader must take responsibility for guiding the vision shared by members of an organization. To achieve this, Senge suggested that the leader must be able to craft a narrative about the organization's purpose which is intensely personal to him or her. He argued that listening to others' visions is an important part of this narrative building, because by learning from and incorporating these different perspectives, the vision can act as a 'calling', through which the goals of an organization's members transcend their self-interest.

3. *The teacher* – in which the leader must empower others to acquire a better understanding of the events, behavioural patterns, structures, and vision which make up their organizational reality. In this way, leaders can teach others how to make sense of how and why change happens. Fostering this kind of understanding requires a leader to show other members of the organization how to challenge their assumptions regarding their own practice, and those of others.

Senge's metaphors for the leader's role are appealing on many levels – they represent an alternative to the 'great man theory' in that they offer a less heroic, more humble way of 'doing leadership'. Nonetheless, there are some practical limitations. Can you think of a leader who exhibits all these behaviours? Once again, it seems impossible that any one leader could exhibit all these tendencies! It soon becomes clear that the literature on leadership behaviours and styles offers as many competing frameworks as does the trait theory scholarship. Nonetheless, these lists of styles and behaviours remain attractive as a way of understanding leadership, due to their practical applications within leadership development. The enduring popularity and growing number of style/behavioural leadership theories owes much to the assumption that, unlike traits, actions, behaviours, and styles can be *learnt* by individuals who step into leadership positions. Leaders are able to measure their abilities against the frameworks set up by theorists like Blake and Mouton (1964) in order to assess their leadership style, and identify the areas in which they need training.

However, similarly to the competing frameworks for leadership traits, leadership style theorists have been unable to come up with a universally applicable model which sets out the leadership styles required in every situation. Put simply, this is why so many models and frameworks of leadership styles exist! Furthermore, as with trait theory, the link to performance is far from proven. There is little evidence that leaders' behaviour, characterized as concern for task or relationships, can impact positively on employee morale or productivity (Northouse, 2004).

While this section has outlined an important difference between theories relating to leadership traits and leadership styles, both the style and trait approaches make two tacit assumptions, both of which stem from the emphasis on the *leader* as the locus of leadership practice.

The first assumption is that, whether we talk about the style or the personality of a leader, trait and style theories are *normative* approaches to leadership, which attempt to describe – or even prescribe – the 'best way' to lead. Very little attention is paid to the influence of context on the style or personality required by a leader. And yet, in different contexts, we might witness very different but equally effective leadership styles. For example, in contexts which demand urgent decision-making, like a battlefield or an operating theatre, we might expect (though not exclusively) a more top-down, autocratic leadership style, whereas within the creative media and advertising industries, a more participatory, consultative leadership style is often employed. Examples like this tell us that leadership is multifaceted and that perhaps there is, after all, no 'one best way' to behave as a leader. This has led to the rise of situational leadership theories (e.g. Hersey and Blanchard, 1993), which are equally prescriptive, but have attempted to set out which leadership styles are most appropriate for different contexts.

The second assumption made by both style and trait theories is that little attention is paid to *followers* in the practice of leadership. The style and behavioural approaches to leadership therefore assume that followers are passive recipients of leadership, who do not actively participate, but who must be simply guided towards a particular goal. Under the style and trait theories, leadership is something which is created solely by leaders and simply absorbed or responded to by followers. The danger is that style and trait theories place the success, or failure of leadership, solely at the hands of the leader. Mintzberg (1999) makes this clear when he rounds on Fortune Magazine's declaration (1998 in Ibid.: 26) that 'within four years, Lou Gerstner added more than $40bn to IBM's shareholder value'. Mintzberg points out the senselessness of this statement, asking: 'Every penny of it? Nothing from the hundreds of thousands of other IBM employees . . . no contribution from luck . . . Just Gerstner.'

According to the trait and style leadership perspectives, if the leader possesses the correct personality traits, or displays the correct behaviours, leadership will be successful regardless of surrounding contextual factors, or how followers behave. Yet we know that leadership does not happen in a vacuum. Successful leaders do not all act the same way or possess the same characteristics. Equally, sometimes, leaders who outwardly display all the characteristics or enact all the behaviours expected of them, fail to lead their community, organization, or team to success.

Our critique of trait and style approaches is therefore twofold. First, we have questioned the assumption that there can be a 'best person' or 'best style' of leading, which works across all contexts and for all leaders. Second, we question the assumption that leadership is located solely within the individual 'leader'. Many of the debates we discuss in this book explore the possibility that leadership extends beyond the leader, to encompass those practices, relationships, and interconnectivities within a wider network of 'leaderful activity' (Raelin, 2003). Focusing solely on the leader's attributes is a synecdoche approach to studying leadership, whereby the 'whole' of leadership (the interactions and relationships with followers and other group members; the cultural, social, and economic context; and so on) comes to be represented by a single 'part' (the individual leader).

Studying leadership, then, is concerned with more than the two questions asked here so far: 'what are leaders like?' and 'what do leaders do?' Yet the leader as an individual is an enduring part of our social reality: we recognize leaders as having a vital role in the dialogues through which groups come to be influenced. It would be hard to deny that some people are undoubtedly more capable and/or committed to achieving particular outcomes than others. Does this mean that, to a certain degree, the trait approach is correct?

The next question we ask in this chapter is '*how* do leaders do what they do?' This involves looking at how leaders maintain their identity in a group, and how this relates to the regulation of the group identity as a whole.

In the next section, therefore, we turn our attention to some of the debates surrounding leadership and identity. While trait theories of leadership assume that the 'self' is relatively stable and measurable over time, other theories of identity are grounded in very different ideas about how our identities are produced and maintained. Looking at leadership by focusing on the individual requires us to turn to these theories now, to explore how leaders enact an identity which is meaningful to followers, and which in itself is a certain '*leadership of the self*'.

Leadership and Identity: Who do you Think you are?

People tend to make sense of their world and the others in it by assigning individuals into social categories, such as class, age, and gender, and by associating individuals belonging to these categories with certain characteristics (Tajfel and Turner, 1979). An individual's sense of self-image, or identity, is informed by their membership of these groups (Sveningsson and Larsson, 2006). As we have pointed out, a 'leader' is a recognizable identity in that everyone has an idea of what it means to be a 'leader'. Often this meaning is linked to the traits and actions previously discussed in this chapter.

The psychological concept of 'social identity' is the foundation of an increasingly influential approach to Leadership Studies (see e.g. Haslam, 2004, Haslam et al., 2010). Social identity, conceptualized by Tajfel (1974), is an individual's recognition that he or she is a member of a certain social group, to which he or she attaches some emotional significance. Each group derives a sense of collective identity by self-evaluating the properties of their own group, in relation to its perception of the characteristics of other groups. By positioning the group of which they are a member against 'other' groups, individuals collaborate in creating a *social reality*, a methodology for thinking, being, and doing, based on group norms and perceptions.

Developed through this perspective, leadership is seen as a form of group-based agency which is made possible through the a priori existence of a shared sense of identity within a group (Reicher et al., 2005). Leaders are thought to emerge within a group because they possess the defining features, known as prototypical characteristics, associated with that group. Thus, Hogg (2001: 186) argues that 'being a prototypical ingroup member may be at least as important for leadership as being charismatic or having . . . characteristics of a particular type . . . of leader'.

It is assumed that prototypical group members are more likely to put forward suggestions for action which are commensurate with the groups' values and critical attributes (Hogg 2001; Reicher et al., 2005), and which are therefore accepted as part of the desired course of action for the group as a whole.

As Reicher et al. (2005: 549) point out, this means that leadership is not a '*zero sum game*' in which leaders are 'agents' and followers are passive recipients of this agency. Rather, leadership emerges from the interrelationships between group members, which give priority to the proposals suggested by prototypical group members, and which construct a social reality through which some proposals for action are mobilized, and some are rejected or foreclosed. In this way, though, leaders are able to influence the construction and transformation of their own, and their followers' identities. A social identity perspective therefore sees leaders as '*entrepreneurs of identity*' (Ibid.: 557).

Additionally, leaders give legitimacy to their proposals, and to their in-group status, by ensuring the construction of material structures which promote the social identity of the group and give it a concrete existence. Reicher et al. (2005) offer as an example of emergent leadership, a 'prisoner' within the *BBC Prison Study*, an experiment in which research participants were assigned to a high-status 'guard' or low-status 'prisoner' identity within a closed environment set up as a 'prison' for eight days. The authors describe how one 'prisoner' set up a forum to promote the shared goals of his fellow inmates and challenge the directors of the experiment. This is an instance of how a leader emerged from an in-group by constructing a shared sense of identity within the group (that of 'prisoners') and establishing this identity in opposition to another group ('those running the experiment'). Setting up a forum to promote quality of life among the 'prisoners' legitimized the group's shared identity by giving it a material structure, and enabled him to mobilize the group effectively to support their shared goals.

Social identity theorists point out that leadership is not an individual process but evolves out of group dynamics. For leadership to happen at all, however, the social identity approach assumes the pre-existence of a shared sense of identity. The theory is based upon a notion of identity in which individuals are thought to possess relatively stable characteristics (similar to traits) which allow them to categorize themselves into groups, and distinguish themselves from others (Tajfel and Turner, 1979). However, the field of Leadership Studies has also been influenced by other, more fluid ways of characterizing identity, which are drawn from sociological and poststructuralist, as opposed to psychological, positions.

BECOMING LEADERS: A PROCESSUAL ACCOUNT OF LEADER IDENTITY

A fluid account of identity within leadership questions to what extent leaders: (*a*) can make sovereign choices, since their ideas are the product of a myriad of competing discourses embedded in power relations; and (*b*) are controlled within organizations by the leader identity they aspire to.

Authors such as Alvesson (1994) argue that we cannot assume the self is fixed and stable, or derived from some interior 'essence'. Rather, maintaining a stable sense of identity is a *process* in which we actively engage throughout everyday life. 'Fixing' our identity by categorizing ourselves and others into social groups helps to reduce anxiety about who we are, where we belong, and how we should behave in the world (Ibid.; Collinson, 2003). Our everyday choices such as what to wear, what kind of music to listen to, or how to interact with others are part of this 'identity work', described by Ashforth (1998) as a process of 'becoming'.

As well as supporting a more fluid view of identity, this perspective differs from the social identity theory perspective in its characterization of power. It draws on a field of literature which argues that selves are constructed (but not determined) through the disciplinary effects of discourses. Discourses are webs of assumptions that set out the ways of thinking, being, and doing that are available to us, while foreclosing alternative possibilities (Foucault, 2002). Conceptions of self are not, therefore, freely 'chosen' by individuals, but result from the power relations which are inscribed in these discourses.

Identity work, then, is the active process of constructing a self-identity which forms a reasonably stable basis for engaging in social relationships (Alvesson, 1994). Identities are never fully secure, but always in progress, actively being made, shored up, and remade during our everyday interactions, as we seek to reassure ourselves *'who we are, and what do we stand for?'* (Sveningsson and Alvesson, 2003: 1164). Given the importance of work in many people's lives, it is unsurprising that job roles such as teacher, secretary, or even 'leader' are identifying categories which form part of the basis for our identity work. A processual account of identity would suggest that by engaging in leadership, individuals are also engaging in identity work, fixing and stabilizing their identity as 'leaders' and struggling to come to terms with competing and inconsistent representations of who they are.

The identity of 'leader' offers the potential for individuals to secure their sense of self, and reduce feelings of tension, by becoming a member of a recognizable social group. However, like any other identity, the leader identity must be constantly striven for, and, being constantly in progress, can never be fully achieved, and therefore is a source of continuing anxiety. Individuals must constantly seek to validate themselves by demonstrating successful leadership, and constantly reflect upon their own ability to adhere to their desired notions of self (Knights and Willmott, 1999). One of the key tenets of this perspective on identity is the struggle individuals face as they negotiate the fragmented, conflicting identities which make up their experiences of work. Sveningsson and Alvesson (2003: 1165) point out that identity work is 'a process in which individuals create several more or less contradictory and often changing managerial identities (identity positions) rather than one stable, continuous and secure manager identity'.

It has already been pointed out in this chapter and elsewhere (e.g. Grint, 2005a) that so many conflicting and competing leadership traits exist that it would be very difficult to find anyone who could embody them all. How easy can it be to constantly measure oneself against such an impossible ideal? (see Jepson and Edwards, 2009). Thornborrow and Brown (2009) use the term 'aspirational identity' to describe how paratroopers constantly strive to embody the ideals of what it means to be part of this elite fighting unit. This ambiguity (the need to shore up one's sense of self, by striving to attain an unachievable norm) means that aspirants are trapped by a somewhat 'illusory goal' (Collinson, 2003: 533).

The constant need to verify oneself by aspiring to become a 'better' leader, or to better demonstrate 'leadership potential', means that the leader identity acts as a form of organizational control which seeks to normalize behaviour among employees seeking to impress senior managers and encourages self-regulation. Sveningsson and Larsson's study (2006), for example, explored how a middle manager positioned himself in relation to the discourses about 'doing leadership' embedded in a corporate culture programme set up by senior managers. They suggest that enacting these discourses was, for this manager, a way of engaging with a fantasy about 'being a leader' which tied in with his own aspirations.

The idea that individuals may strive to enact a more 'authentic' leadership identity is gaining increasing attention. Luthans and Avolio's theory (2003) of 'authentic' leadership, for example, suggests that individuals must develop an awareness of their fundamental values and purpose, which can act as a moral compass, and which can *'positively transform or develop associates into leaders themselves'* (Ibid.: 243). The assumptions behind the concept of 'authentic leadership' are discussed below.

Keeping it Real: The Implications of Authentic Leadership

Authentic leadership has been promoted as a way of overcoming the crises of confidence in leadership practice that have resulted from ethical and financial organizational breakdowns, as happened at Enron (George, 2003), Lehman Brothers, and the Royal Bank of Scotland. It draws on similar assumptions as the social identity approach to leadership, arguing that leaders gain credibility in the eyes of their followers by acting as role models for a social group. This credibility, however, is drawn not from 'developing the persona of a leader', but rather, by 'being yourself; being the person you were created to be' (Ibid.: 11).

Proponents of authentic leadership argue that to enact the kind of moral integrity required by followers, leaders must identify and clarify their personal values and sense of purpose which serve as a framework for action (Kouzes and Posner, 2002; George, 2003; Luthans and Avolio, 2003). Aligning behaviour with personal values, and constantly self-monitoring to ensure consistency, results in a transparency of moral outlook that will inspire followers, first, to have confidence in a leader's ability and motives (Kouzes and Posner, 2002) and second, to develop authenticity in their own actions (Luthans and Avolio, 2003).

As Sparrowe (2005) points out, authentic leadership is framed around four key assumptions. These are first, that self-awareness is key to developing an authentic self (George, 2003). In order to understand our true self, we must look inwards. This proposal is predicated upon the assumption that an 'inner self' exists, drawing on a more essentialist view of self, as opposed to a notion of self as constituted through relationships with others.

Related to this is the second assumption, that the authentic self is relatively stable and enduring. Authentic leadership recognizes the importance of developing self-awareness, meaning that leadership can indeed be learnt, but nonetheless as Sparrowe suggests (2005: 422):

Constancy in the core self is necessary to anchor self-regulatory processes so that leaders are transparent, that is, to insure their behaviours are consistent with their true selves. If the leader's true self is constantly changing, followers will be hard pressed to differentiate what is consistent with a changing true self from what is garden variety flip-flopping.

Third, it follows that authentic leadership is predicated upon 'self-regulation' which ensures that actions are commensurate with inner values (Ibid.; Luthans and Avolio, 2003). This is important to allow consistency in the leaders' behaviour, thought to encourage trust amongst followers. As Avolio et al. (2004) indicate though, little attention has been given to *how* authentic leaders diffuse their values and ideals across members of a group to impact on followers at the levels of attitudes and action.

The final assumption underpinning authentic leadership is its normative character. Authentic leadership is a prescriptive approach, associated with morality and ethical action. In contrast, *inauthentic* leadership is framed by a narcissistic self-interest which leads individuals to 'treat followers as means to their own ends' (Sparrowe, 2005: 423). Sparrowe argues though that the need to look inwards to find authenticity means that authentic leadership is itself based on a kind of narcissism (a concept discussed in greater detail later in this chapter).

By highlighting these four assumptions, Sparrowe points out some of the limitations of the authentic leadership rhetoric, including the idea that individuals have pre-existing, static 'essences' or inner selves, which can be accessed through self-evaluation. As such, authentic leadership locates the practice of leadership solely within the individual leader, who remains distinct from context and uninfluenced by followers.

Authentic leadership asks leaders to act out consistent, internally derived morals in line with a 'higher purpose'. It bears a resemblance to the ideals encapsulated within servant leadership, as discussed in Chapter 2. With its focus on self-regulation, it also has much in common with the 'aspirational leadership identity' critiqued by Jepson and Edwards (2009), which can serve as a powerful mechanism for the control of individuals in organizations. And yet, as these authors point out, aspirational identities are impossible to achieve, entrapping subjects within a vicious circle as they struggle to enact an unachievable norm.

The struggle to enact an unachievable authenticity bears resemblance to Butler's notion (1990) of performativity – whereby subjects maintain their selves by repeatedly calling into being or 'citing' norms associated with a particular identity. On these grounds, authentic leadership is said to be grounded not in an inner, moralistic self, but is invoked through a series of repeated acts and utterances. Leaders enact on the surface, through actions and speech, an illusion of authenticity, a performance of an authentic inner self-grounded in pre-existing values and morals. Authenticity is never fully achieved, so that leaders must continue to discipline their performances, making sure they cite the norms and values which followers will associate with authentic leadership.

Looking at authentic leadership as a mechanism for disciplining the self in line with discourses about 'authenticity' implies that followers also play an active part in leadership. By interpreting and judging the enactments of leaders, they ensure that leaders constantly monitor their own performances of authenticity. Similarly, Sparrowe (2005) argues that authentic leadership must be viewed from a relational perspective, drawing on the concept of the 'narrative self' (Ricoeur, 1992).

He suggests that leaders develop a narrative of the self which justifies leadership actions by relating them to a set of morals, and which is interpreted or 'read' by followers. The consistency of the narrative, as opposed to the leader's core beliefs and inner self, is what matters to followers and what inspires their dedication and commitment. By employing the narrative approach, Sparrowe avoids making an essentialist commitment to a sovereign, static leader identity. His perspective has more in common with the 'identity work' approach taken by Alvesson (1994), Sveningsson and Larsson (2006), and Sinclair (2007), which explores how individuals shape and work on their identities, crafting a sense of self using language, relationships, and material things.

The subject of how leaders develop narratives is a recent addition to debates in the leadership field. It draws on a body of literature which explores how individuals make sense of their experiences of organizational life (e.g. Weick, 1995). In academia, as in everyday life, we often use metaphors to express different ways of looking at organizations. For example, Morgan (1986) shows us how we can look at organizations as *machines*, as *organizms*, or as *cultures*. Each of these different metaphors conveys something different about what an organization is like.

Individuals in organizations are no different from academics in their use of metaphor to help them make sense of their everyday working lives. How often have you heard someone say '*my work was chaos today!*', or '*finishing this job was a breeze!*'?

Leaders, it is argued, play an important role in developing these metaphors, using them as 'devices' or tools which have explanatory power, within what Czarniawska-Joerges (1998) terms a 'meta-device', or narrative. Creating a consistent narrative, to be drawn upon during mission statements, speeches, and organizational documentation, is a way of telling other members of the organization about their collective values, purpose, and goals. The following section is itself an exploration of a metaphor: that of leader as storyteller.

Are you Sitting Comfortably? Leaders as Storytellers

There are two ways in which we can explore leadership through the storytelling perspective. First, storytelling provides us with countless examples and 'role models' which become part of our general framework of reference for understanding leadership. Through the recounting of stories about their lives and heroic activities, leaders become legends. Their actions form part of our social reality – that is, out of their actions, we construct an account of what leadership *is*. For example, the story of Sir Francis Drake playing boules on Plymouth Hoe even after the Spanish Armada has been spotted in the English Channel remains a staple of British school education some 400 years later – a powerful reminder about the value of patience, calm, and timely intervention in leadership strategy.

Stories do not need to have a basis in reality or history for them to have an impact on how we see leadership. Individuals from books or popular culture often make their way into our social consciousness so that we associate them with particular forms of action or ways of doing things. Hawkins (2008), for example, demonstrates how teamworkers in a recruitment consultancy drew upon the heroism, agency, and entrepreneurialism embedded in Ian Fleming's iconic character James Bond. She argues that the consultants identified with *007* because these attributes of his character helped them to make sense of the individualistic, capitalist, action-oriented aspects of their sales work.

Second, as Sparrowe (2005) outlines, a narrative approach to leadership suggests that leaders act as storytellers, or narrators, of organizational events. As Collinson (2003) has pointed out, life in organizations can be fraught with uncertainty and insecurity, as individuals negotiate the competing discourses and assumptions in which they are embedded. The narrative perspective on leadership owes much to this line of thinking, whereby individuals seek to secure their fragile identities by embodying a particular framework of values.

The use of narratives implies a kind of creativity or artfulness on the part of the leader, who harnesses relevant characters, plots, and events to give meaning to a particular situation. Grint (2001) argues that despite the existence of countless analytical 'models' of leadership, the *practice* of leadership itself bears closer resemblance to the arts than to the sciences. He links the art of leadership to the practice of sensemaking as theorized by Weick (1995), in which individuals attribute meanings to complex situations by making sense of them through '*language, talk and communication*' (Weick et al., 2005: 409), to construct their own interpretation of reality. By composing a particular narrative, leaders hope to channel the sensemaking abilities of members of an organization so that they are anchored to a particular course of action, or set of rules and values.

Under the storytelling approach to leadership, then, the creation of a narrative may help leaders to reduce uncertainty and ambiguity in an organization, and offer a guide to organizational values. The leader's role is to formulate, edit, and convey a consistent way of thinking about the organization and its purpose, which individuals can relate to and draw upon as a framework for action (Czarniawska-Joerges, 1998). The narrative becomes part of the sensemaking processes engaged in by those individuals at work (Weick, 1995).

Organizational narratives are constructed partly through language, in the form of metaphors and rhetoric, and also make full use of leaders' physicality, as well as material 'props'. They convey important messages about the kind of behaviour which is appropriate from the members of a community, team, or organization. As Denning suggests (2001), leaders can use stories to varying effect. For example, the parables Jesus told in the Bible were used to transmit the values associated with Christianity, such as being a 'good Samaritan'.

Alternatively, narratives are often employed to incite individuals to action. Helen Mirren's performance of Elizabeth I's speech at Tilbury Docks is a great film example of how a leader can construct a narrative which aims to unite followers around a shared experience. Standing on a platform in front of her soldiers, Elizabeth enacts her identity as queen through *language*, describing herself as a '*weak and feeble woman*' [with] '*the heart and stomach of a king*', who is prepared to stand in solidarity on the battlefield with soldiers. By emphasizing her femininity – also foregrounded by her physical presence and 'difference' from the male soldiers who surround her – she highlights the extraordinariness of her courage, and so incites loyalty, protectiveness, and valour in her followers. While speaking, Elizabeth steps from the platform onto the battlefield and walks amongst the ranks. In so doing, she reinforces her call to solidarity by removing the *physical* hierarchy that existed between herself and her men.

The use of narratives to unite and inspire followers as Elizabeth I does, above, is incorporated into theories of charismatic, or transformational, leadership. As has been pointed out in Chapter 2, transformational leadership differs from transactional leadership in that it acts to change not only followers' behaviour but their *identity* too. Conveying the importance of a shared identity centred on a common purpose is another role of leadership narratives. For example, part of Barack Obama's appeal during the 2008 US presidential campaign was his ability to create a narrative which gave many members of the United States electorate a greater confidence in their ability to create change. This came at a time where many Americans were experiencing a crisis of confidence, fuelled by the perceived threats of international terror-ism and a faltering economy. Obama is a clear example of the storytelling leader. His own story, as the first black United States president, as well as the powerful rhetoric he uses in his speeches, inspired in the electorate feelings of optimism, empowerment, and unity. These values were typified by his 2008 election campaign slogan '*Yes, we can*'.

Within organizations, leaders' narratives often form part of a wider initia-tive to develop a 'strong' corporate culture (Peters and Waterman, 1982), using rituals, rites, and symbols which epitomize the organization's values. Rosen (1985) describes an advertising company's ritual yearly 'staff breakfast', which was followed by a speech given by the organization's leader, who sat at a top table with other directors. The ritual served to legitimize and reproduce existing organizational hierarchies. By emphasizing or prioritizing certain values as being central to an organization, narratives can make some courses of action seem 'natural' or legitimate, and foreclose alternative approaches. As Mumby (1987) points out, narratives therefore can serve an ideological function, reproducing and/or challenging existing power relationships.

As with all leadership theories which focus solely on the actions of the leader, though, the storytelling perspective assumes a certain sovereignty on the part of the leader. Either leadership stories are passively absorbed by the followers who are the recipients of the story, or the narrator has an almost exclusive control over how the story will be 'read' by followers. Admiral Lord Nelson, the naval commander who led the English fleet to victory against Napoleon at the battle of Trafalgar, is a prime example of a leader who actively 'managed' the stories which were told about his exploits (Jones and Gosling, 2005). Perhaps no leader in the world can do without a good spin doctor! Yet today, in the face of 24-hour rolling news channels, would this 'manufacturing' of a legend be quite so simple? Recent televised coverage of events in the English and French camps, at the 2010 South Africa Football World Cup, showing players rejecting the demands of their managers, might suggest otherwise.

It seems that modern-day storytelling is not the product of one individual; it is a collaborative, reciprocal, social process. Stories are not only *told*: they are listened to, interpreted, and recounted by others. The effect a story will have clearly depends on how it is interpreted. Therefore, a leader cannot be certain that the meaning given to a particular narrative is the one which was intended – indeed, individuals will associate their own meanings, developed from their own sources of experience, with the narrative. To this end, stories can be reproduced, reinterpreted, remade, or challenged by alternative 'counter-narratives'.

Additionally, the stories told by a leader will certainly not be the only narrative to which workers are exposed. Sensemaking is a collaborative process, engaged in as workers share their own unique stories about – and argue about – their experiences of work. This means that the process of storytelling is not unique only to leaders. Telling stories about key events, whether through formal presentations, or through informal 'water-cooler' chat, is central to the way we interact at work more generally (Watson, 2000). We encounter dozens of fragmented, conflicting narratives in our working lives which we have to negotiate, and use to give meaning to our workplace relationships. This means that stories do not just have the power to induce commitment to a particular leader or organizational message. Stories are often a source of resistance for dissident or disengaged individuals within an organization.

Leading from the Heart? Leadership and Emotions

Many leadership theories relating to skills and behaviours were developed at a time when organizations were assumed to be rational, bureaucratic places. It was thought that ideally, emotions had no place in decision-making and that emotionality should remain in the 'private', or domestic, sphere. In his theory of scientific management, for example, Fredrick Taylor (1911) aimed to rationalize the work process by standardizing and fragmenting production into separate actions. Under this approach, emotionality was seen as irrational, unnecessary, and as a threat to the standardization of work outputs. While the Human Relations Theorists (e.g. Mayo, 1960) attempted to acknowledge the social aspects of work and explored some of the implications of group relationships on work processes, they continued to view emotions as something which should be managed and contained, rather than harnessed or valued. However, during the later decades of the twentieth century, organization theorists began to question the assumption that emotion could be so wholly removed from public life. As Hancock and Tyler (2001: 128) write:

Emotions represent a juncture between organization and the most personal realms of an individual's experience. They also straddle the cognitive and corporeal aspects of our being and resist the Cartesian mind-body dualism that has dominated Western thought until recently . . .

Increasing attention is now paid to the implications of emotions for organizing. In particular, the practitioner-oriented literature on management and leadership has sought to view emotionality as a source of added value, helping to improve organizational performance. Peters and Waterman (1982), for example, called upon leaders to build 'cultures of excellence' which encouraged employees to develop an emotional bond with, or affinity for, the company and its values. Similarly, the emotionality of employees is harnessed within many organizations to improve customer services. Arlie Hochschild (1983) described how airlines encourage their flight attendants to display an appropriate emotional countenance (attractive, sympathetic, sociable) when dealing with passengers. She termed this behaviour 'emotional labour', highlighting how it involved the harnessing of what had previously been thought of as 'private' emotions for the organization's financial gain. Emotional labour is a key aspect of many forms of customer service work. Many call centres, for example, provide their employees with scripts which tell them exactly what kind of behaviour or language is expected of them as they provide 'service with a smile'.

This focus on emotion, however, is often directed at 'followers' – that is, the employees working at ground level in a customer services job. Similarly, the ability of followers to experience emotion is a key aspect of transformational leadership, which aims to harness the follower's emotions, so that they *feel* connected and committed to a shared goal. Under this approach, leadership involves managing the emotions of *others*.

Other perspectives on the links between leadership and emotionality in the workplace focus on the emotionality of the *leader*. George (2000: 1029) argues that emotions *'play a central role in the leadership process'*. The emotions of leaders have been shown to strongly influence the performance of followers. For example, groups of sales workers were shown to provide increased levels of customer service if their team leaders experienced positive moods at work (George, 1995). George (2000) therefore suggests that the experience of positive and negative emotions can be used to enhance cognitive processes and decision-making, by directing attention to pressing issues, and by helping people to choose between a variety of options (Damasio, 1994). Acknowledging the role of emotions in leadership has led writers such as Goleman et al. (2002) to suggest that a key skill required of by leaders is that of 'emotional intelligence'.

EMOTIONAL INTELLIGENCE: HOW DOES THAT MAKE YOU FEEL?

Northouse (2004: 219) writes that emotional intelligence involves: 'being aware of one's own abilities, needs and feelings, recognizing those of others, displaying trust and self-control, and responding to others in appropriate ways through well-developed interpersonal skills'.

According to the Descartian tradition which separates mind from body, emotions were traditionally thought to 'intrude' upon cognition, or rational thought. As a result, intelligence or intellectuality was thought to be at risk from 'dangerous', 'irrational' emotions. In the twentieth century, however, this line of thinking gradually began to change. As well as analytic capability (the kind of intelligence measured by IQ, 'intelligence quotient', tests), psychologists like Sternberg (1985) suggested that other modes of intelligence existed, such as practical intelligence, ('being streetwise') or creative intelligence ('thinking outside the box'), which gave us different capacities beside analytic skills.

The concept of emotional intelligence (often referred to as EQ) was first established by Salovey and Mayer (1990). They drew on the social intelligence theories of the 1920s (Thorndike and Stein, 1937), which focused on the ability of an individual to understand their social environment. Salovey and Mayer (1990) suggested that far from clouding or disturbing our analytic capability, emotions are central to our ability to make analytical decisions. Emotional intelligence skills, they argue (Mayer and Salovey, 1997), help us to:

- accurately perceive our own emotions and those of others;
- regulate our emotions and those of others;
- understand the implications of emotions in ourselves and others; and
- employ our feelings to motivate, plan for the future, and direct our attention – for example, by channelling our anxieties or feelings of confidence towards a particular goal.

The authors point out (1990) that being emotionally intelligent may well be an important part of being a mentally healthy, empathic individual. Emotional intelligence skills help people to build effective relationships and manage conflict – the implication being that emotional intelligence might be central in helping to foster a harmonious work environment. As a result, emotional intelligence became one of the buzzwords of the 1990s.

Other emotional intelligence models were established by several researchers, including Cooper and Sawaf (1998) and Dulewicz and Higgs (1999), and the term was popularized in a world bestselling book by the journalist Daniel Goleman (1995). Goleman's research (1998) of 188 international organizations suggested that emotional intelligence played a more important role than either technical skills or IQ in workplace performance. So what is it about our ability to manage our emotions, as well as those of others, that might help us to become better leaders?

Harrison and Clough (2006) argue that the importance of emotional intelligence to leadership efficacy is founded upon five key skill sets. These are:

1. *Self-awareness*: the ability to recognize your own moods and understand their effect on others.
2. *Self-regulation*: the ability to control disruptive moods and think before you act.
3. *Self-motivation*: a drive to work, which is not linked to financial compensation and which enables you to pursue goals with enthusiasm and passion.
4. *Empathy*: the skill of understanding the emotions and drives of other people and to treat people according to their emotional responses.

5. *Social skills*: the ability to manage relationships, build networks, and establish rapport with others.

George (2000) identifies similar links between emotional intelligence and leadership, identifying specific skills required by leaders including: the appraisal and expression of emotion, the use of emotion to enhance cognitive processing and decision-making, knowledge about and awareness of emotions, and the ability to manage emotions successfully. George's research is useful in that it explains how these skills fit into leadership practice. She sets out five key aspects of leadership, which she argues draw upon the four emotional intelligence skills outlined directly above. These five leadership competences are explained below:

1. *The development of collective goals and objectives*: emotional intelligence is thought to play a role in helping leaders to process the potential challenges and opportunities facing their organization. It may also help leaders to recognize the impact of emotions on their judgements, causing them to be overly optimistic or pessimistic. Leaders who are emotionally intelligent may also be able to use their ability to regulate the emotions of others, to ensure that followers are emotionally connected to the organization's vision.
2. *Instilling in others an appreciation of the importance of work activities*: emotionally intelligent leaders may be able to subtly manage the emotions of others so that followers experience positive moods when they are participating in tasks which are aligned with the organization's vision.
3. *Generating and maintaining enthusiasm, confidence, optimism, cooperation, and trust*: the ability of a leader to generate excitement requires skills in appraising the emotions of others, and anticipating alterations in mood which may arise from changes in work practices or goals. This skill, George (2000) argues, enables leaders to maintain a collective sense of commitment to a common purpose.
4. *Encouraging flexibility in decision-making and change*: leaders who score highly in emotional intelligence are considered to be better able to 'use emotional input in their decision making' (George, 2000: 1043). They are aware of their emotional state and are able to assess whether or not a particular emotion might need to be discounted during decision-making, in case it proves to be a source of error. By managing their emotions in this way, leaders are able to approach problems with more flexibility, and generate alternative solutions. Additionally, Wasielewski (1985) suggests that emotionally intelligent leaders may have improved change management skills. This is because their ability to understand, react to, and manage their followers' emotions enables them to put forward alternative situations which are commensurate with follower's affective states, and to 'sell' changes in a charismatic way which generates enthusiasm among followers.

5. *Establishing and maintaining a meaningful identity for the organization*: this chapter points out that leaders often maintain organizational commitment using narratives which draw upon cultural symbols, rites, and rituals which signal organizational values to followers. As George (2000) explains, these cultural forms aim to generate emotions and affective commitment among followers. Therefore, as Ashforth and Humphrey (1995: 111) have argued, 'symbolic management is largely dependent upon the evocation of emotion'. Being able to evoke, affective commitment in followers through the creation of corporate culture narratives is thus the final leadership skill which, George (2000) argues, draws upon emotional intelligence.

MIRROR, MIRROR: LEADERSHIP, EMOTIONS, AND NARCISSISM

The emotional intelligence literature therefore sets out a set of leadership skills which seems akin to yet another 'style' of leadership, focusing on the leader's ability to manage the emotions of self and others. However, the effectiveness of emotional intelligence for leaders has been questioned. Maccoby (2003), for example, suggests that while emotional intelligence might well be important for project managers or those who manage the operational effectiveness of people at work, visionary leadership requires different skill sets. He highlights five personality characteristics: eloquence; egotism; control; risk-taking; and aloofness, which contribute to a positive form of narcissism called *productive narcissism*. Maccoby argues that productive narcissists are more likely to have the confidence, innovation, independence, and charisma necessary to establish organizational goals and to encourage others to pursue them to fruition, but that their narcissism means they are not necessarily likely to show an awareness for the emotional drives and states of others.

Whether or not emotional intelligence is necessary for leadership is therefore still a matter of debate. Harrison and Clough (2006: 289) found that of fifteen '*leaders at the forefront of American Business*', two-thirds displayed elements of productive narcissism *and* emotional intelligence. They suggest that the real skill needed for leadership lies in being a: 'complex chameleon . . . [who is] adaptive to situations as needed. For example, they may prefer to be aloof, yet are able to demonstrate effective social skills when necessary. Conversely, they may have strong social skills, but by the nature of their role and responsibilities must isolate themselves at times to think more objectively, thus projecting a sense of aloofness' (Ibid.: 292).

What is also clear is that theories of emotional intelligence in leadership do not successfully eliminate the rational–emotional dualism on which much of Western organizational theory has traditionally been predicated. As George (2000: 1043) points out, emotional intelligence is thought to improve leadership skills in part because it allows leaders to '*discard*' emotions which might '*interfere with effective decision-making*', so that they can think more rationally and objectively. The binary categories of emotional subjectivity versus rational objectivity remain in evidence. Emotions, whether they are seen as having a positive or negative impact on decision-making, continue to be seen as 'separate' from rationality.

The Emotional Intelligence literature therefore seems to take an 'add emotions and stir' approach to leadership. Its value lies in the acknowledgement that emotions *do* play a role in leadership processes. Emotions, and sensitivity towards emotions in others, are involved in decision-making and relationship building, and in the way leaders engender commitment in their followers.

However, emotional intelligence theorists tend to engage with the leadership literature at the level of the individual, advocating a new skill set to add to the many others demanded of successful leaders. As such, the emotional intelligence perspective on leadership is predicated on the same assumptions as other skill-based theories of leadership. Once more, the relational, processual, socially constructed aspects of leadership become subsumed to the primacy of the *leader* himself or herself.

Just Another Set of Traits? Critiques of Authentic and Emotionally Intelligent Leadership

Authentic leadership and emotionally intelligent leadership contribute to debates on leadership because they place emphasis on different behaviours on the part of leaders (ethical integrity and emotional intelligence, respectively) from those encompassed in the traditional leadership models. However, they are more closely aligned with these traditional models, offering another set of leadership skills and/or attributes according to which we can judge the capabilities of our leaders, and retaining the focus on the individual leader. For example, while George (2000) describes how leaders may use their emotional intelligence skills to manage the emotional responses of others, she does not reflect on the implications of this for followers. Are they dupes who can be 'managed' by an omnipotent leader? Do they have any role in the leadership process beyond that of receptors to emotion management?

Furthermore, while 'authentic' and 'emotionally intelligent' approaches to leadership have some normative value (in telling us what leaders *should* be like) and some descriptive value (in telling us *what* they do), little research has been conducted to see *how* they do it. In other words, there remains a gap between the *knowing* and the *doing* of leadership. As Baum et al. (2008) have suggested for the work of strategy, so too is the case for leadership.

Despite decades of research and bold prescription, we do not really know all that much about how strategizing, organizing [and leading] gets done by real people in the day-to-day of real organizations. (adapted from Baum et al., 2008: 8)

We all know that we *should* be authentic and emotionally intelligent and we can probably *describe* a number of leaders who appear to exhibit these characteristics (normally the usual suspects: Mandela; Gandhi; etc.); but it remains incredibly difficult to articulate what constitutes an 'authentic' or 'emotionally intelligent' way of responding to a specific real-life situation, or the likely consequences of engaging in this way or not. Take, for example, the oft-cited question from a loved one of 'do I look good in this?' In formulating our answer, we clearly have to consider a range of factors including the person's temperament, self-confidence, ability to select an alternative item of clothing, and our relationship with them – not to mention whether or not they actually *do* look good in it! In such situations, the most 'emotionally intelligent' response may not necessarily be the most 'authentic' one (and vice versa), and the repercussions of either approach may be long term.

In order to gain a deeper and more intricate understanding of the dynamics of authentic and emotionally intelligent leadership, we need far more in-depth, qualitative case studies which can tell us how – and indeed, whether people engage – collaboratively – in their leadership endeavours.

Chapter Summary

This chapter has explored a number of approaches to leadership which focus on the leader as the central character in the leadership process. This perspective has attracted a great deal of attention within the discipline of leadership studies. Initial theories of leadership have been shown to focus on the innate characteristics of leaders, or their 'styles' of behaviour. These approaches remain popular because they are intuitively appealing and because they enable organizations to recruit and select leaders using psychometric tools like the MBTI.

The chapter has also outlined two of the newest ways of thinking about leadership: authentic leadership and emotionally intelligent leadership. These models reflect some of the shift in focus within organization theory more generally. Authentic leadership, for example, might be related to the burgeoning literature on leadership and organizational ethics, whereas the interest in emotional intelligence and leadership is grounded in the increasing acknowledgement throughout the 1990s of the interstices between emotions and organizations.

As the discipline of leadership studies gathers momentum outside the United States and takes on influences outside the field of psychology, Parry and Bryman (2006) argue that alternative, *process*-based ways of looking at leadership may come to the fore. Theories of leadership which explore the roles of storytelling and identity work in these processes of influencing are steps in this direction, because they suggest that leadership is constructed out of social interactions and shaped by context, rather than resident in one particular individual with 'special' attributes.

Theories relating to identity in organizations (e.g. Alvesson and Willmott, 2002) have the potential to examine more critically some of the implications of leadership. As this chapter has argued, the process of regulating the self is not always a positive experience. Rather, it is steeped in the power relations and underlying assumptions through which organizations set out to define what leadership *is*, and how leaders do it. Chapter 4 therefore sets out some of the implications of leadership within an organizational context.

4 Organizational Perspectives on Leadership

So far, this book has examined the development of leadership theory, with a particular focus on exploring theories and perspectives which situate leadership as the property of the individual – that is, of the leader. As we have pointed out, there are advantages and limitations in looking at leadership in this way. Understanding leadership as the property of a leader is intuitive and deeply entrenched in Western society. We hold leaders in great esteem, as people (often men) who have undertaken great acts. We often see them as the personification of these acts themselves. Yet this approach does not take into account the other variables at play – the individuals, groups, and social trends and movements that enabled that leader's endeavours to come to the fore.

In this chapter, we move on to a more contextualized perspective on leadership, as situated within the boundaries of the organization. We look at the ways in which leadership is defined within organizations as:

1. A factor contributing towards organizational performance.
2. A source of power.
3. A set of competences which can be developed and assessed.
4. A strategic vision setting out the organization's future.
5. A property and product of organizational culture.
6. A practice which is shaped by organizational context.

As we progress through the chapter, our thoughts move away from the universalist approaches to leadership which are epitomized by somewhat prescriptive leadership theories (as discussed in Chapter 3), and reject the objectivist approach which implies that leadership can be determined through a series of attributes or behaviours. Many of the ideas set out in this chapter take a 'sensemaking' approach to leadership which was first examined in Chapter 3 (see section on the 'storytelling leader'). This means that in the following sections, we draw in greater depth on the concept that leadership involves a collaborative process of creating meaning through shaping our interpretations of reality.

We end the chapter by arguing that a more interpretive approach to leadership calls for greater utilization of qualitative research methods in leadership enquiry which allow participants to 'give voice' to the various processes and experiences which characterize their organizational realities.

Leadership and Organizational Performance

Effective leadership and management are widely heralded as key factors contributing to organizational performance and frequently targeted as priorities for development. The following quote from the UK Department for Education Skills is typical of government and organizational policy in this area yet embeds a number of assumptions that are worth exploring.

Our productivity as a nation is already lagging behind our competitors in North America and Europe. By tackling our management and leadership deficit with real vigour, we will unlock the doors to increased productivity, maximise the benefits of innovation, gain advantage from technological change and create the conditions for a radical transformation of public services. (DfES, 2002: 2)

This quote is interesting because it makes two assumptions: first, that a management and leadership 'deficit' exists within British industry, and second that through addressing this deficit (through development interventions in the main) the country will reap improvements in productivity, as well as the optimization of innovation, technological change, and transformation of public services. Yet, despite the boldness of this statement there exists remarkably little consistent empirical evidence of:

1. The nature of any such deficit.
2. The link between management and leadership capability (MLC) and improved productivity etc.
3. That through management and leadership development (MLD) we can enhance MLC and subsequently individual and organizational performance.

As illustrated in Figure 4.1, the relationship between management/leadership development, capability, and performance is largely a 'black box' in which, while we may know a certain amount about the constituent elements, we know remarkably little about how they impact one another, are influenced by contextual factors, and, furthermore, how the manner in which we *conceive* of one will have major ramifications for each of the others.

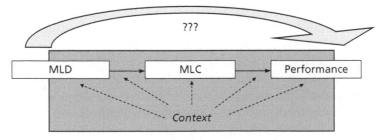

Figure 4.1. The Management Development, Capability, and Performance Black Box
Source: Adapted from Burgoyne et al. (2004: 7).

The difficulty in identifying clear relationships is the result of many factors, not least the significant influence of contextual factors on each variable in the diagram and the high degree of interdependence between factors. In the next sections, we review the evidence for this argument and the extent to which our hopes and expectations for leadership and management may be realistic. In particular, we assess:

1. Whether there is in fact a management and leadership deficit.
2. Whether there is indeed a link between management and leadership development and performance.
3. Whether we can really argue that management and leadership development enhances leadership capacity and organizational performance.

WHERE ARE OUR LEADERS? ASSESSING THE MANAGEMENT AND LEADERSHIP SKILLS DEFICIT

The above quote from the Department for Education Skills indicates that the UK Labour government believed that improved management and leadership were the key to unlocking national productivity, and that poor national performance was directly associated with a deficit of good managers and leaders. An influential report published around the same time, co-authored by the renowned strategy professor Michael Porter, questioned both whether the UK's economic performance was poor and whether management capability was one of the main determinants of economic performance. It concludes that while 'there is always room for improvement... efforts to upgrade management will not however be sufficient to achieve a sustained improvement in UK competitiveness' (Porter and Ketels, 2003: 6).

Research into whether or not there is a national deficit in management skills tends to point more strongly to a qualitative shortfall (i.e. a perception of poor management and leadership within organizations) rather than a large-scale quantitative absence of management skills per se. Both the National Skills Taskforce (DfEE, 2000) and Skills in England (Campbell et al., 2001) reports indicated that skills shortages are more prevalent within technical, generic, intermediate, ICT, and numeric skills areas than in the area of management, even though this was noted as an area of concern.

So despite some evidence of a management and leadership skills gap in the United Kingdom, it is hard to prove that if the gap were closed this would enhance competitiveness and economic performance, because skills shortages would continue to exist elsewhere. The best we can do is to say that the organizational evidence suggests that a region where effective leadership and management are prevalent is likely to outperform the others on a range of indicators. However, this means we need an effective way of assessing the impact of management and leadership development and capacity – not exactly a straightforward activity!

Evaluating leadership development and capacity

The ramifications of MLD and MLC vary, depending on the level at which we assess their influence. For example, the impact of MLD and MLC will appear different, depending on whether we explore at:

- *The individual level*: assessing the capacity of the individual leader through 'hard measures, such as productivity, technical knowledge, or soft measures such as improved communication and strategic thinking' (Bolden, 2004: 19).
- *The group level*: assessing the impact of an individual's behaviour on colleagues and subordinates, again through soft measures such as improved motivation, communication, and morale, and reduced absenteeism and turnover.
- *The organizational level*: assessing the leadership capacity of the organization as a whole, often through quantifiable measures like profit, turnover, job satisfaction, and innovation.

Most consideration of the impact of MLD stops at the organizational level. Yet the commitment of national and regional government to enhance MLC indicates that the potential impact of effective leadership can cross organizational boundaries. By building the capability and performance of organizations within a specific geographic area – regional, national, or international – much larger scale impacts are possible.

Exploring these different levels tells us that demonstrating the relationship between management and leadership development, capability and performance – if there is one! – involves untangling a series of interwoven issues, including the appropriateness of MLD (does it address the right skills? for the right people?) and its impact (does it increase capability? performance? other qualities?). Attention must also be paid to the level at which any effect occurs, situational context, and the range of factors on which they impact.

THE MISSING LINK: EXPLORING THE RELATIONSHIP BETWEEN MANAGEMENT AND LEADERSHIP CAPABILITY AND PERFORMANCE

The difficulty in effectively measuring the impact of MLD on MLC and performance means, unsurprisingly, that reliable research evidence is in short supply. In a review of the literature, Burgoyne et al. (2004) drew together what evidence there was. In what follows we explore their key findings in relation to the level of the individual and of the organization.

At the level of the individual, the evidence is unclear. Managers are sent on development programmes on the assumption that this will improve their management and leadership capability and resultant performance. Yet it seems that the impact of leadership development training is dependent on two factors:

1. The inclusion of opportunities for receiving and discussing individual feedback.
2. The quality of management processes preceding, supporting, and reinforcing development activities.

It appears that providing MLD alone is insufficient to ensure an increase in individual capability and performance, rather it needs to incorporate appropriate opportunities for feedback and discussion, and be accompanied by supportive management processes. *At an organizational level,* there is slightly more evidence of a positive link between MLC/MLD and organizational performance.

In a study of leadership in UK organizations, Horne and Stedman Jones (2001) concluded that where systematic implementation of leadership development existed there was a strong relationship to the perceived quality of leadership in that organization and organizational performance. An international study for the Chartered Management Institute reached a similar conclusion and stated: 'There is strong statistical evidence that management development leads to superior organizational performance across companies of all sizes, sectors and national location' (Mabey and Ramirez, 2004: 9).

At this level, what is most important is to ensure that individuals are encouraged and supported in contributing towards a collective leadership culture within the organization (Burgoyne et al., 2004; Mabey and Ramirez, 2004: 9).

So, in general, the evidence supports a relationship between MLD, capability, and performance at an individual and organizational level. Yet this relationship is not clear-cut, but is mediated by a range of factors. Acknowledging the situated-ness of this relationship within its organizational context requires a holistic approach to the development and implementation of MLD programmes.

Developing an integrated approach to management and leadership capacity

As illustrated in the following quote from the *Center for Creative Leadership Handbook of Leadership Development,* an integrated approach aligned with the strategic Human Resource Management (HRM) objectives of the organization is more likely to be effective than any number of isolated initiatives.

To be fully effective, a development system must be integrated with the organization's other processes: management planning, performance management, job selection, reward and recognition systems, and even mistake systems. The confluence of these processes determines the relative effectiveness of any one development activity. (McCauley et al., 1998: 228–9)

What this means is that the development of skills and knowledge alone is not sufficient to improve performance – it requires the provision of constructive feedback and appropriate support and encouragement to take on management and leadership responsibilities.

These findings demonstrate the importance of considering leadership in the wider context of the organization. In isolation, there is no guarantee that leadership development and/or capability will enhance individual or organizational performance. However, if considered as a key enabler within wider organizational and HRM processes, its impact becomes evident.

Equally, the presence of effective leadership and management processes within an organization increases the likelihood of further training and development being successful. Without a sense of vision, inspiration, and direction, HRM and MLD initiatives will not be integrated with business objectives, and employees will lack the motivation and commitment to work towards shared organizational goals.

There is a pressing need for more extensive research into the relationship between leadership and management development, capability, and performance. It is particularly important to improve our understanding of the manner in which these (and other) elements interact to make them effective within certain situations but not others. All organizations should seek to find ways of evaluating their management and leadership capability and development processes, not in a simplistic linear fashion but as part of a holistic integrated organizational strategy.

So in conclusion, it can be said that effective management and leadership are now widely recognized as key ingredients in the effective performance of individuals, groups, organizations, regions, and nation states. Yet the absence of definitive empirical evidence suggests that we cannot take this assumption for granted. The difficulty in measuring this relationship in simple economic terms indicates the need for more elaborate measures that consider performance in its widest sense and that take account of the interplay of a diverse range of interrelated factors.

Examining organizational performance and leadership indicates some of the complexity of exploring leadership at the organizational level. Yet leadership need not only impact on organizations in terms of their productivity and output. Leadership in organizations has other consequences and functions: it is produced by and reproduces social hierarchies, norms, and values.

To understand leadership at this level, we need other perspectives, which explore the relationships through which leadership is itself produced and enacted. And looking at leadership as a series of relationships necessitates an examination of the implicit power imbalances embedded in the leader/follower binary.

Leadership and Power

Of course, the complicated, interwoven relationship between leadership and power is made more so by ongoing discussion as to how power should be defined. While Weber (1978) suggests that power is the ability to get another person to do something he or she would not otherwise do, Gardner (1990: 55) argues that power is 'the capacity to ensure the outcomes one wishes, and to prevent those one does not wish'. He argues (Ibid.: 56) that 'leaders always have a measure of power', but points out that some individuals are able to exercise power without being leaders. For example, traffic wardens and air traffic controllers are able to exercise power and judgement over situations and people, but are not employed to set goals or create a vision for others.

Yet to say that people 'have power' is an incomplete view of power. Power is also linked to the common sense, tacit assumptions embedded in our everyday culture, which help us to make sense of our lives. This way of defining power has additional implications for leadership practice which go beyond how individuals can 'use their power' to effect change.

This section outlines a variety of ways of looking at leadership and power, from the different 'sources of power' a leader can use, to the ways in which power works on the leader. The overarching argument here is that the leader cannot be seen to be the sole location of power, but is immersed him or herself in relations of power. Nevertheless, a power imbalance is implicit within the concept of leadership, in which a 'leader' controls, directs, guides, or transforms other people, and the situation in which they find themselves.

I HAVE THE POWER! POWER AS A PERSONAL ATTRIBUTE

The most common way of exploring leadership and power is to locate power within the leader as individual. Power is seen to be something leaders possess – a trait, almost – which enables them to influence followers and set direction. As with the trait literature, which sets out frameworks of leadership attributes that leaders should possess, scholars of leadership and power have attempted to identify the different sources of power available to leaders.

French and Raven (1959) established one such taxonomy, based on five different sources of power which leaders can employ to secure the compliance of followers. These sources are known as:

1. *Reward power* – based on the provision of rewards for followers upon compliance. An example of this source of power would be monthly financial bonuses as incentives for sales workers to reach their management-set sales targets.

2. *Coercive power* – based on the administration of punishments for followers upon non-compliance. An example here would be the use of disciplinary procedures for poor or inappropriate behaviour in organizations.
3. *Legitimate power* – based on the followers' belief that their leader's role is legitimate and their orders are therefore rational. This can occur where there are strict hierarchies, where followers acknowledge the 'office' of the leader, as embodied in the rank structure of the military and police service.
4. *Expert power* – based on the followers' belief in the expert knowledge of their leader. For example, within multidisciplinary project teams where different people may 'take the lead' on particular tasks by virtue of their subject knowledge and/or professional expertise.
5. *Referent power* – based on the followers' personal identification with their leader, and their related need to seek his or her approval. This source of power is often linked to the 'charisma' of the leader and/or the extent to which they are seen to embody values and/or qualities to which followers aspire (as in the case of transformational leadership discussed in Chapter 2).

In considering these various sources of power, it is common for reward, coercive, and legitimate power to be collectively grouped under the term 'position power' because they depend on one's formal position within the organization, and hence are only available to the holders of formal managerial roles. In contrast, expert power and referent power are referred to as 'personal power' because of their link to personal attributes, and are available to anyone imbued with such characteristics (French and Raven, 1959). Bratton et al. (2005: 128) suggest that ultimately all leadership may be dependent upon referent power, since 'no individual leader can ever be successful without a network of supporters'. Yet it is sometimes difficult to separate the sources of power and identify which source of power is the cause of compliance. For example, the most experienced member of a project group may not emerge as leader unless they are confident about showcasing their expertise. The group dynamics might mean that a person who is perceived to have more charisma is more assertive, or who best embodies the characteristics of the social group might well emerge instead. In this case, other sources of power would be involved in determining who is considered to be the most 'legitimate' leader.

POWER TO THE PEOPLE! POWER AS LEGITIMIZED BY FOLLOWERS

For power to be effective, then, it must be legitimized – that is, the apparent source of the leader's power must be recognized as legitimate by followers. Weber's writing (1978) on power explores how this legitimating process happens. He argued that a difference exists between power as force or coercion, and power as authority, whereby individuals are not forced, but persuaded, to accept a leader's demands.

Weber suggested that power is given legitimacy because it is grounded in one of the three following sources:

1. *Traditional authority*: the leader has the power to make decisions because of custom and tradition, as in the case of a monarchy.
2. *Legal–rational authority*: the leader has the power to make decisions because followers recognize the rules and procedures which give them this right (e.g. the CEO of an organization).
3. *Charismatic authority*: the leader has the power to make decisions because followers perceive them to have inspirational and extraordinary qualities that mark them out from others. Often, charismatic leaders act as role models who are perceived to best embody organizational values. This is how leaders like Anita Roddick and Richard Branson become synonymous with the organizations they have led (the Body Shop and the Virgin empires, respectively).

Weber's framework shows how leaders can justify their decisions and goals, by grounding them in a source of legitimacy. Yet while legal–rational authority makes decisions appear neutral because they are cloaked in bureaucratic rules and structures, Weber makes clear that leadership decisions remain political: enacted by those with access to these sources of authority.

The meshing of leadership, politics, and power is explored further by Lukes (2005) who argues that power works on three levels. The first dimension of power, according to Lukes, is *the ability to influence decisions*. In other words, we cannot summarize power simply as the ability of A to secure the compliance of B. Lukes argues that this is a 'one dimensional' view of power, and carries within it the assumption that there is some form of visible conflict, whereby B starts off by thinking differently from A, before being persuaded otherwise.

The second dimension of power, according to Lukes, involves the ability of a leader to establish which topics come up for discussion. This dimension, known as the *agenda-setting dimension*, implies that conflict must not necessarily happen for power to be working on people. By influencing which decisions come to be discussed, the leader can exercise power by preventing the occurrence of conflict. In this way, leaders can confine decision-making to 'safe issues' (Ibid.: 22), while other issues are not made overt. Lukes argues that this second dimension is important because it allows for what he calls the 'mobilization of bias' – the conscious or unconscious employment of a system of values and beliefs that work to the benefit of some members of society and to the cost of others. This system affects which issues come to be seen as important and ripe for discussion, and which do not. If issues do not come to be discussed, they cannot be decided upon. These potential issues are therefore prevented from becoming actual because of this 'non-decision-making'. Since they are not discussed, there appears to be universal agreement on the matter as it currently exists, and differences of opinion remain unobservable.

The agenda-setting dimension introduces into the study of power and leadership the idea that how controlling the agenda for discussion can keep potential issues out of the decision-making process. Yet Lukes argues that this dimension retains its focus on power at the individual level. He argues that agenda setting is 'a function of collective forces and social arrangements' (2005: 26), and cannot ever be attributed to one individual. The potential issues that come to be seen as important are governed by the implicit cultural assumptions, the everyday ways of thinking, being, and doing which are dominant in our society. These cultural values shape our social reality. They are internalized by groups and individuals so that people accept and reproduce this form of reality without question. Lukes argues that this third form of dimension – the *institutional dimension* – causes people to accept the status quo even when it is against their real interests. He suggests that groups who have power can control meaning, such that those who are 'powerless' are unable to recognize when something is not in their interest.

THE 'HIDDEN HAND': POWER AS EMBEDDED WITHIN SOCIAL SYSTEMS

Lukes' power dimensions have been criticized, however, because they assume that those in power are able to control power. Power is conceptualized as a possession, which some have, and others do not. Knights and Willmott's analysis (1999: 97) suggests that: 'The fundamental problem with Lukes' perspective is that it assumes a priori knowledge of the "real," objective interests of particular individuals, groups or classes in society; and further assumes that these exist prior to, or independently of, power relations.'

These authors subscribe to an alternative view of power, in which power is not something which can be possessed, like any other leadership trait or attribute. Rather, power is embedded in discourse – the networks of assumptions concerning the ways of thinking, being, and doing which help us to make sense of our everyday lives. This conceptualization draws on the ideas of the French poststructuralist writer Michel Foucault as outlined below.

Foucault's 'power-knowledge' theory (1980) proposes that we can never 'escape' power and hence cannot assume any a priori knowledge which is untainted by power. His work is based on the premise that power produces the ways of thinking which help us to make sense of our world and through which we accept, categorize, and refer to certain things as 'true' or 'false'. This concept of power is inescapably intertwined with knowledge, such that there can be no knowledge that is objective, since all 'truths' are infused with power relations. Power therefore produces the truth effects which help us to make sense of things, and in so doing, forecloses other ways of thinking about the world.

Power is therefore implicit in the construction of our subjectivity, causing us to regulate our conduct to think and act in line with the norms contained within discourse in a largely unconscious manner. To illustrate this point, Foucault (1979) drew on Bentham's 'panopticon' – an architectural design for a prison. The design consists of a circle of prison cells, facing inwards, with a watchtower in the centre. The prisoners in their cells are visible to the prison guard at any time, but the prison guard in his watchtower remains hidden. Foucault argued that this surveillance mechanism was imbued with what he called 'disciplinary power' (Ibid.). He pointed out that the knowledge that the prisoners *could* be watched at any time – and the threat of punishment if they were seen to act out of line – was sufficient to ensure that they regulated their conduct in line with the prison rules.

Organization Studies scholars have drawn on the image of the panopticon and institutional surveillance to explore how power/knowledge is embedded in organizational materiality. For example, Sewell and Wilkinson (1992) explored the surveillance mechanisms in a factory, which had a disciplinary effect on workers: individuals regulated themselves to make sure their work was of the required standard and speed, because they knew they might be observed. Other monitoring systems which have a disciplinary effect on workers in organizations include the performance review process (Townley, 1994) and employee selection procedures (Brannan and Hawkins, 2007), through which workers are expected to demonstrate commitment to organizational values.

Leaders may have more access to the material wealth and privilege which make them better able to impact the actions of others. As the previous chapter of this book has pointed out, leaders can be, to some extent, the producers of 'truth regimes' within organizations through their ability to tell stories and use symbols which are steeped in discourses about how followers should behave and which values they should hold as 'true'. However, leaders are not immune from the disciplinary effects of power. Leadership competency frameworks used by many organizations, for example, are another way of ranking and categorizing leaders' performances according to discursive 'norms'. As suggested in Chapter 3, the leadership identity itself can also be a disciplinary mechanism, which asks leaders to continually regulate their behaviour as they aspire to a norm which they can never fulfil. The leadership competency approach is a core component of leadership development and assessment in many organizations, and is one of the benchmarks which organizations and individuals use to measure leadership ability and behaviour. This perspective is discussed in further detail in the next section.

Leadership Competencies: The Science of Leadership

As we pointed out in Chapter 2, the competency perspective on leadership assumes that there are sets of traits, behaviours, and skills that enable leaders to perform effectively in their role. This assumption is an attractive one for many organizations who seek to build the capacity of their existing leadership and management teams and to recruit newcomers with the appropriate skills for leadership roles.

Throughout the public and private sector, organizations are putting in place the so-called 'competency frameworks' which set out the leadership skills and abilities that are prioritized by that organization. These frameworks are used to monitor performance and analyse training and recruitment needs. They have their counterparts at sectoral level too, in the form of National Occupational Standards (NOS) frameworks. These describe the skills and abilities required within the sector to perform a specific job. They are used to develop training programmes, benchmark performance, and to standardize the skills, or components of competence, possessed by individuals working in a similar job across a sector.

The competency approach is fast becoming one of the dominant models of leadership development, yet it remains the subject of many debates. On the one hand, the apparent objectivity and 'scientific' nature of competencies is highly attractive as a means of measuring, assessing, and developing leaders. On the other hand, the approach has a number of major weaknesses that are yet to be addressed, summarized by Bolden (2005) as follows:

- Leadership competency frameworks tend not to be forward looking. They look at current and past needs rather than what will be required in the future.
- The focus on measurable behaviours and outcomes, or 'evidence-based' performance, comes at the expense of more subtle relational, ethical, and emotional dimensions such as social responsibility. Somewhere in the process, the 'human being' is lost.
- Frameworks, though often designed for developmental purposes, tend also to be used deductively for measurement, assessment, and recruitment. These are competing objectives and can greatly undermine the developmental impact of the tool.
- The focus on individuals underestimates the socially constructed nature of leadership and the role played by others in the organization. Leadership is not a property of individuals, but an emergent, contextually situated, relational process.
- We reap what we sow. By implementing an individualistic, behaviourally focused framework, we run the risk of producing an organization full of action-oriented individuals rather than a culture of shared leadership that values reflection, collaboration, and consideration.

These and other criticisms are reflected in much of the literature on the subject. Authors such as Lester (1994), Bell et al. (2002), and Brundrett (2000) have attacked the competency approach for being overly reductionist (fragmenting the management role rather than representing it as an integrated whole); overly universalistic (assuming a generic set of capabilities no matter what the nature of the situation, individuals, or task); and tending to reinforce rather than challenge traditional ways of thinking about management and leadership.

The implications of such criticisms are quite damning in practice. They imply, in effect, that competency frameworks neither give a realistic picture of the management and/or leadership role nor a credible basis for the selection and/or development of managers and leaders.

Here, we explore the extent to which competency-based approaches to leadership fail to match the requirements of organizations. We do this by comparing an analysis of competency frameworks with the key concerns and issues of leadership today and tomorrow as identified by leaders themselves. To a great extent, the two simply do not match: what leaders identify as important and the language they use to express this is substantially different from that represented in leadership competency/quality frameworks. Our central argument is that while competency frameworks, used considerately, can have an important role to play, they are no more than a map which can be used to explore and navigate the concepts of leadership and management. Like all maps, however, they only represent a fragment of the complexity of the terrain and an over-dependency will fail to engage with the real problems of leading in complex and changing environments (Bolden, 2005; Bolden and Gosling, 2006).

MAPPING THE TERRAIN

We begin with an analysis of leadership competency/quality frameworks currently used in the United Kingdom and overseas. Bolden et al. (2003) collected and analysed a total of twenty-nine frameworks, including nine private sector, twelve public sector, and eight generic frameworks.

Most of these frameworks considered a number of cognitive, affective, and interpersonal leadership qualities, as well as providing prescriptive definitions of behaviours. But while the role of others in leadership may be recognized, that recognition was usually rather simplistic and unidirectional in manner. Leadership was presented as a set of skills, qualities, and behaviours *exhibited by the leader* that encourage the participation, development, and commitment of others within the organization. It is remarkable how few of the frameworks (only eight) referred to the leader's ability to 'listen', and none formally acknowledged the role of 'followers' (Ibid.).

The 'leader' is thus promoted as the source of 'leadership'. They are seen to act as an energizer, catalyst, and visionary equipped with a set of tools (communication, problem-solving, people management, decision-making) that can be applied across a diverse range of situations and contexts. While contingency and situational leadership factors may be considered, they are generally not considered barriers to an individuals' ability to lead under different circumstances.

The leader is also expected to display excellent information processing, project management, customer service, and delivery skills, along with proven business and political acumen. Leaders are said to build partnerships, 'walk the talk', show incredible drive and enthusiasm, and get things done. Furthermore, they are expected to demonstrate innovation, creativity, and be prepared to be challenged and take risks.

Such a representation of the leader is typical of the competency approach, whereby the leader is represented as a multitalented individual with diverse personal and interpersonal skills. Having encountered and challenged individualistic perspectives on leadership in Chapter 3 of this book, we might justifiably wonder whether this is a valid, realistic, or helpful representation. Bolden et al. (2003.) certainly identified a discrepancy between the generalized skills recognized by leadership competency frameworks, and those valued by leaders themselves, who placed far greater emphasis on self-awareness, integrity, and the ethical dimensions of leadership practice (as observed from the comments of participants on programmes by the Windsor Leadership Trust – see Bolden, 2004: 28).

In short, then, the research indicates a worrying gap between the attributes of leadership as identified by practising managers and popular leadership competency/qualities frameworks. Furthermore, if leadership is characterized as a language game (Marturano et al., 2010), this discrepancy becomes yet more concerning: implying that competency-based approaches do not provide an appropriate vocabulary for the construction of effective leadership as determined by practising managers (Holman and Hall, 1996).

MIND THE GAP!

It would seem that in their desire to construct an objective, rational representation of the leader/manager, competency-based approaches dehumanize the individual. Emphasis is placed almost exclusively on observable characteristics and skills sets to the near exclusion of moral and emotional concerns. But it can be argued that it is precisely these dimensions that lie at the heart of true leadership. Indeed, the concept of 'transformational' leadership (which seems to underlie many frameworks) is founded upon a notion of the leaders' moral responsibility to their followers and their ability to engage and inspire them at an emotional level (Burns, 1978).

The competency approach tends to veer away from addressing the moral and emotional aspects of leading. While it may be true that the concept of emotional intelligence (Goleman et al., 2002) has been well received within many organizations, it tends to be treated as a rather impersonal skill set for emotional containment and control of self and others. Yet, when you place a group of senior managers in a room to reflect on and discuss their leadership role the language is rich with emotions. Take, for example, the experience of learning to work with a difficult colleague, trying to reach a decision with no clear 'right' answer, or balancing work and non-work responsibilities – these are the sources of emotions experienced on a daily basis by people in organizations. In the research mentioned earlier (Bolden, 2004), participants spoke frequently of subjective qualities such as trust, honesty, humility, empathy, and intuition, all of which have a strong emotional dimension that tends to be absent within the more rational and objective competency approach.

The tendency of competency frameworks to steer clear of the more abstract and contested dimensions of ethics, emotion, and social relations, however, is perhaps not surprising. Indeed, a fundamental element of their attraction to policymakers, employers, and educators is the manner in which they offer a sense of clarity over the nature of leadership and how it can be measured and developed.

Making reference to the less 'rational' concepts of morality and emotions might be seen to undermine their ability to predict and prescribe managerial behaviour. Yet, at the same time, their failure to do so greatly undermines their utility in the real world.

In an insightful review of the field, Salaman (2004) identified a recurrent trend in the way in which management (and now leadership) has been conceived. He traces early attempts to identify management competencies, the difficulties faced, and the subsequent move towards leadership competencies. Salaman identifies four fundamental characteristics of the competency approach, outlined below.

1. By describing the management/leadership role, the competency approach puts into place a framework for measuring, monitoring, comparing, and regulating the behaviour of managers. This point is also made by Brewis (1996), who argues that competency frameworks seem objective and neutral, but are embedded with disciplinary power and can become a mechanism for control. Leaders and aspiring leaders must regulate their own conduct in order to be perceived as 'competent' according to the standards outline in the prescriptive framework.

2. Competencies require a translation from strategy, to organization, and to individual manager; frameworks thus disguise or assume key organizational assumptions, objectives, and priorities, which may remain hidden and unquestioned.
3. As well as defining qualities of the new manager, competencies also emphasize ongoing improvement.
4. The competency approach expects much more of managers than before, transferring responsibility for maintaining motivation and development, from HR specialists to the individual manager.

Salaman concludes by proposing that, like management competencies, leadership competencies will fail to deliver their promise: 'the problems it promised to resolve are not capable of resolution and its promise consisted largely of a sleight of hand whereby organizational problems were simply restated as management responsibilities' (Salaman, 2004: 75).

Thus, leadership cannot be dissociated from the temporal and situational context. In the presence of an incompatible organizational system or culture, a leader may remain powerless to achieve what is expected of them. Likewise, failure to consider the broader social context of leadership is to miss the significant role played by followers and other actors in the leadership process.

This, then perhaps points to the true problem with the competency approach. Leadership occurs in situ and cannot be distilled into a number of constituent elements. It is in a constant state of flux and hence can never be captured within a static framework. In the same way as Magritte's famous painting of a pipe with the legend '*ceci n'est pas une pipe*' (this is not a pipe), we should remind ourselves that competency and quality frameworks are simply a representation of leadership rather than the real thing (if, indeed, a concrete leadership entity could ever be argued to exist).

A competency framework is like a map. It is a two-dimensional representation of the terrain. Like all maps, however, it shows only selected features, becomes rapidly outdated as the terrain changes, and is only useful for interpreting the data from which it was created (a road map is no use for predicting the weather!). Furthermore, to be useful it requires the user to be educated in the process of map reading, should be used alongside other measures, and is dependent on a number of environmental conditions. Thus, for example, if it is dark, foggy, windy, or raining it becomes difficult to use the map effectively. Likewise, with leadership, in the face of uncertainty and change it is experience that counts.

THE MAP IS NOT THE TERRAIN

Our aim here is not to argue that competencies are valueless, but to recognize that they are just one way of looking at and developing leadership. When used with care and consideration, alongside other approaches, they can be useful for opening a dialogue and discussion on the nature of leadership and what leadership means within different organizational settings.

When used as the primary or sole vehicle for leadership assessment and development, however, they are limiting and potentially damaging. The competency approach then becomes like a repeating refrain. It continues to offer an illusory promise to rationalize and simplify the processes of selecting, recruiting, and developing leaders, but it reflects only a fragment of the complexity that is leadership. Taken in abstraction a competency framework says little of how leadership occurs in practice. It is too general, fragmentary, and impersonal to speak of the lived experience of leading, either from the perspective of leader or follower.

Extended versions of the ideas presented here can be found in Bolden and Gosling (2006) and Bolden et al. (2003). In summary though, one way of interpreting the core of our argument is this: leadership competencies can be likened to the skills of map reading and orienteering. They describe the features of the terrain, but they cannot explain the experience of exploration nor provide the skills necessary for it. To survive, the explorer also requires the skills of 'bushcraft' – learnt from experience and an appreciation of the environment. So it is with today's managers and leaders, trying to survive in an increasingly unpredictable global business environment and who require emotion, intuition, and moral judgement as well as competencies in order to do so. Competencies provide a map they can use as a guide, but they should never be mistaken for the terrain.

Despite the fact that trait and behavioural theories of leadership have proved unsuccessful in isolating a definitive set of leader characteristics, the competency approach to leadership development and assessment is becoming increasingly widespread. Leadership standards, qualities, and/or competency frameworks now form the basis of the management development and review processes within most large organizations.

One of the reasons the competency framework has been so successful is that it provides organizations with a way to develop a leadership training programme that is apparently aligned with business strategy, by focusing on measuring and developing the skills and competences that are perceived to be crucial to organizational success. The assumption is that for leadership development to be successful, it must be aligned with long-term business objectives (Clarke et al., 2004). In the following section, we explore the interstices between strategy and leadership. Are all leaders necessarily strategists? Is strategy separate from leadership practice, or embedded within it? We engage critically with these issues, as well as question the assumption that leaders can impose and control change according to their wishes.

Setting the Direction: Strategic Leadership

Defining and implementing a strategy that propels an organization towards a successful future lies at the core of many conceptions of leadership, yet this topic has been relatively poorly understood. This is in part due to the continued complexity surrounding the concept of leadership, with some authors perceiving leadership as a separate discipline from strategy (Barker, 1997). This section explores some of the elements involved in strategic leadership, including designing organizational visions and implementing change. The section also sets out a more critical approach to strategic change leadership, drawing on work by Levy et al. (2003) to suggest that attempting to secure an organization's future may be part of an existential quest to secure our own identity in an increasingly insecure world. We also suggest that strategic leadership often presumes that change can occur without reference to the past. Strategic leadership involves layering visions of the future over faded memories of the past. We cannot separate the past, present, and future within our understanding of change and leadership in organizations.

WHAT DO WE MEAN BY STRATEGIC LEADERSHIP?

Achua and Lussier (2010: 370) define strategic leadership as:

A person's ability to anticipate, envision, maintain flexibility, think strategically, and work with others to initiate changes that will create a viable future for the organization. It is a process of providing the direction and inspiration necessary to create and implement a firm's vision, mission and strategies to achieve organizational objectives.

They go on to suggest that effective strategic leaders are skilled in building core competencies, team building, communicating, and goal setting – phew! Once again, we come across a long list of behaviours and tasks which locates strategic leadership within the individual. Yet we know that much of the purpose of strategizing lies in its attempt to unite the beliefs, goals, and activities of a whole group of people, by presenting a view of the future, a 'vision', which must be embodied by all members of a group or organization.

Vision is perhaps the starting point for much talk about strategic leadership. The leader is expected to set out, for the rest of the organization's members, a clear, desirable representation of what the organization will become in future years (Zaccharo and Banks, 2001). Examples of strategic visions include President J. F. Kennedy's aim to put a man on the moon before 1969, and Henry Ford's dream of a world where everyone could own a car. The vision provides a motivating force which will unite followers in pursuit of a future with which they identify with and to which they aspire. Leaders then establish concrete, achievable tasks which guide the organization in this direction. The point of strategic leadership, therefore, is to turn the vision from the idealistic to the specific, via a process of strategy formulation, implementation, and evaluation (Achua and Lussier, 2010). Strategy implementation is often set out as a pathway, or series of stages, which can include the following:

- *Analyse the environment*: what is happening right now, economically, socially, and culturally? Strategic leaders are expected to interpret and adapt to the complexities in their environment, and use this as a basis for strategic decision-making.
- *Develop a vision statement*: what will the organization be like in the future? As suggested above, the vision is usually ambitious and challenging, but fairly unspecific. Instead, it sets out a picture that everyone in the organization can aim for, together.
- *Develop a mission statement*: this statement draws upon the vision to suggest how the organization will differentiate itself from its competitors. Rather than answering the question '*who are we, in the future?*', the mission aims to explain '*what business are we in?*' (Achua and Lussier, 2010: 377).
- *Establish goals*: what needs to happen to achieve the vision and mission? Establishing goals helps the organization narrow down its ideas for the future into smaller, actionable targets to be achieved in both the long and short term.
- *Set up actions*: how will the goals be achieved? These actions are the practices by which the organization aims to achieve its goals. They are specific, measurable, and are related to the long- and short-term targets set out in the previous step.
- *Strategic reflection*: what are the results? By evaluating the impact of the strategic process, leaders can establish whether measurable targets have been met, and make decisions about what aspects of the strategy need to change. This evaluation has to take into account the external, environmental changes affecting the strategy's effectiveness, as well as organizational factors. Achua and Lussier (2010) point out the need for leaders to encourage reflection and feedback across all levels of the organizational hierarchy, in order to ascertain where changes should (and should not) be made.

Strategic leadership visions must therefore be actionable – that is, they must tap into an organization's existing strengths, abilities, and sense of purpose. Yet imposing a vision onto employees and expecting them to identify with and implement the changes it implies is not without risks. Members of organizations often apply very different logics to situations, and may have very different ideas about what the future will be like. This is increasingly important in modern industrial society, where outsourcing, subcontracting, and corporate social responsibility schemes mean that organizations have vast numbers of stakeholders, and are thought of as having permeable boundaries (Rubery et al., 2004). This is why Senge et al. (1994) argue that organizational visions cannot be the product of one leader, but must emerge out of a process of negotiation and discussion:

Visions which tap into an organization's deeper sense of purpose, and articulate specific goals that represent making that purpose real, have unique power to engender aspiration and commitment.... The content of a true shared vision cannot be dictated: it can only emerge from a coherent process of reflection and conversation. (Senge et al., 1994, cited in Gill, 2006: 109)

This statement implies a more evolving, collaborative, and reflexive view of vision, which has to be shared to be effective. Without an effective consultation process, a vision can become a tyranny, the dream of a dictator, imposing their will on the organization and its members.

GOING WITH THE FLOW: EMERGENT STRATEGIES AND STRATEGY-AS-PRACTICE

Mintzberg and Waters (1985) have pointed out that to understand what strategies *are*, we have to understand how they are shaped within organizations. They argue that the concept of strategy as a process of establishing long-term goals is incomplete and inadequate. Rather, they take the view that strategy is a 'pattern in a stream of decisions' (Mintzberg and Waters, 1982). Within this conceptualization, different kinds of strategy processes take place and interconnect with one another. Some of these are part of the intended strategy – the result of precise, deliberate intentions. These are called 'deliberate strategies' (Mintzberg and Waters, 1985: 257). Yet by themselves, deliberate strategies are inadequate – it is so time-consuming and expensive to carry out such detailed forms of planning that the authors argue it is only found in its entirety in contexts where there is very little likelihood of change (Ibid.).

In other, more unstable contexts, other processes also form part of the realized strategy, which are not the product of deliberate intention. These actions are not part of the intended strategy, but are the means by which an organization responds to a situation as it unfolds. The authors have termed these processes 'emergent strategies'. They argue that openness to emergent strategy is vitally important, because it allows organizations to be flexible in the face of a changing reality (Ibid.). Figure 4.2 demonstrates how the deliberate strategy process and emergent strategy processes both contribute to the eventual strategy which is adopted by the organization.

The key point made by these authors is that strategy is not simply a process by which managers can impose their goals on organizations, when they exist in a fluctuating context. They argue that:

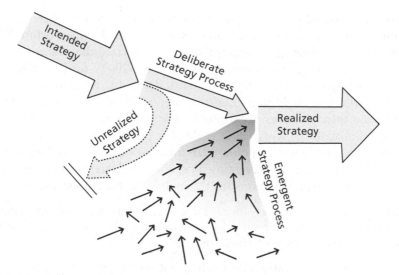

Figure 4.2. Deliberate and Emergent Strategy
Source: Adapted from Mintzberg (1987: 14).

Strategy walks on two feet: one deliberate, one emergent... managing requires a light deft touch – to direct in order to realise intentions while at the same time responding to an unfolding pattern of action. The relative emphasis may shift from time to time but not the requirement to attend to both sides of this phenomenon. (Ibid.: 271)

The implication here is that strategic leadership is not solely dependent upon following policy. Rather, is an emerging, iterative process of action and response. The need to understand the subtleties that take place inside the apparent 'black box' which constitutes the 'doing' of strategic leadership has been the focus of what is termed the 'practice turn' in strategy research. This perspective, also known as 'strategy-as-practice', treats strategy as something people *do* (Jarzabkowski, 2004). As such, as Whittington (2006) argues, it must take account of both intra-organizational and extra-organizational contexts.

Whittington (2006) identifies three principle strands of practice theory: the notion of 'relationality' (the interconnection between the individual and the social); the notion of 'practice' (the *how* of social action); and the 'actors' (on whose activity practice depends). These principles, he argues, give rise to three interdependent concepts: strategy praxis (what people actually do), practices (shared routines and behaviours that guide and shape activity), and practitioners (the various social actors). He concludes that:

The essential insight of the practice perspective is that strategy is more than just a property of organizations; it is something that people do, with stuff that comes from outside as well as within organizations, and with effects that permeate through whole societies. (Ibid.: 627)

Strategic leadership is not just the product of the leader, therefore, but requires a process of cooperation and a sense of shared values, before it can make sense to anyone. However, authors have criticized the strategic leadership approach on other grounds, too. Levy et al. (2003), for example, point out that strategic management is a political project, whereby leaders can employ a vision to establish a discursive framework which causes employees to regulate their identities according to the prescriptions embedded in it, in ways similar to the storytelling leadership model outlined in Chapter 3. Visionary leadership has the potential to foreclose other potential representations of the future, and to prevent members of organizations from identifying these alternative representations for themselves. As the authors suggest:

Thinking 'strategically' routinely invites a degree of top-down control, self discipline and the freezing of goals. Inherent in such means-end thinking is a restrictive or even an anticommunicative element. (Ibid.: 106)

Strategic leadership cannot be neutral, but reflects the aims of those who occupy positions of power within organizations. The risk is that this will give legitimacy to, and perpetuate, existing organizational inequalities and hierarchies. While Senge et al. (1994) suggest a more inclusive approach to the development of leadership visions, in reality it is often difficult to marry the vastly different perspectives held by organizational members into an integrated, shared picture of the future.

Regardless of how inclusive and emergent the vision development process has been, for a strategic vision to be credible, leaders have to be seen to 'walk the walk', not just 'talk the talk'. A poorly enacted vision can be very embarrassing once it does not match commonly held perceptions of the organization. The search engine Google risked this situation in China recently. Google's stated mission is '*to organize the world's information and to make it universally accessible and useful*'. Yet Google's Chinese search engine had to function according to strict Chinese regulations, meaning that search engine results from *google.cn* were restricted and therefore far from 'universally accessible'. Google has tried to reconcile this problem by redirecting traffic to its Chinese search engine via servers in Hong Kong, thus escaping the censors.

Attempts to redress these tensions are not always successful, however. Hatch and Schultz (2003), for example, point out that British Airway's strategic goal to be the 'world's favourite airline' was severely at odds with public perception of the company as an '*icon of Britishness*'. The new series of tail fin designs accompanying the vision were rejected by the public and were never implemented, and the aim to be the 'world's favourite airline' lost credibility in the face of disappointing financial results. Visions offer a moral imperative to employees to think and act in certain ways which display identification with organizational values, but this morality is only justified if the leader can act as an example for others to follow. In the case of British

Airways, the 'global' vision was not matched by changes inside the cabin. British accents, styles of dress, and traditional silver tea services were still in evidence. For a vision to remain credible, it also has to be seen to be embedded in organizational procedures including recruitment, training, customer service, and product development.

ANOTHER FINE PROGRAMME! THE LIMITS OF STRATEGIC CHANGE

Perhaps it is unsurprising, then, that despite growing numbers of courses aiming to teach corporate strategy to leadership professionals, the practice of strategic leadership is more difficult than it first appears. Quirke (2008) cites a survey by Deloitte and Touche (2003) which discovered that only 22 per cent of employees felt their leaders provided adequate direction, while the CEOs of these companies said that they could seldom find time to communicate with their employees! Unsurprisingly then, organizational change is hard to achieve, particularly at the level of employee identity. Some change programmes become seen as managerial attempts to join another bandwagon. Senge et al. (1994) describe how at Harley Davidson, workers use the term 'AFP', short for 'another fine programme', to describe management change efforts!

Ezzamel et al.'s case study (2001) of restructuring processes at a US-owned automotive factory in the north of England revealed how a vision which required a programme of change towards leaner manufacturing processes failed to achieve employee 'buy-in' because the employees identified so strongly with the autonomy encapsulated within their previous work practices. Similarly, the factory workers in McCabe's case study (2000) interpreted the top-down implementation of teamwork as their leaders' attempts to 'brainwash' them into adopting a managerialist agenda. In a separate study, Terry and O'Brien's analysis (2001) of employee responses to an organizational merger further highlights the political aspects of support for and resistance to change. They found that support for the merger was affected by in-group – that is, that the group of employees from the lower status pre-merger organization felt more threatened by the merger, had less job satisfaction, and were less likely to perceive themselves as sharing a collective identity with other members of the organization.

What these case studies show is that change, whether it is strategically developed or not, is never imposed on a neutral work environment. Any work context is always steeped in evolving values and assumptions which characterize 'the way we do things around here' (Schein, 1992). This means that the standard, linear approach to change, advocated by Lewin (1947) – implying a pre-existing fixed state, followed by a process of change, leading to a 'new, improved' fixed state – is inadequate.

The linear approach is unsuccessful for several reasons. Firstly, we cannot assume that organizations ever exist in a fixed state. Organizations, their practices, and relationships are constantly evolving and emerging. This is why Senge et al. (1994) refer to the process of leading change as a dance, made up of intricate, collaborative, coordinated manoeuvres, a certain amount of repetition, and a healthy level of improvisation.

Relatedly, we cannot always predict the impacts that change processes will have on an organization and its members. Many consequences of strategic change programmes are unintended. As the case studies conducted by Ezzamel et al. (2001) and McCabe (2000) demonstrate, even after the change strategy has been implemented, some elements of the pre-existing workplace mentalities may linger on. It is much harder to change the collective identities of a workforce than it is to introduce a new name or logo! Leaders, when they develop and implement strategic visions, cannot expect to wipe the slate clean. Organizations are not just neutral structures – they are held together by memories, values, and assumptions associated with its past which are entrenched deep in the collective identities of its members. Strategic leadership therefore involves the managing of continuity as well as the introduction of change (Gosling and Mintzberg, 2003; Gosling, 2008). It must find a way to integrate these previous inscriptions into a vision for the future.

From a psychoanalytic perspective, French (2001) argues, change requires what has been termed 'negative capability' – the ability to tolerate the uncertainties, conflicts, and 'half knowledge' (Ward, 1963: 161) that are part of the change process. French argues that leaders with negative capability can work alongside people and help them to contain, address, and face their anxieties about an uncertain present and future. Where leaders do not effectively exert negative capability, he argues that employees are likely to 'disperse' their unmanaged feelings by denying the need for change, engaging in activities such as postponing meetings, or exhibiting emotional responses like increased levels of stress and dissipating organizational commitment.

This perspective presents negative capability as a further 'competence' which organizations require in their leaders – and it is therefore subject to all the criticisms faced by the competency/leadership skills literature identified in this chapter and in Chapter 3. The negative capability interpretation demands much of leaders and very little of followers. The leader is placed in the position of having to 'manage' the emotions of employees who are deemed incapable of responding adequately themselves. Alternatively, perhaps negative capability is a shared exercise, a process by which members of an organization can collaborate to negotiate the chaos of change. Collaborative attempts to introduce change, which take into account the values of stakeholders, are perhaps more likely to achieve this process of continual integration and learning.

SOME FINAL THOUGHTS ON STRATEGIC LEADERSHIP

This section has examined various perspectives linking leadership and strategy. It has engaged critically with the notions that:

- Leaders can impose their vision on an organization without unintended consequences.
- Strategies can be translated effectively into reality without any unintended consequences or tensions.
- Strategies are politically neutral projects, separated from the actions, practices, and interests of groups and individuals who are in positions of power in organizations.

So what does the role of strategic leader really look like? The arguments put forward here suggest that strategic leadership involves admitting that the future is complex and unknowable. As such, it requires direction and participation – a new challenge for leaders unwilling to relinquish control. As Pedler et al. (2004: 268) put it:

Leadership will ever be about purpose, clarity of vision and direction setting, but in the face of complexities, the best response is openness about the uncertainty and ambiguity and the commitment to share the responsibility for choosing the next step.

Senge et al. (1994) point out the vital importance of a learning organization culture, which allows individuals to work together, to put forward innovative ideas, and even to make mistakes without fear of recrimination. Certainly the values and assumptions held by an organization's members, and which are enacted – consciously and unconsciously – in their practices, have a bearing on how change takes place and how successful it might be. Yet instilling new values in the form of an organizational culture is itself not a straightforward exercise. In the following section, we examine leadership in relation to organizational culture.

Rites, Rituals, and Belonging: Leadership and Organizational Culture

Have you ever heard someone in your class or workplace talk about 'the way we do things around here'? This is a common, everyday phrase people use to describe their organization's culture. They are referring to ways of behaving which draw upon often tacitly held values and assumptions which are loosely shared by individuals belonging to an organization or group. Culture, as a metaphor for describing organizations, and as a way of describing the forms of symbolic production that go on in organizations, is a growing topic of discussion within Leadership Studies. One of the first and most well-known theorists who wrote about leadership and culture is Edgar Schein. He described culture as: 'a pattern of shared basic assumptions that the group learned... that has worked well enough to be considered valid and therefore, to be taught to new members as the correct way to perceive, think, and feel in relation to those problems' (Schein, 1992: 12).

Schein (1992: 5) believed that leaders were central to organizational cultures, arguing that 'one of the most decisive functions of leadership is the creation, the management and sometimes even the destruction of culture'. He argued that one way of differentiating between leaders and managers is that the latter live within culture, while leaders create and alter them.

But are leaders really 'outside culture' enough to control culture? And do all members of a culture have to share values about what it means to be a member of the organization? Some authors (e.g. Smircich, 1983) would disagree with this perspective on the basis that leaders themselves also live 'within culture' but have greater access to the resources which enable them to influence other organizational members. These are the debates that we engage with in this section of the chapter.

IN THE CLUB: LEADERSHIP AND CORPORATE CULTURISM

In the early 1980s, the concept of 'strong organizational cultures' came to the fore of popular management thinking. Writers like Peters and Waterman (1982) and Deal and Kennedy (1982) suggested that companies could achieve greater commercial success if they employed symbols, rituals, and narratives to transmit organizational values in a way which made employees feel emotionally committed to the organization and work hard to pursue its goals. We can think of 'strong cultures' like organizational brands. Modern organizations often transmit their brand values internally, so that employees are expected to identify with the characteristics of the brand that is promoted outwardly. Ulrich and Smallwood (2007) argued that this process is about developing a 'leadership brand' which will inspire employees and consumers alike.

Many organizations like Virgin, Apple, and Google have developed this kind of 'strong culture', and focus on ensuring that employees demonstrate their commitment to values through their behaviour. There are lots of Youtube clips which take you on a tour of the Google headquarters in the United States. Employees can wear whatever they like, are able to take their dogs to work with them, can book a massage at work to ease their aches and pains, and eat free food in the canteen. The corporate culture at Google is designed to make us believe that, hey, suddenly it is cool to be a geek! Designer corporate cultures have an effect at the level of identity – the implication being that if you work at a 'cool' place, perhaps some of that 'coolness' will rub off on you too.

Schein (1992) argued that there are three levels to organizational culture. These are:

1. *Artefacts*: artefacts are the phenomena we can see, hear, and feel, which symbolize the organization's culture. They include objects like the organization's buildings and products and material manifestations of organizational values, like company slogans, training programmes, and newsletters. The also include the legends, myths, rites, and ceremonial rituals (like organizational award ceremonies) which are part of the social life of the organization. Artefacts are the means by which leaders can embed the values they wish to encourage, within the material and social fabric of the organization. The symbolic meaning of cultural artefacts, however, is contextual and must be interpreted. Even within organizations, employees can possess different ideas as to what a particular artefact represents.

2. *Espoused values*: espoused values reflect the 'rhetoric' of the organizational culture. Let's take the example of Google again. On its website, Google has provided a statement containing '*ten things that we know to be true*'. They include things like '*fast is better than slow*' and '*it's better to do one thing really, really well*'. '*As we keep looking towards the future*', says Google, '*these core principles guide our actions*'. They comprise the strategies, goals, and philosophies which justify the organization's processes (visions, goals, targets), and form a framework which aims to justify and legitimize action. These values are *validated*, Schein argues (1992: 20), when they are 'confirmed only by the shared social experience of a group'. As he points out, if leaders' actions do not corroborate their espoused values, members are not likely to see the values as being important or legitimate.

3. *Basic assumptions*: these are the commonly held, taken-for-granted assumptions, thoughts, and feelings which influence the preferred course of action within the organizational culture. To be effected, the espoused values set out by leaders must be 'reasonably congruent' (Ibid.: 21) with these assumptions. This is because the basic assumptions are so ingrained that any other way of behaving does not only appear irrational, but actually becomes inconceivable. These values are rarely articulated in writing, because they appear so obvious to the members of an organization that there is no reason to set them down in the form of 'commandments'. Since other ways of doing things are rarely debated or conceived, basic assumptions are often very difficult to become aware of, let alone change.

Often, linking the corporate culture assumptions and values to specific symbolic artefacts involves the kind of storytelling approach to leadership which was discussed in Chapter 3. The leader is seen as an architect or designer of 'truths' about the organization. Followers participate in the reproduction of this culture by telling and retelling stories about themselves and their colleagues which imbibe the cultural symbols with certain values.

Critics of the so-called corporate culturism have argued that this process can act like a form of 'cultural cleansing' (Strangleman and Roberts, 1999). By this, the authors mean that corporate cultures can remove or prevent alternative systems of values and assumptions from existing in the organization, giving employees little choice about what to believe and how to act. Sometimes this even takes the form of a 'script' from which employees are not allowed to deviate – as Bain and Taylor (1999) effectively described in their study of call centre operatives in the United Kingdom.

More often, the corporate culture values are embedded in the stories, symbols, rites, and rituals which make up organizational life. Casey (1995) studied an organization which introduced a corporate culture centred around the values of 'team and family' to encourage employees to retain close relationships with one another despite the introduction of a flatter, less obviously hierarchical corporate structure. She describes the unease that employees felt about this culture, and suggests that those employees who were seen to disagree with the culture were asked to leave the organization, or chose to leave of their own accord. This suggests that corporate culture is not always the force for good that management gurus like Peters and Waterman (1982) have claimed it to be.

BRANDING OR BRAINWASHING? CRITICISMS OF 'DESIGNER' CORPORATE CULTURES

Corporate culture represents, according to Willmott (1993), a sinister attempt to control not only the actions but also the emotions of employees that represents 'nascent totalitarianism'. The implication is that corporate culture is not always a benign technique aimed at making workers feel happier and more engaged with their work. The values embedded in corporate cultures are not neutral and equally accessible to all employees. Some individuals will find themselves better able to identify with their organization's values than others. For example, assumptions about the relative qualities, skills, and functions of men and women employees have been identified as core to some corporate cultures, especially in the service sector. Hochschild (1983), for example, points to the requirement for female flight attendants to provide 'service with a smile' and to embody the glamorous, sexy role of 'air hostess' in an appropriate way. The 2009 Virgin Atlantic television advertisement, celebrating twenty-five years since the airline first took to the skies, draws upon the image of the Virgin Atlantic flight attendant as female, immaculately dressed, perfectly made up, and at the heart of the airline's cultural values. Adkins

(1992) took Hochschild's argument further to suggest that within the tourist industry organizations she studied, the corporate culture values proclaimed that women were expected to provide 'sexual services' for customers. These services took the form of flirting when pouring drinks for customers, and wearing figure-flattering costumes and high heels. In contrast, the dress rules for men were far more relaxed, and men were placed in less obviously customer-facing job roles where 'flirting' was not considered necessary. More about the relationship between leadership and gender is covered in Chapter 6.

These arguments suggest that designing a corporate culture is not a politically neutral project. Rather, they suggest that corporate culturism can oppress and even 'brainwash' employees into believing in and behaving according to certain values. Yet these criticisms are often based upon the same assumption made by the proponents of corporate culture. This is the assumption that for an individual to be a member of a culture, they must share the same values as other members. As Smircich points out (1983), this assumption has two implications. First, any individual who subscribes to alternative values is somehow considered to be 'outside culture', and second that the values of a culture are static and pre-existing, such that new members have to adopt these values wholly in order to 'belong'. Smircich (1983) suggests an alternative perspective taken from the discipline of anthropology, in which culture:

- emerges and is reproduced from within the interactions and relationships of a group of individuals; and
- draws upon a variety of values which can incorporate differences of opinion, contradictions, and tensions.

Culture therefore involves a network of fractured values and assumptions, reproduced, resisted, and renegotiated through practice, which are at best only loosely shared, but which nonetheless help members of an organization to define themselves as a group (Adarves-Yorno et al., 2006). Culture is clearly an embodied, shared experience which cannot be reduced to a 'backdrop' of symbols and assumptions. Equally, it cannot be the preserve of leaders, just as leaders cannot be said to exist 'outside culture'. Even where leaders are able to employ the symbols and rituals of their choice in an organization, they cannot be sure how these artefacts will be interpreted and used by employees.

Studies employing ethnographic research techniques, which examine cultural interactions within their 'natural' context, reveal how employees attribute new meanings to corporate culture artefacts so that they can be used to alternative ends. Hawkins' ethnographic research (2008) within self-managed teams of recruitment consultants has reflected on this process. While senior managers imposed a James Bond/Miss Moneypenny fancy dress theme on workers in the hope that it would inspire them to engage in heroic selling activities, the consultants took the opportunity to reappropriate the 'James

Bond/Miss Moneypenny' corporate culture theme to their own ends. By acting out the 'undercover secret agent' role during team jokes and banter, they were able to escape the monotony of the working day.

Studies like this highlight the importance of contextual specificity in understanding cultural practices and interactions, yet the complex relationship between leadership and context remains under explored. The developing literature on the role of context in leadership practice is examined in the following section.

Setting the Scene: Putting Leadership into Context

Context is increasingly cited as a key dimension within leadership research, yet remains somewhat under represented in theoretical accounts other than in a simplistic manner such as the significance of 'task' and 'followers' in models such as Hersey and Blanchard's 'situational leadership' (1977). In a review of the literature, Porter and McLaughlin (2006) found only 16 per cent (373) of articles on leadership published between 1990 and 2005 in twenty-one leading journals took account of organizational context to at least a moderate extent as a factor affecting conclusions. They conclude that:

> In the field of organizational behavior generally, there has been a relative lack of attention to how the larger organization context affects specific areas of individual and group behavior. These areas would include, among others, motivation, communication, teams, and, as emphasized here, leadership. (Ibid.: 559)

In considering contextual factors they highlight a number of dimensions that are likely to impact upon leadership – including: culture/climate, goals/purposes, people/composition, processes, state/condition, structure, and time – and propose three recommendations:

(1) In the future, our understanding of leadership could be improved by making a concerted effort to focus directly on the nature of the organizational context as a primary object of interest, rather than treating it as almost an afterthought...

(2) In the future, not only is there a need for increased emphasis on the organizational context of leadership, but there is also a need to study the effects of interactions among two or more components of that context...

(3) In the future, we believe there is a strong need for the leadership field to focus on the dynamic aspects of organizational context relationships. In effect, there is a need to build more movies rather than just snapshots. (Ibid.: 573)

Osborn et al. (2002) make a similar case for a 'contextual theory of leadership', in which leadership is conceptualized as embedded within a specific temporal, spatial, and historical context. They suggest that leadership, as a social construct, takes its cues from contextual factors, which serve as the grounds within which human agency can occur. This means that different contexts require different definitions, or ways of looking at leadership.

The authors argue that where conditions are most stable, traditional, hierarchical forms of leadership are produced which employ systems of rewards and punishments. In contrast, where conditions are thought to be 'at the edge of chaos' (Ibid.: 822), organizations must engage with the highest levels of unpredictability and non-linearity. The authors draw upon complexity theory to highlight the possibility of infinite unintended consequences for each interaction, causing a so-called 'butterfly effect'.[1]

Under these conditions, leadership cannot be thought of as less tightly controlled and centralized, since any and every interaction has countless effects and implications. Understanding leadership therefore requires an understanding of: 'the co-evolutionary dynamics among the environment of the firm, its viability in the setting and its collective leadership' (Ibid.: 823).

POWER AND PRESCRIPTION: CRITICISMS OF CONTEXTUAL LEADERSHIP THEORY

One of the criticisms which can be levied at these 'contextual theories' is that they rarely take into account the implications of how power shapes the context out of which leadership emerges. As discussed earlier in this chapter, power is embedded in the material, structural, bureaucratic, and cultural elements of an organization, and has a constraining and enabling influence on the ability of leaders to pursue their goals and the ability of followers to accept or resist these goals.

Supporting this point, Ray et al. (2004) highlight how context, which the authors refer to as the *'stable sensemaking conditions'* (Ibid.: 321) informing the tacit knowledge shared by members of an organization, affects how forms of leadership are perceived and enacted. They explore how leadership is interpreted differently in a Japanese organizational context which privileges the group over the individual. The authors use this context to highlight how Japanese organizational processes like lean manufacturing and self-managed teamwork have not always transferred successfully to Western companies. They suggest that leadership practices cannot make sense to academics unless they are studied in their natural context, where they are embedded in tacit knowledge structures. An understanding of context is vital because: '. . . it provides the subtle, implicit, tacitly interpreted cues for enacting everyday actions that become the data for social scientists to interpret . . . the active process of "doing things" in practice is always shaped by the reflexively automatic use of "here and now" tacit knowledge that is deployed locally, in situ, by the actors themselves' (Ibid.: 332).

The *Quest for a General Theory of Leadership* (Goethals and Sorenson, 2006) was a five-year study by leading scholars into some of the commonalities across perceptions of leadership among academics and practitioners. It identified context as a key factor in leadership studies, but made links between context and power, by proposing that context offers a 'framework for action' that offers both opportunities and constraints for individual action. Context is linked to power because it allows room for individual agency yet shapes what is most likely to be successful; it both shapes and is shaped by individual actors; and combines elements of subjective perception and more concrete, observable features. In a recent special issue of *Human Relations* on the context of leadership, Fairhurst (2009: 1611) goes one step further to highlight the sequential and temporal form of leadership (and other human interaction) to propose that 'what is "text" one moment becomes "context" the very next'.

Yet within leadership theory and practice, we see a tendency towards prescriptive, normative ways of thinking about leadership which do not necessarily take the *uniqueness* or the *temporality* of each organizational context into account. Even Osborn et al.'s contextual leadership theory (2002) attempts to place the infinite possibilities for leadership contexts into four categories!

Like leadership, then, context can be hard to pin down in that, while it is often presented as having an essence of its own, the very act of describing it is socially constructed. As Grint (2001: 3) argues: 'What counts as a "situation" and what counts as the "appropriate" way of leading in that situation are interpretive and contestable issues, not issues that can be decided by objective criteria.'

What matters is not so much the objective nature of the situation but rather the 'story' constructed by each candidate and how this is interpreted and conveyed by others. Grint (2005b) shows how the events leading up to the second Gulf war, enabled George W. Bush to construct the situation as a 'crisis' which, he argued, justified a command response (war). Other constructions of contexts demand alternative responses. For example, under the so-called 'tame' conditions, in which the context is constructed in a similar way by various parties, Grint argues that problems require a managerial response – a known solution to an existing problem. In contrast, extremely complex problems with high levels of unknown variables are often constructed differently by parties with opposing interests. Finding solutions to problems like the global economic recession or climate change is therefore much more difficult. These problems are termed 'wicked' and are argued by Grint (2005b) to require a 'leadership response'. By this, Grint means that a leader is required in order to unite the different perspectives surrounding the problem, thus allowing everyone to pursue a shared goal.

The accounts of leaders, as they justify the decisions they make, represent attempts at sensemaking that give meaning to the associated actions they propose. Indeed, as the historian E. H. Carr explains, an account of history (and/or context) is always a view from somewhere, as illustrated in the following quote:

The facts of history never come to us 'pure', since they do not and can not exist in a pure form: they are always refracted through the mind of the recorder. The facts are not at all like fish on the fishmonger's slab. They are like fish swimming about in a vast and sometimes inaccessible ocean; and what the historian catches will depend, partly on chance, but mainly on what part of the ocean he chooses to fish in and what tackle he chooses to use – these two factors being, of course, determined by the kind of fish he wants to catch. By and large, the historian will get the kind of facts he wants. History means interpretation. (Carr, 2002: 19)

Context therefore not only encompasses the situation within which leadership takes place but also the framework of assumptions, beliefs, and practices through which we come to know what leadership *is*.

Researching Leadership in Organizations

Before we conclude this chapter, we should point out that our understanding of leadership in organizations has, in the past, largely been constructed through the quantitative, questionnaire-based research methods which have historically dominated the field of Leadership Studies. These are important sources of knowledge, but can only take us so far. To complement these perspectives, researchers are increasingly calling for the kind of qualitative research which is more applicable to studies of leadership in context.

Quantitative research has made and will continue to make a huge contribution to our understanding of leadership. It has the capacity to provide a wide-ranging picture which *describes* and ranks leadership and leaders according to various categories and attributes. Yet qualitative data arguably provides a more *in-depth* view of leadership, with the power to *explain*, not just describe (Bryman et al., 1996). Interviews offer participants in leadership to tell researchers, in their own words, what is most important to them in the leadership process. Historical documents like the minutes of meetings and participant observation can tell us about the *practice* of leadership as it emerges in context.

Qualitative methods support a move away from attempts to generalize, objectivize, and universalize leadership. Rather, as Bryman et al.'s analysis (1996) of the England and Wales Police Service demonstrates, these methods highlight the nuances and subtleties which prevent a universal approach to leadership from being entirely successful. The authors' interview data demonstrates how attempts to introduce prescriptive charismatic leadership ideals into police training programmes were undermined by a continued belief in directive, instrumental leadership approaches. The authors suggest that the police service context, where levels of certainty must be sustained under often difficult circumstances, meant that police officers saw the need for leadership '*from the front*', with its greater emphasis on certainty and structure. Particularly on the ground, officers continued to reject the '*vision thing*' as '*soft*', irrelevant, and ineffective (Ibid.: 365–6).

Bryman et al.'s article (1996) is important because it highlights how context shapes the social reality of organizational members, from which they make sense of leadership practice. They emphasize the need for 'dialogue ... between quantitative and qualitative research in such a way that the respective contributions of each approach can enhance our overall understanding of a domain like leadership' (Ibid.: 356).

Qualitative approaches are commensurate with the perspective of leadership as a social process, which has dominated this chapter. A qualitative approach requires scholars of leadership to recognize that leadership interactions must, first, be studied as they occur *in practice*, and *in context*. Second, it demands the acknowledgement that the study of leadership is dependent upon the researcher's *interpretation* of events.

Following Alvesson (1996), we call for a more reflective approach, which does not attempt to pin down interpretation in the form of 'truth', but which opens up avenues which could lead to new ways of understanding. Providing 'thick descriptions' (Geertz, 1999) – detailed contextual information about the context and culture in which leadership occurs – can help to convince the reader that the academic has sufficient understanding of the accomplishment of leadership within a particular organizational setting.

Chapter Summary

This chapter sets out a range of debates surrounding leadership in organizations. It traces the movement away from traditional ways of understanding leadership as a set of traits which can be measured and categorized within the individual, towards acknowledgement of the cultural assumptions and discourses which surround leaders of organizations. Some of the perspectives we have covered here – such as the competency frameworks beloved of many corporations and industrial sectors – nonetheless hark back to the 'great man theories' we have covered in previous chapters. They are presumed to set out a comprehensive set of skills and trainable behaviours thought to improve leadership performance within and across different industries – yet as we have noted here, these frameworks, like leadership, are in themselves social constructs, defined by the 'ways of knowing' (Foucault, 2002) which delimit how leaders should behave in the specific circumstances in which they operate.

Like other aspects of organizational life, competency frameworks are not politically neutral or objective. They form part of the 'way of knowing' what it means to be a leader. Like corporate cultures and organizational strategies, competency frameworks are embedded in relations of power which can encourage individuals and groups to regulate their actions. Their function is to control, as much as it is to improve organizational performance. Indeed, as we have noted here, the link between leadership development and performance is tenuous at best.

Our arguments here have focused on examining the underlying assumptions that comprise the contextual framework through which we come to understand what leadership 'is'. Yet these assumptions are not contained solely within the walls of an organization. The social construction of leadership is not just influenced by organizational factors but is also permeated by the ways of thinking and doing which are valued elsewhere in our society. What might leadership look like when it does not take place inside an organization? Chapter 5 extends these ideas by exploring leadership from a societal perspective.

[] **NOTE**

1. A term coined by Edward Lorenz to illustrate how a small and seemingly inconsequential change in one part of a system can trigger a chain of events that lead to a major event elsewhere or, as he put it, 'does the flap of a butterfly's wings in Brazil set off a tornado in Texas?' (Lorenz, 1972).

5 Societal Perspectives on Leadership

In Chapters 3 and 4 we have explored leadership from individual and organizational perspectives. In this chapter we will expand our horizons to consider leadership from a societal perspective. Organizational scholars and leadership practitioners often espouse the benefits of trying to see the 'big picture' – to 'helicopter' up and down between the fine details of a particular situation and a broader perspective of the wider context. In this chapter we explore how the social context in which we live shapes and informs our understandings and expectations of leadership. We begin by looking at the idea of 'community' and the extent to which leadership in communities is similar to and/or different from that in organizations. Next, we consider how national culture impacts upon leadership and the extent to which 'globalization' may be fuelling a tendency towards conformance to a Western leader-centric ideology. We then turn our attention to the physical environment and how a concern for 'sustainability' might promote more 'responsible' forms of leadership. The finer things in life then become our focus as we consider what the areas of aesthetics, beauty, and culture might tell us about how we create and maintain 'value' through leadership. Finally we consider the moments when 'leadership' might not be the answer to the questions we ask.

Being 'One of us': Leading in Communities[1]

This section addresses two questions:

1. What if anything is special about community leaders (leaders in and of communities)?
2. Is communityship more valuable than leadership?

Leadership in local communities provides numerous theoretical and practical challenges. Apart from the intrinsic difficulties in defining the identity and boundaries of communities, leaders within them are both creatures of their surroundings and instruments of political and personal interests. Yet some members of communities come to exert extraordinary influence, and this becomes legitimized by association with particular institutional roles. For example, the local vicar, councillor, residents' association chair, and school governor are roles which potentially – but not necessarily – offer a base for community leadership.

This suggests that community leadership is exerted through some kind of organization; but is this the case – or can we think of ways in which leadership is done in 'community' ways, rather than in 'organized' ways? This section will therefore begin with a review of what is implied by these two terms: organization and community. Then we will examine what happens (from a leadership perspective) when organizations are described as communities, or when communities are approached as if they are organizations. Finally, we will consider the trade in benefits each way: what would we gain by seeking 'communityship' (Mintzberg, 2006, 2009a, 2009b) rather than leadership; and how does leadership theory help us to understand community.

First a word of caution: If it is fruitful to think of organizations as communities (or vice versa), it is only in specifically qualified senses (Gosling, 1996; Parker, 2002). By examining how leadership is exerted in communities, we may discover concepts and processes of use beyond the community setting itself. But there are clearly some significant ways in which communities differ from organizations (see next section), and these should not be overlooked. Despite this, it is becoming increasingly common to find networks of individuals and organizations referred to as 'communities', for example, in the notion of 'local health communities'; 'on-line communities'; and 'communities of practice'. What does leadership mean in these contexts, how is it done, and who does it?

Which comes first: organizations, the activity of organizing, or the principle of organization? Look out of the window now and what do you see? Whatever it is, it is likely to appear organized in some ways; not total chaos. It is possible that the world you see adheres to natural laws by which everything is ordered, thus expressing a principle of organization. If you decide to rearrange things – for example, to rearrange your room – you will be taking apart one manifestation of organization and imposing another. It is you doing the organizing, but the formative idea or principle that you are working to is that of organization. One of your most significant considerations will be 'where things fit', or in other words how all the items in your room relate to each other, taking into consideration your purposes and your aesthetic sense of beauty or order. So we already have three key aspects of the principle of organization: purposes, interrelations between things, and a sense of order. We also have evidence of unequal power – you took the initiative and had the resources and ability to rearrange all those things. If some of those things had been people, and had their own purposes and relations to each other, you would have had a harder time persuading them to reorganize according to your sense of order; if you succeeded we might say that you exerted leadership. Even if you compromised a lot, and the new arrangements were not quite what you had in mind, you might still be the leader in that organization for all sorts of other reasons (such as your standing in the wider network of stakeholders, your status or position, your ability to represent the identity or interests of the group). In any case, in this example you can see the distinctions between organizing, organization, and organizations; and also the connection to power and leadership. Some of the key ideas are purpose, interrelations of parts (to a whole and to each other), and a sense of order.

Can we say the same about 'community'? Not quite, because there is no verb of 'community-ing'. But as the following subsection will argue, the juxtaposition of community and organization helps us understand some of the subtler challenges facing leaders.

ORGANIZATIONS AND COMMUNITIES: SIMILARITIES AND DIFFERENCES

The terms 'community' and 'organization' are often taken to refer to quite different aspects of social life. Organizations have goals, tasks, formal structures, and overtly sanctioned authority: this is the world in which we generally look for leadership. 'Community' on the other hand refers to a more general sort of belonging, often associated with a place, and characterized by informal relationships. Private and even public sector organizations are owned, and can be bought and sold; communities cannot be owned by outsiders, and do not 'employ' their members.

There is often a tendency to idealize community life in opposition to life within formal organizations (Pahl, 1996). In such comparisons, organizations – especially those in which we find employment – are identified, rightly or wrongly, as sites of alienation and inauthentic relations. The reasons for this are fairly straightforward: companies and public services want us to work for them in roles requiring aspects of ourselves, but not the whole self. In the old days they wanted 'hands'; these days it is our knowledge and intelligence, and also our feelings, and even our spiritual commitment (but not other aspects of our humanity, such as our desires, phobias, neuroses, illnesses, perversions, and other assorted quirks) (Casey, 2002; Bell and Taylor, 2003). Commercial organizations make profits by extracting from labour a 'surplus value' over and above what it costs to employ and reproduce that labour: that is how capitalism works, including its post-industrial varieties. Community, on the other hand, is remembered as a place of belonging (but not, significantly, of ownership).

However, the distinction is becoming less clear. Several influential writers argue either that organizations should be more like communities (Handy, 1994; Mintzberg, 2009a, 2009b), or that communities should be more organized (e.g. Etzioni, 1993). Both these imply nostalgic images of authentic relationships, self-evidently meaningful activities, permanent containing social structures, and continuities. When referred to in organizational contexts under the banner of community, these images engender a sense of belonging to a transcendent unity: to be part of a community is more inclusive than to be part of an organization. Are community leaders concerned only with the organized mobilization of community resources? Do the other values implied by the term community have any use for leadership? And conversely could these values, summed up by the term 'community', bring something important to organizations (perhaps something better than leadership)?

CONSIDERING ORGANIZATIONS AS COMMUNITIES

Maybe organizations *are* becoming more like communities; and maybe they *should* become so. This section will examine such propositions by considering significant trends in contemporary organization. It is structured into the following four subsections: localization and federation; simulated communities; virtual organizations and the problem of trust; and collegial values.

Localization and federation

Federal political structures tend to emphasize allegiances to localities, in tension with the union of states or units. The principle of subsidiarity suggests that decision-making powers and resources should be located as close to those affected as possible – that is, devolved rather than centralized. But in reality the appropriate level of devolution is seldom clear-cut. For example, giving GPs the power to control health spending enables them to call on services that their patients need. But some kinds of health care require large-scale planned investment, ahead of local demand. The same tensions affect multinational companies: for a while in the 1990s, Cable and Wireless PLC operated as an explicit federation of its sixty-nine companies, and Unilever described itself a 'multi-local' multinational corporation (Unilever, 1996). One purpose is to be closer, more in touch, and responsive to local product and labour markets; another is to foster a local sense of ownership and commitment among employees, and the 'empowerment' of managers. The idea is that a business should be associated with locality, and be of a small enough scale to be comprehended in its entirety – more or less – by its members. But there are shadow sides to this. A large company organized as a collection of local communities could miss economies of scale and scope; there might be duplication of functions, and a myriad of local practices that get in the way of coordination and learning across the whole. Local communities can easily become fiefdoms of those who control the resources that others need. The same dynamics affect cities, for example: richer boroughs protect their interests against possible shifts of resources towards poorer areas. The leadership exercised by City Mayors can be crucial in mediating the competing interests of more local communities; and of course mayors compete with their peers for national resources and influence. Thus, we see that community leadership is intrinsically political; and so is corporate leadership as soon as one moves beyond managing a single project or unit, and has to contend with a plurality of interests.

Also relevant here is the argument for local specialization. In the corporate context this is expressed as the need for a company to focus on its core competences (Prahalad and Hamel, 1990), the things that it is especially good at, and in which it has a competitive advantage vis-à-vis others. Some suggest that communities are the same: they have a particular character for which they are known and which tends towards certain activities. One might be laid-back and relaxed – so should specialize as a holiday destination; another might be wired and frenetic, great for new-tech developments. So far so benign. Some communities might be poor, the people desperate for employment: this makes them a great location for sweatshops and low-cost production. But poverty and exploitation are unlikely to be characteristics that local people cherish (notwithstanding the solidarity and interdependence necessary for survival in these conditions). This example shows how commercial interests are not identical with community interests; they might work in tandem, and they might be in conflict: they should always be juxtaposed.

This is because the 'core competences' argument rests on a logic of concentration and focus, in which the characteristics of the community are valued for what they bring to the process of wealth creation, and not the other way around. A community leader should be concerned about the prosperity that organized work can bring to the community; and business leaders will value the community in so far is it is instrumentally useful for the business.

Finally, while localization and federation may permit greater diversity between provinces or business units, if they become too specialized and their leadership parochial and particular, there is less space for peripheral, experimental, or other 'non-core' activities – and perhaps also less tolerance of countercultural sympathies, 'deviant' behaviour, and so forth. Ironically, therefore, localization may effect deterioration in the kind of generous inclusive qualities that it is supposed to enhance.

Simulated communities

Where knowledge and intelligence become central to the work of an organization, it is people and their networks, rather than tangible assets, which form its core value. Leaders are therefore expected to create positive 'corporate cultures' to bind people together in a shared and mutually supportive sense of what matters. The very fact of the attention and labour required to generate and maintain such enthusiasm exposes the simulation of community, and also points to the work of 'communityship' involved in sustained collective enterprise. Is this work – communityship – the responsibility of organizational leaders? The paradox is that the more leaders believe it is they who create a sense of community, the less likely they are to succeed. From the perspective of community, leaders are members, not creators.

Virtual organizations and the problem of trust

The ubiquity of information and communication technology (ICT) introduces a spatial distancing in organizations, and even where colleagues work physically close to each other they may seldom meet face-to-face, as communication is conducted through email, video and voice telephone. Various symbolic forms representing the organization in its (physical) absence, such as TV adverts aimed at employees as much as at customers (an early example was a British Airways' transmissions on TV networks around the world as part of its employee empowerment campaign entitled 'the world favours the brave', *BA News*, November 1995). In virtual organizations many people who represent the organization and deliver its services are distributed around the world, and many are on short-term or part-time contracts. They have to be trusted to act in the best interests of the firm, and this has obviously led to speculation about the conditions for engendering trust. Charles Handy (1995) outlined some implications for organizations, based on the assertion that 'you can't trust someone you do not know, you can't trust someone who is not committed to the goals of the organization, and you can't trust someone who lets you down' (Ibid.: 213). So:

- Choose the right people – so make use of probationary contracts.
- Keep units small enough for people to know each other.
- Promote talk – and get people to meet whenever possible (hi-touch as well as hi-tech).
- Reinforce common goals, vision, mission.
- Reward loyalty and performance – and be tough on those who let the organization down.

These may be wise prescriptions, but they also tell us something about the social construct of trust. Handy takes it to be an aspect of a relationship between individuals, secure only in a network of people known to and answerable to each other. Larry Ray (1996) argues that need for this arrangement of trust-engendering relatedness is typical of contemporary conditions of 'hyper-differentiation'. This term refers to the way in which the collectivities to which each of us belongs are now categorized in minute classes: instead of referring to mass class-culture groupings, modern market taxonomies, for example, identify individuals in very small groupings of like-minded consumers. Niche marketeers aim at ever-smaller populations – and are able to do so because of better information about individuals, and hence more accurate targeting. This process of breaking down membership boundaries to more detailed levels becomes 'hyper-differentiation' when the defining terms of such membership are constantly changed and hence reconfigured: using a real-time search engine to do this is the basis of Google's business model. In effect, the boundaries defining groups of people multiply to the extent that they explode and dissolve, leaving individuals to form their own networks of contacts with whom they have enough in common to share some degree of trust. This is exactly what social networks do (Facebook, LinkedIn, etc.). Leadership of these constantly evolving networks seems to coagulate when there is something to be done: an event to organize; a petition to distribute; and so forth. At these points, the medium of the social network becomes a channel for communication, and the network assumes familiar characteristics of organization and leadership.

In more traditional modern societies, institutional regulations provide at least some of the conditions for trust and confidence – but these depend on confidence in professional and juridical procedures, and in the state to manage these procedures. If such confidence prevails, trust among strangers is unproblematic at the personal level because it is looked after by state and professional establishments. Alternatively, a more generalized morality may characterize social relations, in which there is shared confidence in good will, that agreements will be kept. This is the traditional notion of community, defined by shared values and expectations. However, Ray also posits a situation of generalized *dis*trust with little confidence in systems and institutions. He argues that individualized market relations generate such mistrust, because each actor is seeking his or her own advantage. The response to such conditions is generally to form and maintain networks of contacts which act as havens of comparative trust in the midst of a multitude of anonymous market relationships. This latter seems to be the kind of solution that the term 'community' implies, pointing once more to the manager's crucial task of defining and maintaining a sense of boundedness for those on the inside – of being contained psychologically, of being able to trust one another commercially and professionally, and of being allied to something greater than themselves that justifies self-control.

Figure 5.1 shows a continuum of 'belonging' from market relations to community. In each of these, the function of leadership must be quite different. Furthermore, most situations are contestable: they could be shifted more towards one or other of these characteristics, or described as several at the same time by people with different interests. For example, a Facebook

Market relations	Networks	Community

Figure 5.1. A Continuum of 'Belonging'

friends group might be a community for some of its members, a network for others, and a location for market exchange all at the same time.

Collegial values

There are some organizations that nominally at least think of themselves as communities: universities are a prime example, often defined as 'a community of scholars'. Managers, in this scheme, administer mundane resources on behalf of the scholars in such a manner as to preserve opportunities for scholarship. But this is by and large now a nostalgic fantasy. The production of academic goods is as regimented and managed as any other intellectual knowledge production process, and one can observe the same tendency to form tight personal networks, organize in small groupings, move frequently between institutions, and pay more attention to the terms of individual employment contracts than to collegial values. It may be, of course, that the knowledge creation process requires a form of collaborative work that could be seen as a form of community – there are certainly language communities defined by those who speak a particular jargon. It might even be that, taking an ecological view, academics as a whole, or some local populations of the species, are endangered communities. But this is taking us into the next section, in which we will discuss the ways in which communities can be conceived in terms of organization.

CONSIDERING COMMUNITIES AS ORGANIZATIONS

Images of community are necessarily diffuse, ambiguous, particular, and generally suited to being conjured with. Sometimes these images are crystallized into ideals, and act as ideological touchstones for political programmes; and the reality is that 'community' is too complex, idiosyncratic, and laden with unconscious meanings to be captured in any single theoretical or descriptive frame. Nevertheless, it is possible to identify several ways in which the term is interpreted; following Jacobs (1995), we list these as six:

1. *Communities of ascription.* Local neighbourhoods and their social structures, focusing especially on people's shared experiences and outlooks, and on how social networks operate. It is often this image of community that is referred to as 'traditional'. A salient feature of such social networks, however, is that membership of them, and of subgroups within them, is generally by ascription rather than choice.
2. *Elective communities of interest and commitment*, defined by shared characteristics other than locality. Although these shared characteristics may be more or less freely chosen (e.g. being a vegetarian on the one hand, or being disabled on the other), defining oneself as a member of such a community 'Community of practice' (Wenger, 1998) is an existential choice. The

proliferation of communities of interest can be taken as a sign of increasing value pluralism and of de-traditionalization. They are often seen as emancipatory in comparison with traditional local communities, which tended to be oppressive towards some subgroups – particularly in-comers, etc.

3. *Communitarianism* (especially Etzioni's version (1993)), which returns the focus to the 'social contract' in local communities, emphasizing reciprocal responsibilities and duties. Individuals cannot be allowed to do whatever they want (in opposition to libertarianism), while communities can do things for themselves (in opposition to statism) (Grint and Holt, 2011).

4. *Social-ism.* Another version of communitarianism arises from the argument that people can only be conceived of and understood in a social context. Societies have to flourish in order for individuals to do so; attention must therefore be given to the development of society as a whole, as well as to choices for individuals (Avineri and de-Shalit, 1992; Mulhall and Swift, 1992; Bell, 1993).

5. *Common sympathy.* Beneath much of the above lies the desire to see community as a distinct means of describing social relations. Such relations are based on common sympathy, voluntary reciprocity, and mutual respect, precisely the qualities emphasized by attachment theory (Bowlby, 1969) as promoting secure and trusting relationships. These are rather different categories to those used to describe social relations as markets (with a focus on exchange) or as fixed by hierarchies of state and employing organizations (focusing on authority and force).

6. *Community development and self-management,* voiced mainly by practitioners (e.g. Atkinson, 1994) in opposition to market forces and state bureaucracies. In practical terms it has given rise to co-ops, credit unions, development trusts, and numerous self-help and voluntary sector organizations. This is the stuff of civil society, in the defence of which campaigning groups, such as the '*Citizens Organizing Foundation*', are mobilized (MacLeod, 1995).

In each of these definitions, communities are arenas for organization – of social networks, of social identity, of interest groups, of a social contract of rights and obligations. Calls for communities to be revitalized and for organizations to become more like communities share this perspective: a notion of membership experienced via organizational roles; of communities constructed by organization. In this view, community members not only share a dependency on pre-organized organizations such as shops, schools, utilities, etc., but they also construct a network of organizations in which the community is enacted – from baby-sitting circles, dinner parties, and self-help groups to churches, clubs, political parties, credit unions, and so forth.

The community is thus seen as a summation of conscious goals, a multitude of small organizations expressing both the particular interests and the empowerment of its members. A 'healthy' community is one replete with organizations. It is a place in which people recognize a *'community of interest'* as a basis for organizing. When they do so as consumers of goods or services, or as residents, they identify themselves as stakeholders in specific enterprises. The ability of people living in an area to identify a common interest and to organize around it can have important consequences for more formal organizations – as demonstrated by resistance to wind farms in rural areas, and many other 'NIMBY' (Not In My Back Yard) pressure groups.

It is precisely these kinds of activities that break down in areas affected by large-scale changes. Although a frequent response is to call on professionals to take over responsibility for these matters, an alternative is to organize a new, indigenous way of dealing with the issues. Thus, organization becomes an explicit means for rebuilding a sense of community, which gives plenty of opportunity for leadership.

MEMBERSHIP AND BELONGING

In the previous sections we have assumed that membership of a community is desired, consciously chosen, or at least acquiesced to. But often we are placed in categories by other people in ways that exclude us from particular groups. Other people's assumptions about our motivations, political beliefs, and other characteristics effectively classify our membership of – or exclusion from – communities of various sorts. Thus, as well as belonging to communities of interest and of organization we belong to communities defined by individual prejudice and shared social constructs. These are the communities to which we have 'been committed' in the more pejorative, passive, sense of the word.

These kinds of groupings are formed at least partially out of unconscious desires to hive off and distinguish parts of the 'whole' of society or of organization. Communities thus come to represent split-off parts of society into which we project the more undesirable and frightening aspects of humanity that we would rather disown. These excluded groups then become objects of guilt and aggression (and even envy at the dependent positions afforded them). In this state – or rather in this kind of relatedness to other social groupings – communities find it difficult to be empowered, or to speak with their own voice, or to alter their behaviour and experience, because their definition and characterization is not in their own hands. An example is the 'community' of the 'underclass'.

In conclusion, one might elaborate a clear distinction between being included and 'belonging' on the one hand, and excluded and alienated on the other. However, each exclusion is by implication an inclusion of an 'outgroup', even if one has not selected it as such (Rioch, 1979; Giddens, 1990; Tönnies, 2001/[1887]).

RHETORIC, RELATIONSHIPS, AND AN ETHIC OF CARE

We have seen that communities are almost universally defined in terms of organization, and often by the number, types, and relationships of formal organizations within them. Members of both ascribed and elective communities seem to have a lot to gain by becoming organized, and this is an obvious role for leadership in the old-fashioned sense of organizing and directing collective aspirations and efforts.

So what do we hope to evoke with the hazy concept of community? One possible answer is that an 'ethic of care' – as distinct from one of justice – is struggling for a voice in this particular discourse (Gilligan, 1982). Conjuring with 'community' may be an attempt to voice a concern for people's needs (as well as their rights and duties). Even the most successful have needs for attachment, and in spite of all the apparent autonomy and independence of the contract culture, it certainly brings home the insecurity of attachments. Talk about community in organizations, and about organization in a community context, may in fact allude to the desire to talk about relationships in a way which is not possible in the dominant discourse of either. Leadership of community might thus be identified in actions that encourage these sorts of conversations; it is the practice of caring.

Being Global, Being Local, and Being Worldly

The previous section has illustrated how individuals within a society are connected to, and separated from, one another by their membership of communities. But what about our interconnectedness with people from other parts of the world? How do the forces of 'globalization' and multiculturalism impact upon leadership? These are issues we will consider in this section.

Management, leadership, and the economics of globalization are two of the most widely written about topics of recent years. Books, scholarly papers in peer-reviewed journals, textbooks, popular books – for a while it felt as if anything academics wrote had to contain a section on globalization, preferably at the beginning. Scholars of management and organization, sociology, anthropology, religion, geography, all contributed to the debate. Advertising and marketing reflected the trend as well – slogans such as 'think global, act local' or 'the world's local business' tell us that this is a serious company, with ambitions that stretch beyond just one little country, beyond continents, to encompass the entire planet we live on.

How did this happen? When did managers and leaders in organizations start to think about the globe as their potential market, rather than limit commerce to an urban area like Exeter, a region like Devon, or a country like the United Kingdom? How did we all become global instead of local? Why has globalization generated so many countermovements, protest groups, and demonstrations?

If we start to think about the idea of globalization in more depth, and especially if we think about it historically or in terms of research evidence, then we find that globalization is not as complete or novel as marketing departments and advertising companies suggest. This is especially the case if we only think about globalization as an economic phenomenon. This section is an encouragement to think about globalization beyond the usual ways of economic or trade statistics. It is time to think about the globe in different ways, especially if we are also thinking about leading people. We are looking at the roots of global organization and globalized management through a key case, McDonald's, but then we look at an alternative, worldly leadership. This does not involve returning to a romantic idealized notion of local; instead it is a way of thinking about our worldwide context as diverse, as a source of creativity rather than as something to be homogenized or controlled.

GLOBALIZING, McDONALD'S BY McDONALD'S

The first company many think of when asked to name a global organization is McDonald's. Although the story of the company is familiar from promotional materials, books, and films, it is worth reiterating to emphasize the speed of its spread around the globe and its centrality to the process of globalization. Founded as a one-off local diner in 1940s California, the two McDonald's brothers quickly developed a set of products and a production process that would satisfy key customer requirements – speed of service, low price, and predictability. Their strictly rational, mechanized ethos, supported by colourful branding and a robust attitude towards employees and competitors, underpinned rapid growth. First, McDonald's popped up around north and central America, then gradually all over the globe. You can now buy McDonald's products in more than a hundred countries – around 45 million of us choose to do so every day. The company and its products have become so globally pervasive that its most famous burger is used by the British newspaper *The Economist* as a way of measuring whether national currencies are accurately valued against each other.

It is, of course, an extremely controversial organization. Its products have been criticized for their salt, fat, and sugar content; employment practices are frequently ridiculed, notably through the term 'McJob', defined as a low-skill, low-wage position with little or no opportunity for development; and the sourcing process, especially for potatoes and meat, cause considerable protest.

McDonald's is interesting for us here because of its business model. Sociologist George Ritzer has spent many years analysing this, coining the term

'McDonaldization' along the way. Ritzer (1996) defines this process (and way of making a business global) through four ideas. First, a McDonaldized organization has efficiency as its key aim; second, everything has to be calculable, or quantifiable, preferably in economic terms; third, a McDonaldized business process and product must be predictable; and finally, this kind of organization seeks control.

The model of leadership this implies is probably not one that most of us reading this book would be very happy with. Control, predictability, calculability, and efficiency all point towards a very transactional form of leading, based on extensive sets of rules and regulations, always oriented towards the fast output of an unvarying product. Managers and leaders will also be subject to the same ways of working – McDonald's expanded mainly through franchising, a tightly controlled way of starting new branches of an organization. There is little space here for creative leadership or different ways of thinking about the business.

Alongside this, McDonald's business model and Ritzer's notion of McDonaldization also imply a particular way of looking at the world as a place – as one place, to be precise, in which all customers want exactly the same thing, produced in the same way, with the same packaging, to be consumed in similar surroundings. American journalist P. J. O'Rourke once wrote 'if people were dogs we'd all be the same breed' – this idea is supported when you find yourself in a strange city or country and you look into, or eat in, McDonald's. It can be a curiously reassuring experience.

BEING TAUGHT OR EXPERIENCING

A British academic, Martin Parker (2002), has noted George Ritzer does not simply want to observe that McDonald's is a global organization based on four key organizational practices. Instead, Ritzer builds on this to argue that McDonald's, and the managerial ideals it has made into such a successful business model, leads to a form of cultural poverty. He holds up traditional, local, higher quality, more emplaced food and lifestyles as better, more real, more socially rewarding than yet another burger and fries made to a recipe developed in a warehouse in the United States. (Parker is highly critical of this 'bourgeois liberal' attitude, but that does not concern us here – what is important is that the two ways of living, the global and the local, are contrasted.)

We can also think about leadership in this way. Some organizations, especially the very large, try to develop leaders that can move anywhere and implement the same procedures or processes. Expatriate assignments are the most common form of this approach, with high-level personnel assigned to a country for two or three years then moved on to another, perhaps on another continent. These people may be supported in two ways (Ng et al., 2009):

didactic training programmes that are designed to transfer information about cultures and business systems; or through 'intensive cultural experiences', perhaps as part of the expatriate assignment, perhaps as preparation for it.

These two approaches to developing globalized leaders map well onto the contrasting approaches to doing business that McDonald's and George Ritzer outline. Sending people from the home base of a large organization to manage 'locals' according to prescriptions developed in Anglo-Saxon business schools, or to make 'them' behave and work in such a way as to ensure predictable production, can be seen as a kind of McDonaldized leadership. Encouraging managers to engage with the culture they live and work in, on the other hand, could be seen as more rewarding for everyone involved. The second approach draws on the academic discipline of anthropology, by taking culture seriously as a means of understanding people, ways of living, and work.

In their research, Ng and her colleagues emphasize two aspects of an experiential approach to developing leaders with an ability to work in a globalized organization or a global market. First, that it is a developmental process that takes place over time, sometimes a long period, not always visible in short-term appraisals of performance; and second, that the competence of leaders should be assessed or judged through their learning effectiveness, rather than their work performance. Their recommendations contain a different understanding of globalization from that of McDonald's and the way that organizations such as McDonald's require managers and leaders to work: less globalized, and more of a recognition that we all live and work in a varied, complex world. This approach suggests a more 'worldly' than global attitude.

TOWARDS 'WORLDLY' LEADERSHIP

One of the authors of this book, Jonathan Gosling, developed the idea of worldliness with his colleague Henry Mintzberg in an article published in *Harvard Business Review* in 2003. They share a fascination with what managers and leaders actually do and how they think (in contrast to most academic researchers in this field, who prefer to tell managers and leaders what to do and how to behave). Drawing on their experiences of researching managerial work and designing post-experience management education programmes, Gosling and Mintzberg (2003) identified five 'mindsets' that they think managers work with. For us here, the important mindset relates to managing context, leading with reference to the world that work happens within. There are two approaches available to leaders in contemporary organizations: global and worldly. The global we have already thought about; Gosling and Mintzberg characterize it as defined by generalization, primarily concerned with financial performance, travel, and commonality of cultures.

The worldly perspective, on the other hand, emphasizes specific responses to local conditions; the local consequences of managerial actions, socially and environmentally as well as financially; being in a place rather than travelling through it; and recognizing that the world is patchwork, not homogeneous.[2]

This echoes the anti-McDonaldized approach described above, with an extra twist. Gosling and Mintzberg argue that if leaders take a more worldly approach to being in 'other worlds', they will be able to know 'home' in a more reflective, thoughtful way. They will be able to be strangers at home, to see themselves and their own cultural contexts as outsiders do, acquiring the gift that Scottish poet Robert Burns so desired, the power to see themselves as others see them.

Saving Our Planet and Ourselves: Leading[3] for Sustainability

While we have concerned ourselves so far in this chapter about how our changing relationship with local and international communities is impacting upon leadership and management practice, what about our relationship to the physical environment? In particular, how are our working and lifestyle practices contributing towards climate change and the degradation of the natural world, and what, if anything, can leaders do to resolve this? This is a hot topic these days – a veritable tsunami of leadership books, workshops, and conferences threatens to swamp low-lying areas of thought, so we are forced to scramble for higher ground to get a sense of what is really going on.

Is there something special about leadership that is aiming at sustainability – rather than, for example, profit, growth, community cohesion? Or is this best bunched together with what we might call 'values-oriented leadership', to distinguish it from 'value-free' leadership, presumably concerned only with effectiveness and efficiency (for example) and ignoring any longer term, altruistic, or communitarian values?

Are there special challenges arising from climate change, which will require distinctive kinds of leadership or make new demands on people in leadership roles?

We consider here two principal ways to address these questions:

1. To whom are leaders responsible?
2. Is there a kind of sensitivity, a way of being in the world, consonant with sustainability?

First a brief word on definitions. Sustainability is as difficult to pin down as leadership itself. Any activity or way of life is sustainable only under specific circumstances – change and adaptation are inevitable; and the myriad of interacting factors mean that effects can never be known for sure. Best practice today might turn out to be less than that, or worse, in the future. So leading sustainability cannot be about adopting a predetermined set of behaviours or techniques; it is not at all like learning how to do management accounting, how to articulate a vision, how to convince people, be responsive to them, represent them…or how to do anything in particular. Rather, it must signify a readiness to constantly reconsider and adapt; and to do so in ways that give the best chance of long-term well-being, as far as we can determine it at the time. But in reality, a person's well-being is not simply a trade-off between short-term gains and long-term options; it is subject to competition with others, who may want the same resources and options, or who might understand the situation – and the science – quite differently. Leading sustainability is inevitably political and involves us in debates about values, about what really matters to us. Much less can be simply taken for granted. The two questions above take us into this territory, to which we now turn.

WHAT DOES IT MEAN TO LEAD RESPONSIBLY?

'With great power comes great responsibility.' Such are the wise words Spider-man remembers from his uncle. But what does it mean to be 'responsible' and how might one avoid the corrupting influence of power?

Clearly, leaders should act responsibly – we have seen the effects of irresponsible leadership in successive global financial crises, in developing countries, and transition economies. Legal regulations, voluntary codes of conduct, and rigorous audits all have a part to play, but we cannot get away from the need for leaders to exercise responsibility. These words are chosen carefully: responsibility requires exercise, and the challenges summed up under the banner of 'sustainability' make this abundantly clear. The physical impacts of climate change (biodiversity loss, water shortages, rising sea level, etc.) require innovative responses fraught with political choices; and the existential and moral anxieties evoked by such uncertainties will place extraordinary demands on leaders. We know from previous epochs of radical change that people – individuals and whole societies – respond to such upheavals in complex ways, often searching for salvation in totalitarian regimes, or escapist fantasies and a desire to opt out of responsible citizenship (Cohn, 1970). Leaders will be boosted by unconscious dynamics stirred up by the pace and intensity of change and also attacked for failing to provide the solutions, for taking sides or for not taking sides, and for promising too much or too little. Leading will become, increasingly, a practice of ethics (Ciulla, 2004) and the rigorous exercise of responsibility.

There is extensive literature on responsible leadership (for summaries and reviews, see Maak and Pless, 2006a; Maak, 2007; Waldman and Galvin, 2008). Maak and Pless (2006b, 2006c), in common with many authors focusing more on the analysis of complexity rather than responsibility (Stacey et al., 2000; Uhl-Bien et al., 2007), conclude that responsible leadership involves interaction among numerous elements and is thus inherently *relational*. It cannot be seen as a simple dyad of leader and followers; and even more fundamentally, leadership cannot be divorced from the context in which it is enacted – it is always leadership *of* some specific activities; among specific populations; and involves beliefs and ideas about purposes, reasons, actions; in other words, leadership always expresses shared meanings. Implicit within these are theories (not necessarily well spelt out) about what a leader is responsible for, and to whom. This has immense significance for questions of sustainability, and is the underlying concern of the worldwide movement towards 'corporate responsibility'. In the next subsection we will consider whether stakeholder theories of the firm offer a significant alternative to classical neoliberal models, and the implications for leadership.

Each model, interestingly, also assumes a quite different set of assumptions about the basic character of firms: At the core, what are the defining features of firms? From the perspective of society at large – which in various ways through laws and governments grants them licenses to operate – what are the distinctive mandates of businesses? And correspondingly, what then are the basic responsibilities of leaders who operate these businesses?

The word 'responsibility' refers not just to tasks and job descriptions. Fundamentally, to exercise responsibility is to act ethically. Often we misidentify or too narrowly identify the practice of ethics with knowledge and compliance with codes, the development and use of certain kinds of philosophical arguments, and/or attempts to live personally virtuous lives. While the practice of ethics is indeed related to each of these activities, fundamentally it involves the efforts to consider and assign priority to all of these and many other normative and value-laden claims; to consider as well the interest and claims of others involved; and then, in communication with others, to exercise judgement and take action. The practice of ethics is a skill-based, emotionally informed, relational (Maak and Pless, 2006b, 2006c), intellectually rigorous individual, communicative, and social activity (Bird, 1996).

HOW DO ASSUMPTIONS ABOUT THE BUSINESS OF BUSINESS SHAPE ASSUMPTIONS ABOUT THE RESPONSIBILITIES OF LEADERS?

What are a leader's basic responsibilities? For the leaders of commercial firms, the answers depend largely on presuppositions about the nature of firms and their place in society as a whole.

The classical view of the firm

Let us assume that a firm is something like a person, acting in its own interests and legally accountable for its actions. It belongs to its owners, and the managers who run the operations on a day-to-day basis do so in the interests of the owners – much as the organs of a body serve the interests of the person who 'owns' the body. My managers are not responsible for the welfare of your organization, any more than my heart is responsible for pumping your blood. In this set of assumptions, the purpose of a firm is primarily economic, that is, to produce, market, and sell goods and services for which there is a demand, and in so doing to generate profits for the owners and investors. It is the responsibility of the managers to ensure that resources (labour, raw materials, finance, contacts, and so on) are efficiently used so that the profits retained by the owners are as high as possible.

As Milton Friedman, perhaps the most prominent exponent of free-market, neoliberal economics, argued, 'the social responsibility of business is to increase its profits' (Friedman, 1970). Of course, firms must work within legal and social norms, but they should generally be encouraged to pursue their own interests in as inventive and cunning ways as possible. These assumptions have been promulgated almost uncritically by most business schools, and it is easy to see how the values of self-interest underpin the MBA market, which has been so lucrative for business and management schools. Students are taught technical skills in accounting, finance, operations, HRM, and marketing, and prepared to apply these in an integrated way through strategy and policy classes. Through all this, generally speaking, the purpose is pretty clear: to be ready and able to do whatever it takes (within the law) to further the financial interests of their employers. If there are ethical questions, they are about the process, not the purpose, of business. A manager might face a dilemma in choosing between personal and organizational interests; or mediating different norms when working across cultures. The question of responsibility becomes almost exclusively administrative, to do with method: and most significantly, these assumptions about the morality of self-interest carry across from the firm to the person, so that individual people are assumed to be like mini-corporations, properly interested only in their own profit, in garnering a return on their investments (of money, effort, love, . . .) that exceeds whatever they put in. If a person happens to have feelings of altruism, disinterested generosity, or sheer exuberance, these are private irrationalities, or misguided aberrations that should not be allowed to influence their actions as manager or leader.

Not surprisingly, there are many critics of this model. First, it does not adequately value vital resources such as trained labour, social cohesion, and cultural goods, all of which it treats as externalities to the firm, although in fact every organization relies on a daily basis on these goods. Similarly, the environment is taken for granted, as if it is an endless free source of water, clean air, and pollution-absorbing capacity (Daly and Cobb, 1990). Second, this model accepts a clear divide between capital and labour, treating workers simply as factors of production worth only as much as their employers are willing to pay. This, it is argued, leads both to psychological ills of alienation and material ills of inequality. Third, the model is criticized for encouraging greed and self-interest, and a readiness to exploit other people as well as nature (Bakan, 2004). Fourth, this model considers ethics to be limited to matters of personal virtue, public relations, or compliance. It does not allow that leadership might be intrinsically ethical – that is, about establishing and championing ideas about what counts as good and valuable, at all levels and in every practice of organizing.

The CSR/stakeholder model

The neoliberal model privileges owners and investors; critics of this model have focused on the interests of a wider sphere of stakeholders, all of whom have real interests in the conduct as well as the success of the firm. They argue that these interests are actually reciprocal, and that managers owe some responsibility to their social and natural environment (Freeman, 1984, 2004). Hence the term 'corporate social responsibility' (CSR) and the assessment of firm performance on a triple bottom line – financial, social, and environmental (Elkington, 1998). This model offers a number of distinctions from the classical view. First, the fate of firms is seen as intrinsic to their environment, and they are therefore held accountable to several stakeholders as well as their owners. Who counts as stakeholders may be defined narrowly or widely to include anyone affected – potentially including non-humans or future generations (Freeman, 1984). Second, the outcomes of managerial actions are to be evaluated in social and environmental terms as well as financial. This model has a long history in countries such as Japan and Germany, where workers, creditors, and local communities have a substantial voice in company governance; nevertheless, it is still spoken of as 'impossible' or 'irrational' in countries more rooted in neoliberal values.

The responsibilities of leaders are considerably extended in this model. Most importantly, they are expected not to leave their consciences at home – to develop and enhance their moral sensibilities and to encourage others to do so too. Leading is seen as the exercise of moral faculties, responding to the need to make judgements and choices, the consequences of which might be judged by standards other than simple profitability. At the very least, managers should make sure their firms act as good citizens and abide by codes developed by their industries or other pressure groups (Jackall, 1988).

In practice, this model is often not radically different from the classical model. It reminds managers to bear in mind the wider context of their businesses, but does not really threaten the primacy of the owners' interests nor the rationale for their actions. Variations of this model have been proposed and supported by groups like Businesses for Social Responsibility, the UN sponsored Global Compact, the Global Reporting Initiative, the banks championing the Equator Principles, and the wide-spread CSR movement (McIntosch et al., 2004; Webb, 2004, 2005).

CSR has now become a normal feature in many business school courses, mainly in recognition that managers need this additional set of competencies and concepts. However, the CSR/Stakeholder model has also been widely criticized. Some argue that firms are now expected to act like social work departments, for which they are ill equipped, and that we will all suffer if they are distracted from their core mission of making money. In any case, many firms seem to do what looks good, and continue their exploitative ways if they can get way with it. Even if they genuinely try to benefit wider stakeholders, this is too often piecemeal and uncoordinated because it does not connect to public provision. In some situations the perspective might still be too narrow: a desire to do some good social actions may fall short of the opportunities to invest in (and contribute to) economic and infrastructural development in an area (Bird, 2004a, 2004b; Whiteman, 2004). Although this model calls for a more socially responsible vision of the firm, it tends to reduce ethics to rules and compliance with rules.

The interactive, revised stakeholder model

Rather than viewing the firm as an agent with many relationships to think about (as in the classical and CSR models), some people – including prominent business leaders such as Narayan Murthy of Infosys – perceive the firm as integral to an environmental, social, and economic ecosystem, a part of a whole. Leaders are akin to the moral faculty of the system, and their deliberations are intrinsically ethical – even when apparently instrumental and narrowly focused. One example is the 'Moral Capitalism' espoused by the Caux Roundtables (Young, 2003). Like the CSR model, this assumes that firms must be viewed always in relation to their stakeholders. However, in distinction from the CSR framework, this model assumes *not* that firms *have* stakeholders, as groups in some ways independent of firms of which they should take account, but rather that firms are constituted by their ongoing interactions with their stakeholders. Correspondingly, a firm is best understood as a nexus of negotiated, risk-bearing, asset-creating interactions. It is only by virtue of these interactions that firms are able to operate and do business (Bird, 2001). Firms are correspondingly expected to maximize their overall worth (assets) gauged not just in relation to the residual returns due to shareholders/owners but also in terms of assets variously brought into play by their interactions with all of their relevant stakeholders: investors, creditors, suppliers, customers, employees, leaders, relevant governments, etc. Firms are expected to cultivate and maintain fair, reciprocating, and mutually beneficial (albeit typically asymmetrical) relations with their diverse stakeholders and to integrate and balance these diverse relations in the interests of the firm as a whole.

In this model, morality and economics are not separate concerns. The generation and distribution of goods and services are morally significant and it is the responsibility of those with power – leaders and managers – to think broadly about the nature of the value they create. Advocates of this perspective refer to it as 'asset developing', because the focus is on growing asset values rather than returns to investors. Assets might include goodwill and employee commitment (e.g. manifest in low absenteeism), rare materials preserved for future generations, and the legacy uses of infrastructure investments (Mowday et al., 1982; Glisson and Durrick, 1988; Bird, 1999). This model might be a more accurate description of how firms actually behave in situations where they have to balance the interests of many stakeholders, and where many of the people making decisions in the firms are part of the local community and prone to assess the overall contribution of the firm's effort, investment, and use of market position (Bird, 2006a).

A core concern of this model is to assess the ways in which firms add to or deplete the human and natural resources they use in their operations. How much do they augment or reduce the assets with which they interact? If firms deplete any resource (human, technological, financial, and/or natural), if they 'mine' any of these resources in practice, then what kinds of additional contributions do they attempt to make up for these losses? These questions are precisely those asked of BP by the Obama Government following the 2010 deepwater oil rig explosion and the subsequent massive oil spill in the Gulf of Mexico.

In this model, a leader's responsibilities extend beyond the firm – which remains central, of course – to a wider citizenship. In this context the assets of the firm are understood to include the human, natural, and social resources they use and build upon. These are the assets for which leaders have a fiduciary responsibility, and this is recognizable where there are public institutions able to demand such accountability – as in the case of the BP oil spill. If one were to ask 'what kind of leadership is this', one answer might be that it is genuinely 'worldly leadership' (Gosling and Mintzberg, 2003; this volume above); that is, they are expected to be realistic about their particular situations, their cultural contexts, current exigencies, past experiences, and future possibilities (Bird, 2009).

This interactive model addresses criticisms raised with respect to the other two models in several ways. Like the neoliberal model, it assumes that leaders primarily are responsible for furthering the good of their businesses but it then identifies this good much more broadly in relation to a firm's stakeholders. Like the CSR model, it draws attention to the interdependence of firms and their environments, but it is much more specific about the asset-development criteria by which the firm's social responsibility should be guided and assessed.

Beauty and Aesthetics in Leadership: Cultural Leadership

So far in this book we have considered how organizational and national culture impacts upon leadership, but what about culture in its broadest sense – art, literature, music, etc. – the various forms of expression that mark us out as human?

In Britain today, and in many countries around the world, culture is firmly linked to, and justified by, its benefits to society (diversity, identity, life enrichment, social cohesion, etc.) and its impact linked to statistical data on its contribution to the economy. Culture may be seen not as intrinsic to human life, but as an objectively assessed addendum. This objectification of collective human identity does not go unrecognized by individuals working in the cultural sector. Tessa Jowell, a UK member of parliament, stated while Secretary of State for Culture, Media and Sport that '[t]oo often politicians have been forced to debate culture in terms only of its instrumental benefits to other agendas' thereby avoiding 'investigating, questioning and celebrating what culture actually does in and of itself' (Jowell, 2004: 8).

According to Sutherland and Gosling (2010), cultural leaders see culture as able to 'open doors locked to mere words' that it is 'about everything', about 'quality of life'. They are not only committed to intrinsic cultural value but are committed to culture as an agent for 'good' in the world, a desire to help individuals and society through cultural engagement paralleling Greenleaf's arguments (1977) about *Servant Leadership* which were outlined in Chapter 2. The way cultural leaders describe culture indicates a belief that 'it' can *do* something for individuals and society in addition to the instrumental socio-economic benefits described above. The belief that culture has beneficial emergent properties for social well-being (expressing diversity, creating unity, etc.) is clearly present in the rhetoric of government and cultural organizations, along with statistical economic data.

Leaders of cultural organizations certainly employ this instrumental language, but invariably speak of aims that are more subtle, nuanced, and dynamic than measurable outcomes. One such leader refers to cultural leaders as 'salesmen' of culture, that cultural leaders have to be 'savvy' in packaging cultural products or ventures to say 'well what you get here if you buy this nice shiny thing ... is this nice social economic package', but embedded in this package is the real immeasurable benefits of culture, the 'magic'. For cultural leaders it is not the statistical outcomes that are important; it is about 'trying to get people interested in and involved in culture' (Sutherland and Gosling, 2010).

These cultural leaders work from a belief in the intrinsic value of culture, that its intangible emergent properties are resources for positive agency in the world. They describe two major activities in their leadership roles: (*a*) advocacy and (*b*) facilitation.

CULTURAL LEADERSHIP AS CULTURAL ADVOCACY

A significant part of the work of cultural leaders is pushing cultural events and values on policy agendas, fired by a belief in the inherent value of culture, at local (neighbourhoods, villages, towns), regional (counties and other geographic regions), and national/international levels (government agencies, ministries, funding bodies) in a bid to keep culture at the forefront of society.

This gives us a picture of cultural leadership as a distributed affair across many facets of society. Leadership is not confined to leading organizations; leadership is a more pervasive activity, a zeal to promote culture anytime and anywhere. Leading is exercised across wide segments of society in a praxis better described as leading a *belief* in cultural value and benefits, leading a *concept* that cultural engagement provides intangible benefits to the engaged.

Integral to this is *getting people involved* with cultural products and events, a facilitative mode of leadership practice.

CULTURAL LEADERSHIP AS FACILITATION

In and through their own organizations and communities, cultural leaders are engaged in a process of facilitation of culture, creating space and making resources available for others to engage. This aspect of cultural leadership practice is not usually overtly directive. It is characterized by listening, 'gently tweaking and encouraging people to develop it for themselves', and enabling others to 'step forward' while knowing when to step back. This is an approach very different to more directive modes, often described in terms such as 'encouraging', 'tweaking', and 'suggesting' rather than directing or controlling (Sutherland and Gosling, 2010).

They see their work as part of a project of social enrichment but one much more subtly nuanced than the instrumentalization of culture characterized in policy documents. Quite the reverse: cultural leaders often perceive themselves to be engaging in creative processes that are larger, more powerful, and longer lived than any individual – processes that are transcendent and transpersonal. This is significant: although cultural leaders often define themselves through their work, they do not see themselves as the originators of results or outcomes; rather they are participants in transcendent processes of culture. Where there are tangible results, these emerge through interactions of individuals in, with, and through culture. What they lead is bigger than themselves and those involved.

They are thus doing more than creating space and encouraging others to make use of it; they are opening the doors of the imagination, affording the opportunity to touch and be touched by knowledge, insights, and experiences that are the very substance of life. This is famously described by theatre director Peter Brook as follows:

I can take any empty space and call it a bare stage. A man walks across this empty space whilst someone else is watching him, and this is all I need for an act of theatre to be engaged. (Brook, 1993: 5)

Nonetheless, cultural leaders approach culture as a 'tool' (resource, catalyst) for individual and social betterment. 'I do actually see cultural leadership as using cultural tools to bring people to a better place' says one informant in a recent study (Sutherland and Gosling, 2010). What are 'cultural tools'? Is there something inherent in cultural artefacts that magically enhances, transforms, and extracts potential out of individuals, groups, and communities? For example, does Beethoven's *Eroica* symphony naturally have beneficial powers? It is difficult, if not impossible, to identify any inherent property of a musical work (or any cultural artefact) that has definable and predictable beneficial outcomes. However, *participation* in events surrounding cultural artefacts like Beethoven's *Eroica* symphony – whether as musician, audience member, or any other capacity – *can* have beneficial powers. A young violinist tackling such a work for the first time *may* learn new teamwork skills, new musical skills, or gain a sense of pride and confidence. But these outcomes are not predetermined by the symphony itself. There is some causal relationship, but it is not tightly coupled. One way to think about culture as a tool, and the way that leaders use it, is to recognize that it has affordances: that objects and events have emergent properties arising through interaction with them by individuals and groups.

The term 'affordance' was coined by Gibson (1966, 1977, 1979) in relation to cognitive processes in visual perception but more recently has been used by cultural sociologists to contextualize the dynamic nature of culture in our everyday lives (see DeNora, 2000, 2003). As DeNora (2003) has concluded, referring specifically to music, the emergent properties of culture are affordances for *world-making* activity – culture as resource for action, motivation, thought, and imagination. Culture is a resource for doing, thinking, and feeling where culture in and of itself does not do anything or make anything happen but acts as a dynamic resource for activity based on the way agents respond and orient themselves – how they appropriate culture.

Leadership as the creation of affordances is not, as Bennett et al. (2003: 3) put it, 'something "done" by an individual to others', but is the facilitation of resources that allow the emergent potentials of others to develop.

Cultural or creative experiences can impact an individual's view of the world, they can lead to transformation. Culture affords these things and it is leading this concept, more than leading individuals or organizations or being advocates for cultural value or facilitating cultural experiences, that cultural leaders do.

Cultural leadership at its base is as its Latin root suggests *cultura* – cultivation. Is this not what should be at the root of leadership itself, the cultivation of individuals and groups, followers and leaders, in recursively reflexive processes distributed in the interactions of individuals and groups as they dwell in the world? (Sutherland and Gosling, 2010: 13)

Margaret Wheatley has recently called for a shift of focus 'from hero to host' (2006) in leadership theory, and this might be another way to describe leadership roles that largely consist of receiving and welcoming others into the discursive and symbolic spaces for which they are responsible. So in examining the excellences to which they aspire, we would be mistaken if we expect them to exemplify planning or control; but is our only alternative to see them as facilitators? How might we recognize their passion for beauty in all this?

First, we might want to recognize an aesthetic rather than an ethical or rational sensibility (Ladkin, 2006a). If they enjoy the arts, it is for the sheer pleasure of producing a great performance, not only the doors that might be opened for others, let alone the mere efficiency of resource allocation or grim progress towards management objectives and achieving targets.

The love of beauty has been poorly theorized in organization, management, and leadership studies. A number of recent articles focus on so-called *aesthetic* leadership (Ladkin, 2006b, 2006c; Schroeder, 2008), but these address the perceptions of the audience, those who respond to the action of leaders, or who perceive in unfolding events the patterns and moments that they recognize as 'leaderful' (Wood and Ladkin, 2008). Atkinson (2004) pursues the metaphor of management as an art, arguing that craftwork is the language of art, employed in and speaking to an 'artworld'. However, he concentrates on the art object, the process of its creation, and of its reception. Here we are concerned with a different ontological position – that leadership is – at least in the context we have described in this section – a beauty-making phenomenon.

If there is a science to this, and if it needs a Greek name, it would be *kalology*. Platonists have always venerated the three ideals of Truth, Goodness, and Beauty (Hutcheson, 1969 [1738]). The first two have had a good run in Leadership Studies; on reflecting on the nature of cultural leadership, we advocate bringing the enlivening pleasure of Beauty to the centre of our attention.

When 'Leadership' isn't the Answer

Anyone who has seen the film *Monty Python and the Holy Grail* will remember the scene where as King Arthur approaches the castle he meets a group of peasants who claim to be living as an autonomous collective. 'Here we see the violence inherent in the system ... look at me being repressed' shouts one of the characters as Arthur tries to assert his authority which, as they point out, is 'based on some farcical aquatic ceremony' in which the Lady of the Lake presents a sword to the king.

While this clearly is designed as a comedy, it does encourage us to reflect on the manner in which our countries and organizations are governed and the extent to which leadership – particularly the singling out of an overall 'leader' – can seem a rather unnatural act. Even in nations such as the United States and the United Kingdom that pride themselves on the democratic election of their political leaders, the successful candidate is far from the ideal choice of much of the electorate. Take Obama's success in the 2008 US Presidentials, 'more than 58 million of the nearly 125 million Americans who had cast a vote, voted *against* the winning candidate' (Gronn, 2009: 382, initial emphasis), and in the 2010 UK elections the Prime Minister David Cameron received just 36 per cent of the overall vote (BBC News, 2010). Such observations suggest the value of considering the alternatives to such a system and when, if ever, 'leadership' might not be the answer.

In this section we outline three alternative perspectives that suggest different ways of approaching these challenges.

SUBSTITUTES FOR LEADERSHIP

In an influential paper, Kerr and Jermier (1978) suggested that there are times where structural and cultural factors act as 'substitutes for leadership', thereby reducing the need for a formally designated hierarchical leader. In this paper they argued that previous theory was based on an incorrect assumption that '*some* leadership style will *always* be effective *regardless* of the situation' (Ibid.: 375, initial emphasis). Instead, they proposed that there are a number of characteristics of the subordinate (e.g. ability, experience, training, knowledge; need for independence; professional orientation; indifference towards organizational rewards), task (e.g. unambiguous and routine; methodologic-ally invariant; provides its own feedback concerning accomplishment; intrinsically satisfying), and organization (e.g. formalization; inflexibility; highly specified and active advisory and staff functions; closely knit, cohesive work groups; organizational rewards not within the leader's control; spatial distance between superior and subordinates) that may well 'substitute' for, or 'neutralize' the effects of, leadership. These suggestions were supported by their own empirical work, from which it was concluded that in more than half of the scenarios explored the factors outlined above either act as significant moderators of, or replace the need for, hierarchical influence from a nomin-ated leader. In conclusion, they proposed, that 'if we really want to know more about the sources and consequences of guidance and good feelings in organizations, we should be prepared to study these things *whether or not* they happen to be provided through hierarchical leadership' (Ibid.: 401, initial emphasis).

Subsequent work has explored how, for example, 'self-managed teams' (Manz and Sims, 1980), 'leadership couples' (Gronn, 1999), 'shared leader-ship' (Pearce and Conger, 2003a), and even active 'followership' (Kellerman, 2008) can replace the need for a nominated individual leader. Each of these literatures suggests that in many scenarios, leadership is 'distributed' or 'shared' across many people (see Chapter 2 for further details) rather than being the exclusive responsibility of a single person. Indeed, they suggest that where leadership is widely dispersed, attempts by an individual to exert a degree of hierarchical control over the situation are likely to diminish rather than enhance overall leadership effectiveness.

An illustration of the tension between individual and collective leadership, and the tendency for the latter to not always be described as 'leadership' by those involved in it, can be seen in a recent project on leadership in partnerships (Bolden and O'Brien, 2009). In this research we explored the experiences of participants in an executive development programme based upon the notion of pairing NGO (non-governmental organization), independ-ent, and corporate partners to work together on an NGO-based project over a period of up to twelve months. When asking participants about their experi-ences of 'leadership' within these partnerships, they generally described it as collaborative and cooperative, and sometimes struggled to equate this with their understanding of leadership, as illustrated in the following quotes.

I believe the project has been jointly led throughout. Clearly as I am the one with the time and space to work on the projects that we identify it tends to be me who leads the execution but in terms of setting objectives and reviewing performance this has been done throughout as a collaborative process between all partners. (Corporate partner A)

I have a feeling we're equal partners on this project and none of us has really taken on a leadership role...So no real leadership in this partnership, but rather a cooperation...Leadership is not really relevant for us (unless I've understood the meaning incorrectly...). (Independent partner A)

Our partnership is of equal nature. There is no obvious leadership in the partnership however preference is always given to corporate partners when it comes to business plan...[we] remain the main contact and spirit of this partnership...it was more a team work – we have worked as a team.... (NGO partner A)

Here we see some division of responsibilities between members of the partnership based on time, expertise, and resources rather than a clear 'leader/follower' distinction. This appeared to be a relatively general pattern within successful partnerships and contrasted with accounts from those projects that had struggled and faltered. In the latter cases, there were a number of descriptions of where someone had endeavoured to intervene as a 'leader' and often failed to have much impact, as described below.

I think this project was a difficult one because the partners were not strongly engaged. Each party was waiting for the other to be told what they have to do. As a facilitator, I took the leadership to make things moving but I did not see any commitment from both sides. (NGO partner B)

Lacks common focus...I must admit a leadership failure as no meaningful meetings have taken place. A visit by [one of the programme organizers] helped redefine the project perspective, but again not sure how this is progressing as I have not heard of the current progress. (Independent partner B)

We experienced a lack of leadership from the partner...it was as if they were not actually asking for support...from our part it was difficult to lead the project without support and dedication from the local partner. (Corporate partner B)

In these instances we see 'leadership' being offered by particular individuals but not embraced by other members of the partnership. It is a prime example of attempted leadership without authority that founders due to the lack of shared direction, alignment, and commitment that appeared to exist in those groups that were engaging effectively (precisely what Drath et al., 2008 suggest should be considered as leadership).

The ultimate success of such partnerships, therefore, may be more dependent on mutual collaboration and a genuine appreciation and respect for what each partner brings than the best efforts of any particular individual to intervene as a 'leader'. In such situations talk of 'leadership outcomes' may simply muddy the water and fuel a desire to search out 'leaders', 'followers', and a 'common goal' in a way that fails to account for the complex and emergent role relationships that exist within true partnerships.

To conclude, a 'substitutes for leadership' approach encourages us to look for situations where the leader/follower distinction breaks down and to consider alternative ways of mobilizing collective engagement rather than assuming direct influence from a nominated or recognizable 'leader'.

The methodological implications of such an approach are outlined by Gronn below.

When undertaking research in a school, for example, a more parsimonious approach (in keeping with the spirit of the leader substitute idea) might mean *not* taking the presence of leadership (or its absence, for that matter) for granted. Instead, it would be more helpful if researchers were to inquire of prospective informants: first, whether they perceive leadership to be manifest in the case study site; next, what they understand by 'leadership'; then, what form that leadership takes (i.e. is there one leader, more than one leader or is leadership distributed between, say, couples?) and, finally, why leadership might take this form. In these ways, the aggregated raw material generated by a leadership researcher would comprise empirically grounded knowledge of contextualised perceptions and understandings, as well as some measure of the extent of informants' agreement about those matters. This material would then provide a useful starting point from which to construct an analysis of the processes that have helped to determine these working assumptions and the causal contribution made by leadership in accomplishing organizational outcomes, relative to other candidate siblings in the family of terms. (Gronn, 2003: 285–6)

ALTERNATIVE WAYS OF ORGANIZING

In the account above we suggest a number of situations in which leader-centric perspectives on leadership fail to explain how groups of people manage to work together in pursuit of a common goal. In this section we reflect on how alternative forms of organizing may also reduce or eliminate the need or desire for 'leadership'.

Take, for example, a professional law firm or general practice surgery. In both these environments there are a range of people, in a range of roles, delivering a range of services. Unlike traditional hierarchical organizations, however, there is not a single 'leader' (although such organizations often nominate a 'senior' or 'lead' partner) but rather a number of 'partners' who manage their own workload and that of the people working for them. While there are clearly a number of day-to-day activities that can be coordinated centrally, the strategic development of the practice is a joint endeavour, with a fair degree of independence and autonomy afforded to each partner. While it is entirely possible to frame professional work such as this as 'leadership', it may be that alternative descriptions work just as well and may even be more desirable for those involved.

Higher Education is another context in which individuals can be considered as relatively autonomous professionals (particularly research-active academics within research-intensive universities) whose work does not fit neatly within the bounds of organizational hierarchies (despite these being some of the most bureaucratic organizations you can find!). Research projects, for example, may well involve a number of partner HE institutions, and the content, structure, and process of the initiative are largely left to the discretion of the investigators, with the institution providing support for technical and administrative functions. The responsiveness of academics to a discourse of 'leadership', however, is variable between and within institutions. At the heart of this issue lies an apparent tension between experiences of 'managerialism' and 'collegiality', with the former being associated with top-down, hierarchical leadership, and the latter with participative, shared leadership as illustrated in the following quote by a Head of School in a recent study of leadership in UK universities (Bolden et al., 2008a).

I feel that a lot of my authority and capacity to lead arises out of the fact that my colleagues chose me to do it and did not want to do it themselves, which is both a negative and positive point. And ultimately, there is actually a way of doing things collegially which gives you great powers of leadership, therefore, I have been always resistant to adopt a managerial role like 'I am a Head of School and the VC made me run the school', because I think it would be much harder to run the school if I was like that. I don't have to do it, but it's lurking in their minds that they gave me the job and I am getting on with it and they don't want to do it. If we were in a different structure, where clearly there was a top-down thing and/or my job was a managerial one for life and I was just their head, I actually think that I would be in a weaker leadership position, not a stronger one . . . I think although I might have some of the managerial style, but I am a part of the collegial culture.

In Higher Education, and across much of the public sector, while there is much talk of the need for improved leadership to enhance organizational effectiveness, reduce costs, and secure future business, it needs to be done in a way that is sensitive to the culture and values of people working within these organizations. While talking about 'leadership', however, much of the evidence points towards a desire for better management, administration, and governance (and a shift away from traditional 'collegial' forms of organization), as illustrated in the following comments from a Registrar and Vice Chancellor (VC) respectively (from different universities).

You know, collegiality as an old organizational construct is dead now really. We all want to be collegial and work in a collegial way, but you can't run a £[XXX] million corporation in a very fast changing world in a collegial way. So, we have to be managerial, but hopefully, in a way that takes people along with us. It's not about telling people what to do, but you do talk to people and then you form a view – this is what we are going to do. (Registrar)

[Collegiality] is important in terms of the culture but I think it's probably problematic in terms of management because it's fine when you're spending money but it's useless when you're trying to save money. A classic example is what has happened in

[University Y]. The VC and his team there suddenly announced that they were going to close [x department]. It was then halted in its tracks by the senate who then referred it to the board of governors who then asked for a review. That may be wonderful as a collegial example, but if you've already worked out that that's the only choice you've got then where does that leave the management? It's a hopeless way of managing anything. I feel very sorry for the senior management team down there. (VC)

Such comments illustrate a tendency for the holders of senior organizational roles to bundle together concepts of leadership, management, and administration yet, in so doing, they may fuel scepticism about the true motives of organizational change and a reluctance of academics to become actively engaged in such work due to the very real tensions that it may create in terms of their professional identity. The following quote clearly indicates this tension as experienced by a Head of School during a period of industrial action within their university.

[The strike] has made me very isolated because [my academic colleagues] are all Union members... there was a wall of silence, they have not been able to talk to me about... I had to resign [from the union]. It got to a point where my position was just untenable. I couldn't be seen in their eyes to be undermining my colleagues, which is what I was effectively having to do trying to protect the students. I found the situation just simply untenable so I publicly told them I was resigning, and have done so. That was much more liberating then because I felt freer to take actions that I felt as a HOS I have to take... But I didn't go into this with a view to seek a career in management, which others might have done... so it puts me in the slightly odd position where yes I am management, but no I'm not. You're slightly caught between the two, and the strike has made me feel that very acutely.

The examples above illustrate how, in certain contexts, a call for more or better 'leadership' may actually distract attention from the real need to engage as an active member of a partnership or to enhance the effectiveness and efficiency of management functions. Perhaps, as Mintzberg (2004a) suggests, we have 'enough leadership' already and simply need to find better ways of working together. What alternatives then might there be to the dominant model of organizational hierarchy so prevalent in Western nations?

In a Centre for Leadership Studies seminar entitled '*Into the Bewilderness, Anarchism, Leadership and Groups*' (February 2007), Dr Lesley Prince espoused the virtues of anarcho-syndicalism as an alternative form of organization. Anarcho-syndicalism is based on the principles of 'workers' solidarity, direct action, and workers' self-management (http://en.wikipedia.org/wiki/Anarcho-syndicalism, accessed 27 July 2010) and challenges the dominance of both capitalism and the state. According to Noam Chomsky, a renowned professor of linguistics and self-professed anarchist, anarcho-syndicalism offers a means for creating a more equitable and just society, as articulated below.

Now a federated, decentralized system of free associations, incorporating economic as well as other social institutions, would be what I refer to as anarcho-syndicalism; and it seems to me that this is the appropriate form of social organization for an advanced technological society in which human beings do not have to be forced into the position of tools, of cogs in the machine. There is no longer any social necessity for human beings to be treated as mechanical elements in the productive process; that can be overcome and we must overcome it, be a society of freedom and free association, in which the creative urge that I consider intrinsic to human nature will in fact be able to realize itself in whatever way it will. (Chomsky and Foucault, 2006: 38–9)

The principles of solidarity, direct action, and self-management offer an intriguing parallel to the idea of shared leadership described in Chapter 2 and, arguably, offer an alternative to the notion of the individual or heroic leader. It promotes an environment in which all participants are regarded as equals, and each is held personally responsible for supporting the group in achieving its aims.

An alternative example is provided by Martin Wood (2002) in his paper 'Nomad leadership and the corporate war machine' in which he reflects on (amongst other things) what the US coalition could learn from the flexible and networked organization of Al Qaeda – an organization that despite the distinct lack of visibility of its leader Osama Bin-Laden managed to mobilize and coordinate a sustained assault and resistance to the far more mighty United States and allied military. Central to Wood's argument is a concern for how people relate spatially to the world around them and the extreme challenge of truly embracing an alternative world view. A compelling example of this is given through reference to the experience of Australian aborigines in the face of white settlement. According to the author Bruce Chatwin, aboriginals had no way of understanding the concept of land ownership and, hence, found it difficult to mobilize in response to acquisition of their territory: 'Aboriginals, it was true, could not imagine territory as a block of land hemmed in by frontiers: but rather as an interlocking network of "lines" or "ways through"' (Chatwin, 1998: 56, cited in Wood, 2002: 9). Such a difficulty was not the result of being 'primitive' or lacking intelligence, but rather the result of thousands of years of adaptation and survival.

Most of Outback Australia was arid scrub or desert where rainfall was always patchy and where one year of plenty might be followed by several years of lean. To move in such landscapes was survival: to stay in the same place suicide. The definition of a man's 'own country' was 'the place in which I do not have to ask'. Yet to feel 'at home' in that country depended on being able to leave it. Everyone hoped to have at least four "ways out", along which he could travel in a crisis... Territory is not necessarily the place you feed in, it's the place in which you stay... where you know every nook and cranny... where you know by heart every refuge... where you are invincible to the pursuer. (Chatwin, 1998: 56/113, cited in Wood, 2002: 9–10)

Nomadism is a very different way of understanding the world and holds some interesting considerations for those people concerned with leadership and the mobilization of collective endeavour. The British Army officer T.E. Lawrence (celebrated in the movie *Lawrence of Arabia*) understood these principles and put them to good use in his role in quelling the Arab revolt during World War I. In describing his approach, he referred to 'seven pillars of wisdom' (Lawrence, 1935) founded on the principles of a nomadic lifestyle and summarized by Wood (2002: 13) as follows:

1. Operating from an unassailable base
2. Enjoying autonomous movement
3. Tactics of detachment and disengagement
4. A process of continuous speed
5. A collective ideal of freedom
6. Recognizing the limits of leadership, and
7. The active constitution of democracy.

Within this work, Lawrence clearly extols the virtues of self-organization and collective engagement, warning against a simple attempt to draw a cause–effect relationship between the acts of individual leaders and the outcomes of battle as illustrated below.

The public often gave credit to Generals because it had seen only the orders and the result: even Foch said (before he commanded troops) that Generals won battles: but no General ever truly thought so. The Syrian campaign of September 1918 was perhaps the most scientifically perfect in English history, one in which force did least and brain most. All the world, and especially those who served them, gave the credit of the victory to Allenby and Bartholomew: but those two would never see it in our light, knowing how their inchoate ideas were discovered in application, and how their men, often not knowing, wrought them. (Lawrence, 1997: 582)

A final set of observations on alternative ways of organizing that we would like to mention draw on the concepts of 'complexity' and 'emergence'. Within the field of organization studies, these ideas are closely linked to 'systems theory' which has its origins in the field of systems dynamics, a branch of engineering founded by Jay Forrester in the mid-1950s that attempted to explore and model social systems. In his seminal book *Industrial Dynamics*, Forrester (1961) presented the results of his work computer modelling management processes within General Electric, demonstrating how instabilities in GE employment were due to internal processes rather than external factors such as the business cycle. Such ideas are central to many recent advances in computing, in particular artificial intelligence and neural networks.

These ideas have been applied to the study of organizations particularly through the focus on 'complex adaptive systems' (CAS) (see Anderson, 1999 for a review) and are gaining increasing attention within the field of leadership studies (see e.g. Wheatley, 1994; Goldstein and Hazy, 2006; Uhl-Bien et al., 2007; Lichtenstein and Plowman, 2009). In considering the organization (or any social group) as a CAS, the systems perspective enables a progression from analysis of individual actions to the recognition of higher order processes, particularly the emergence of self-organization. In a similar way to the analysis of the growth patterns of leaf mould or ant colonies, a systems-level analysis enables the recognition of macro-level organizational processes that may be perceived as evidence of intelligent design, yet are actually the consequence of far more basic-level adaptive responses.[4]

From such a perspective leadership, where present, 'should be seen not only as position and authority but also as an emergent, *interactive dynamic* – a complex interplay from which a collective impetus for action and change emerges when heterogeneous agents interact in networks in ways that produce new patterns of behaviour or new modes of operating' (Uhl-Bien et al., 2007: 299, initial emphasis).

LANGUAGE GAMES

In the sections above we see that there are times where traditional conceptions of leadership as something done by individual leaders simply do not work and, furthermore, may even adversely affect our ability to work together effectively. Throughout this book you will note that we often put the term 'leadership' in speech marks to illustrate that it is a contested concept with variable interpretations and boundaries. In this last section we will consider the discursive nature of leadership (as outlined in Chapter 2) and the extent to which it can be considered as a 'language game'.

In a highly influential paper, Pondy (1978) suggested that leadership is a 'language game' in that it is enacted through language. He proposes: 'The dual capacity to make sense of things and to put them into language meaningful to large numbers of people gives the person who has it enormous leverage' (Ibid.: 95). Fairhurst and Sarr (1996) suggest that this capacity is based on the ability to 'frame' things in a way that motivates and mobilizes others to take action or, as Bennis (1996: 154) proposes, 'effective leaders put words to the formless long-ings and deeply felt needs of others. They create communities out of words.'

It has already been remarked, in Chapter 2, that in its origins leadership is a particularly Anglo-Saxon concept – what, then, might this mean for leader-ship in countries where English is not the dominant language?

In German, the word for leader is 'Führer' – a term appropriated by Adolf Hitler in his role as Head of the Nazi party and which has acquired somewhat negative connotations since then – and the word for leadership, 'Führerschaft', is equally problematic. In French there is no direct translation and leader is often translated simply as 'dirigeant' and leadership as 'direction' (similar terms are also used in Italian and Spanish) – both of which highlight just one aspect of leadership: that of giving and setting direction, rather than nurturing, fostering, and developing a more collective approach.

If language shapes the ways in which we understand the world then we need to be very careful about how we use it. In an article about translation, Pavel Palazhchenko (2009) makes some interesting observations about the challenges of translating the word 'leadership' into Russian.

Take the word leadership, which is often translated into Russian as 'rukovodstvo'. In nine cases out of 10, it is a mistranslation, as this Russian word means guidance, management, or even control. So when a phrase frequently used by American politicians – U.S. global leadership – is translated, sometimes deliberately and maliciously, as 'amerikanskoye rukovodstvo mirom', which is something very close to American control of the world. It conjures up all kinds of nasty associations in the minds of most Russian readers. (Ibid.)

More than this, however, even where translations are made correctly people from a different cultural background may struggle to understand them if they do not correspond to common interpretations within their own culture.

The American concept of leadership is difficult for many of us to grasp even when the word is translated correctly. I have seen Russians perplexed when they were told that a college somewhere in Virginia has a program in leadership studies and even students majoring in leadership. They thought it was something too vague to be an academic subject. 'What is there to study, or to learn? You either have it or you don't', they said. (Ibid.)

This is a problem for those of us studying and teaching leadership, especially if we want to effectively engage with people from different backgrounds and cultures. It is problematic enough trying to persuade someone from our own society that leadership is a shared social process if they remain convinced that it is the property of particular individuals, let alone if we do not have a full grasp of the subtleties of their language and cultural background. The problem, however, may go even deeper than this if we take on board a social constructivist understanding of leadership. From this point of view, as leadership is constructed *through* language (rather than simply described *by* language), the important question is not 'what is leadership?' (an essentialist perspective) but 'on what basis do we label certain phenomena, and not others, as leadership?' (a constructivist perspective). Kelly (2008), building on from Pondy's work on language games, terms this the 'categorical mistake' of most leadership research in that there is a tendency to look for 'evidence' of leadership rather than the logic upon which practitioners (and others) categorize certain things, and not others, as leadership.

Consider, for example, a receptionist who, noticing that certain important arrangements for an event have not been put in place by their line manager prior to going off on annual leave, takes it upon themself to pursue a course of action to rectify the situation before it gets out of hand. Is this an example of leadership? Perhaps, or perhaps it is just a case of doing a good job. If the line manager had allocated the responsibility to the receptionist themself in advance, however, it may well be considered as an example of leadership . . . why might that be so and what difference does it make whether we call it leadership or not? In this book we would suggest that it makes quite a lot of difference as by choosing to call one thing leadership and not another we privilege certain things and downplay others. By referring to the response of the receptionist as an example of leadership we potentially empower and encourage them to act in a similar way on another occasion. By brushing it aside we risk devaluing their vital contribution and attributing any eventual success (or failure) to the formal leader.

Does this mean that we should call everything leadership in the hope that it will motivate and inspire our staff? Almost certainly not as people can be quite sceptical and even resistant to such aggrandizement. We need to choose our words carefully and follow them through with appropriate actions as illustrated in the following two quotes from mid-senior-level personnel in the postal service and air force, respectively (Bolden and Gosling, 2008).

When you do a leadership forum with this group I don't think people like standing on ceremony. They don't like big words. They don't like the bullshit stuff. They want to know where we are, where we're going, and how we're going to get there. They don't want namby pamby visionary stuff that's not real to them. Leadership for me is giving people something that is real. My leadership style is very earthy. It's not something that you'd get out of a textbook. It's around the interaction with people. (Postal service manager)

I do consider myself as . . . an Officer as a leader, but not in the charging forward mould, if you like. I don't think of myself naturally as a leader; I think of myself in terms of someone who wants to do a good job for the people that work for her and that's what leadership is to me – that's the leadership aspect for me. It's directing my people to achieve what I want to achieve but at the same time ensuring that they come in to work feeling valued, feeling that they can add value. And I am comfortable that if they are enjoying themselves, they feel motivated and they feel valued, even though I might be, as is the case on occasion, thinking 'crikey, this is really hard work' and there are times when my staff will come and see me and I think 'this is the last thing I want to do, given everything that I've got on my plate', but I know it's important. So it's the people aspect. (Air force officer)

Chapter Summary

In this chapter we have explored leadership from a societal perspective. We have reflected on the similarities and differences between leadership in organizations and communities, suggesting that attention be given to the manner in which we create meaningful and enduring relationships with others and a sense of belonging and being cared for. We have also considered how, while our world is becoming increasingly interconnected and 'global', we still embrace and value local differences. Geography affects leadership and leadership affects geography – we suggest a 'worldly' approach to leadership practice and development that enables us to see our place in the wider scheme of things while also embracing the richness and diversity of local contexts. The worldly agenda is extended further through consideration of the challenges of climate change and leading for sustainability. It is suggested that being 'responsible' in the manner in which we engage with our environment, both physical and social, is the key to ensuring that we (and our descendents) will still be around to enjoy the fruits of our labours. North American Indians reputedly have one key principle that informs their leadership decisions: that we should do nothing that harms the children, and the New Zealand Maori suggest that we must consider the impacts of our actions on future generations. Would either group intentionally engage in business practices that harm the environment? Almost certainly not, and why should we?

The chapter concludes by considering leadership from a cultural/aesthetic viewpoint, followed by reflecting on instances where 'leadership' might not be the most appropriate way of framing our experience of the world. At the core of these and other parts of this chapter are questions of value – what we value, what we give value to, and how we create and sustain value. These are notions that will be returned to in the following chapter from the perspectives of gender, well-being, ethics, and spirituality.

⬚ NOTES

1. This section draws substantially an arguments made in Gosling (1996).
2. The Leadership Trust has now established network and series of events on Worldly Leadership. For further details, visit: http://www.worldlyleadership.org
3. This section draws particularly on Fred Bird's proposals for how firms could value their contributions to socially useful assets, and Peter Case's commentary of the responsibility of managers. These were updated and summarised in a paper to the European Business Ethics Network in London, March 2010. See Bird, 2004b, 2001a; Bird, Case and Gosling, 2010.
4. Perhaps the most well-known example of this is Darwin's theory of natural selection which demonstrated how complex life forms could evolve through genetic mutation and 'survival of the fittest'. Engels (1987) also drew on similar ideas in his analysis of the social evolution and structure of cities.

6 Emerging Perspectives and Enduring Dilemmas in Leadership

Now that we have laid out the main arguments and considerations when looking at leadership from an individual, organizational, or societal perspective, we turn our attention to some emerging and enduring challenges and dilemmas within the field of Leadership Studies. This chapter has three aims. First, to do what the title promises – explore emerging and enduring dynamics or debates in the study and practice of leadership. Leadership Studies, as this book and others emphasize, is rather like a supermarket in the range of products you find. (A medium-sized UK supermarket offers the consumer around 20,000 separate product lines; fortunately the range of leadership theories is more limited than that, but textbooks or handbooks can be overwhelming in the variety they offer.) Each passing year brings new models, new fashions, new ideas, and new ways of seeing and thinking, vigorously promoted by consultants, gurus, academics, and the publishing industries surrounding them. This leads into the second task of this section – to be selective. British employee-owned retailer John Lewis is described by senior managers as performing a 'choice editing' function for prospective customers. Customers should have confidence that whatever they find there, whether electrical goods, clothing, or shoes, is all of an assured quality or standard. Not all ideas about leadership are equal, so we provide a similar service with this chapter.

Finally, we want more than anything to return to our original promise way back in Chapter 1 – to locate leadership and leaders as activities and as people embedded in a wide range of social and cultural contexts. Throughout this book we propose that you cannot understand or be confident in your knowledge of leadership unless you see it in relation to, for example, gender, globalization, embodiment, technology, ethics, or ultimate concerns of meaning. To convince you of this, we draw here on sociology and anthropology, academic disciplines that place the relationship between human and society or culture at the centre of analysis. This chapter should be read as an opening up, to indicate the most recent branches sprouting from the leadership tree (and those that keep resprouting despite the best attempts of certain parts of the leadership community to prune them away). It is followed by a final chapter, to summarize and conclude the book.

Why can't a Woman Behave like a Man? Leadership and Gender

A short exercise in politics:

1. Think of a leader.
2. Think of a political leader.
3. Think of a female political leader.

Did you get to a name? If you were born in the United Kingdom you probably came to Margaret Thatcher, or maybe Barbara Castle if you were born before 1960. If you are German or interested in Germany, then you most likely got to Angela Merkel's name quite quickly – you might even have got there before stage 3. If you are French, maybe you thought of Segolene Royal or Rachida Dati. If you are American, Hillary Clinton. Australian, Chinese, Indian, Japanese...well, we struggle to think of political leaders in those countries who are women, which may mean that (*a*) there are not very many; (*b*) there are some, but not known outside of their own societies; or (*c*) we have a very Euro-centric attitude to politics. Most likely a combination of all three.

Should we care about this? Is it important whether leaders are men or women? The battle for equality of opportunity has been fought and won, surely. Women are entitled to equal pay for equal work in most countries and the majority of occupations. Men can and do work with women without any difficulty; there are even countries and organizations where women are favoured, recruited, or promoted before men because they are women. Take Sweden, for example. The Swedish government passed a law recently that obliged private and public sector organizations to actively work towards a gender-balanced board. This is known as 'mainstreaming', meaning that gender equality is embedded in all aspects of work and leadership rather than seen as a separate issue. Was there a protest? Of course. Loud protest? Yes. Predictions of economic catastrophe, objections about state interference in private business concerns, and a lot of men unhappy that they were being discriminated against.

And yet...it has happened. There are many more women working at board level in Sweden now, and the economy has not collapsed. Men seem to be surviving as well – there have not been any reports of increased sexual harassment on men, nor any significant cases of women getting together to make men feel uncomfortable enough culturally to leave organizations. But the change did not happen on its own – the Swedish government had to legislate, had to intervene in the 'private affairs' of Swedish organizations, to make sure that women are represented in positions of leadership in the twenty-first century. So maybe the battle for equality of opportunity and treatment is not over, has not been won (or lost, depending on how you feel about equality). Perhaps the best indicator of the success of this initiative is that politicians in other countries generally seen as more socially conservative, such as France, are now talking seriously about similar legislation.

This is the issue we are thinking about in this section. Does gender or sex matter? Is (what some people see as) the battle over? Are women and men on an equal footing when we talk about and do leadership? Should we care whether a person has X or Y chromosomes, a three-piece suit or a skirt, lipstick or cufflinks, a womb or testicles? We are also thinking about a fairly radical perspective on this issue, in which gender is detached from the physical person – so we start to think about gender as a process that everyone performs or accomplishes every day, a process in which masculine and feminine behaviours are available to all of us, whatever our biological sex. But to get a clear sense of leadership and gender we have to go back in time a little, to the beginning of the story.

THE BEGINNINGS OF GENDER?

The story of leadership and gender begins in various places and times. Most of us are familiar with the beginnings of modern leadership theory in the idea of the 'Great Man', in the mid-nineteenth century (see Chapter 2). Shortly after this idea was popularized, the suffragette movement began in the United Kingdom, when a small group of radical, mainly middle class, women decided to challenge the assumption that they should not have the same social standing or economic opportunities as men. This movement led directly to women being granted the right to vote on equal terms to men, in 1928.

We could also start with what is known as the 'second wave' of feminist ideas and action in the United States and Western Europe, in the 1960s. Iconic figures such as Betty Friedan, Germaine Greer, and bell hooks published books and made speeches that would set political, economic, and social agendas for change in the status of women. It is worth remembering that at this point, well within living memory, many women in the United Kingdom and other industrialized nations were still subject to a 'marriage bar' at work – that is, if a woman got married she had to leave her job.[1]

Alternatively, we could look to research into management, leadership, and the question of gender. As you know, academic research can seem slow to acknowledge or recognize changing workplace practices. This is definitely the case with gender; despite all of the activity during the twentieth century and especially in the 1960s, the academic research story of leadership and gender only really starts in the late 1970s, with the development of a field known as 'women in management'.

WOMEN IN MANAGEMENT

The title of this research field gives a clear sense of the approach researchers were taking – looking at women as coming into management, entering a male world that 'they' should adapt to culturally and practically. This way of understanding gender in workplaces is still popular in many fields of research, such as entrepreneurship. If we take this perspective, women are defined as odd, 'other', and under an obligation to adapt. However, it has been challenged as a way of thinking. British academic Judi Marshall was among the first to think differently about gender; her ideas are set out in two books published about ten years apart.

The book titles indicate their content and approach. *Women Managers: Travellers in a Male World* (Marshall, 1984) analyses the stories of thirty women managers. They were working in publishing and retail, ten years after legislation had been passed to encourage/ensure equality. The key step that Judi Marshall took in her analysis of women's experiences was to note, and emphasize, that workplaces were designed, structured, and controlled by men, for men. At a practical level, this meant a series of things. Women were pressured to adopt working hours and patterns that were reliant on having a home-based partner to do the domestic labour and look after children. Women also reported feeling they should adopt masculine identities, to become more aggressive or dominating than they felt comfortable with, and feeling pressure to drive a certain kind of car to demonstrate belonging in the male managers' club.

Both books present alternatives and suggest actions that women could take to make this experience better or more bearable; in the first, Marshall proposes that women 'develop and respect their own themes within their own culture before attempting to engage with men' (Ibid.: 220), in combination with personal development that openly acknowledges the different experience of women as physical, social, and ethical agents. The second book, however, *Women Managers Moving On* (Marshall, 1995), is in some ways more radical. Telling the stories of sixteen women this time, Marshall revisits the experience of male-dominated cultures, but focuses on the option of leaving rather than coping or adapting. All of the women involved in the research either leave their jobs, are forced to leave, or think very seriously about leaving. Reading the stories in this second book, it is difficult to imagine why anyone would make the decision to stay in the workplaces described, man or woman, but it is entirely clear that the experience of women is different from men.

WOMEN IN LEADERSHIP, LEADERSHIP IN WOMEN

A little after women began to be included in analyses of management, scholars of leadership began to explore gender as well. Women began to be noticed in positions of power and authority during the 1990s especially, as some broke through the 'glass ceiling' and climbed over the 'concrete wall' (Parker and Ogilvie, 1996). The previously dominant 'Anglo-male' model of leadership, manifest in a variety of theories of leadership from 'Great Man' through psychometric and trait approaches, was being challenged by 'distinctly female' theories. As you might expect, this perspective characterized women leaders as better able to express feelings and emotions, more intuitive, better at personal relationships, more empathetic and collaborative, and generally better able to work in the 'network organizations' that were beginning to develop then.

There is a controversial issue embedded in this intuitively appealing idea. If the argument is set out in its most basic form there is an obvious point at which to object:

- women are different from men;
- so women leading will be different or behave differently to men; and
- women will be likely to construct different kinds of organization.

But, what if 'being a woman' is not something that is essential to being born with two X chromosomes? Are men and women somehow essentially different? Are we not obliged to at least acknowledge that becoming a woman, in the sense described in 'feminine leadership' theory, being more emotional, intuitive, and empathic, may be the result of cultural and social norms and practices? That gender, as some theorists (e.g. Butler, 1990) suggest, is constructed and performed? Is it possible that we 'do gender' every day, as we speak, work, move around, and lead?

PERFORMING GENDER AND FALLING OFF THE GLASS CLIFF

Alice Eagly and Linda Carli, in a journal paper published in 2003, work with this idea. In their reading of 'sex-typed' theories of leadership, which suggest women and men consistently behave differently, they emphasize that 'perceivers' impose stereotypical judgements on those being observed, rather than actually observing with an open mind. In terms of leadership, this means we tend to perceive it as a masculine activity, associated with men, and therefore discriminate against women we find in leadership positions because we do not expect to see women there as it challenges our expectations.

This idea is taken further by two researchers based in the psychology department at the University of Exeter, Alex Haslam and Michelle Ryan, in 2008. In a journal paper published in 2008, they note significant changes to gender distribution in large organizations; simple observations tell us that there are definitely more female executives, directors, and managers. However, they also note that change is uneven – women tend to occupy mid-level positions, women are paid less on average, and equality is concentrated in certain industries. In other words, top leadership remains largely a masculine sport and some workplaces are still segregated. A researcher in the geography department at the University of Cambridge, Linda McDowell, explores the extreme masculinity of the City of London in great depth in her 1997 book. It makes for shocking reading, especially if you are used to more gender-equal or female-friendly organizational cultures.

Haslam and Ryan take our thinking on this a significant step forward, building on the idea that individual attributes are not the most important part of the story of why women and femininity remain minor characters in leadership. They argue that the types of leadership position women achieve are different. This is the idea of the 'glass cliff' (see also Ryan and Haslam, 2005) – their archive research on board-level appointment in FTSE 100 companies shows quite clearly that when a company is performing poorly, a woman is more likely to be promoted to the board. This means, they argue, that women are promoted to the highest positions of leadership under distinctive circumstances – when an organization is struggling. This apparently systematic practice, of promoting those usually excluded from positions of power into those positions when things are going badly, was summarized in the headline on the US-based satirical newspaper the morning after Barack Obama was elected president in the middle of a terrible economic crisis – 'Black man given worst job in America'.

This is where this section ends, on a rather pessimistic note. All research on gender and leadership, whether from an essentialist or performative perspective, acknowledges the enormous progressive changes that have happened over the last forty years or so in Western organizations – the numbers tell us this. However, organizational cultures, professional norms, and other less visible barriers are considerably more difficult to break down.

Leaders Make me Sick! Leadership and Toxicity

Does the title of this section make sense to you? Do you want to read it? If you read it and thought, 'Yes! Leaders make me really angry, they make me want to shout, they even make me feel queasy sometimes', then this section is for you. On the other hand, if you thought, 'Terrible title. Don't understand it. Leaders make me feel happy, they give me a warm feeling inside, they make me feel full of life', then it may also be worth reading.

Academics have been writing about emotion in the workplace for a surprisingly short time (in terms of scholarship, i.e. where the base measure of time is decades rather than months or years). The roots of most of our thinking about management are in rationality, logical models of personality, behaviour, and organization – emotions, like independent thinking, were something to be hung up on a peg by the door as you arrived at the door of your workplace or the business school where you were studying. Good thing too, you might be thinking – the workplace should be a context where rational thought and reasonable behaviour are the norm, I get enough emotion and strangeness at home, I do not want to be dealing with all that at work as well. Well, yes – but organizations are full of people, people behave irrationally or illogically sometimes, and emotions come through the door with people whether we like it or not. (A bit like sex – for a long time organizational analysis was written as if companies were sex-free zones, as if sexuality did not happen at work. Given how many of us meet partners or have sexual relationships at work, it was a strange oversight. But that is another section, not this one.)

Whatever we prefer, emotions are with us when we work, lead, and follow (see Chapter 3). Leadership, interestingly, is one area where this is broadly accepted, perhaps because of the inherently emotional nature of a key concept in Leadership Studies, charisma. Interestingly, the idea of charisma is one of the few ways of understanding leadership that has always acknowledged its potential for damage and destruction. This section is not about charisma, however – it is about things called toxic emotions, and the closely related notion of toxic leadership. One of the darker sides of leadership, related to psychological and physical well-being, or lack of well-being. The question we are going to think about is, how do the emotions inevitably generated in the leadership process become toxic or damaging, and is there anything we can (a) do about this and (b) do to protect ourselves and others.

TOXIC EMOTIONS

The study of toxic emotions builds on the idea of work being both a rational and emotional activity. In the late 1970s, American sociologist Arlie Russell Hochschild (1983) was conducting research on two occupational groups in California: debt collectors and air stewards. As she collected data she began to notice that the people she was observing and interviewing worked very hard emotionally in their jobs. They were not necessarily working hard physically in the way that, say, builders or factory workers do. What they were doing was stretching themselves at work emotionally, being polite to difficult or rude customers, smiling, or feigning amusement. It is working hard – one of the stewards tells a story that makes this clear. A passenger is sounding off about how easy her job is, just serving a few drinks and being nice to people. The steward listens patiently, then asks the passenger to smile. 'Now, hold that for the next 10 hours', she tells him.

For Hochschild, the idea that emotions had become part of managed working life was interesting because it challenged the idea that workplaces demand only rational labour, that work was a process dominated by cold, hard-edged logic. Her argument has turned out to be one of the most influential of recent years in the study of organizations, in academic circles, and popular writings about work. It has been verified, replicated, adapted, refined, and challenged in many different organizational contexts and cultures. The development of it we are interested in here is the notion of 'toxic' emotion. This idea is also very closely associated with one academic, Peter Frost (Frost and Robinson, 1999; Frost, 2003).

HANDLING TOXINS AT WORK

In the late 1990s, Frost was elected head of department in the business school where he worked at the University of British Columbia. During his time as Head of Department, Frost observed (and experienced) an expectation to behave as a kind of sponge, absorbing conflict, ensuring that people working with him were happy whatever the circumstances, and generally taking responsibility for all the bad things that might happen in his organization (and sometimes the world). Drawing an analogy with people who worked in chemically toxic work environments, Frost argued that certain emotions at work could also be toxic to one's self and colleagues. The analogy Frost draws, with people who work with dangerous or carcinogenic chemicals, is especially powerful when he tells us that he has been diagnosed with an aggressive cancer.

Despite his early death, Frost's work in this area continues to exert a powerful influence. He argues that while leading his colleagues he took on a role as a 'psychic sponge', a 'sin eater', handling emotional toxins generated by organizational dynamics and behaviours. Toxins and toxic emotions might be generated inadvertently, or by dynamics that are beyond anyone's control, or maliciously; whatever the source, they are going to have a significant effect. People cannot work as well as they should; they argue or fight, become ill, suffer from stress and get burnt out, leave, and die.

THE PSYCHOPATHOLOGY OF LEADERS AND ORGANIZATIONS

Although, as a lot of pieces in this book emphasize, Leadership Studies tends to focus on the positive, scholars and organizational leaders have found Frost's ideas very meaningful and helpful. By the standard academic measure, how many times other scholars refer to your work, Frost's work is influential; it also appears in most leadership textbooks, another sign of its influence; and it is generating a considerable number of research studies, that both confirm and challenge it. Alan Goldman brings together a lot of the ideas that come from Frost's work, putting work organizations 'on the couch' to analyse their pathological tendencies. (This is similar to what the book (Bakan, 2004) and documentary film *The Corporation* do.) The really interesting thing about Goldman's journal article (2008) is his argument that apparently minor injuries, if ignored or belittled, can reach high toxicity levels. It is obvious when people are behaving really badly, generating a lot of toxic emotion, bullying, or playing nasty micro-political games; it is more important, Goldman argues, to identify mild misbehaviour, 'normal' toxicity, and work to make sure it does not contribute to seriously dysfunctional behaviours and cultures.

He suggests that consultants can play a central role in identifying potentially toxic behaviours, and then help to handle them and heal organizational divisions. Even if you are hostile towards the therapeutic process or touchy-feely personal development programmes, Goldman's analysis and experiential descriptions are very convincing. He also emphasizes that these issues are inevitable in work organizations – a message that may not always be welcome. Have you ever worked with a leader who rejected anyone bringing this kind of idea?

In another article published in the same journal, Gallos (2008) works from the other end of this problem. Her focus is organizations where a high level of emotion is acceptable; interestingly, her case example is also a university, where she worked as an academic dean in the 'toxic trenches' of the organization. Once again, her analysis and recommendations may be read as idealistic, psychotherapeutic, or woolly – but if you have ever worked in an organization which is dominated by blame, scapegoating, secrecy, or revenge, then you will appreciate the need for action to protect and encourage a better standard of behaviour.

Finally, there is a second sense in which the toxic and leaders come together. In contrast to Peter Frost's image of the leader as toxin handler, Padilla et al. (2007) provide an altogether more frightening vision – the leader as toxic in himself or herself. Some scholars of leadership prefer to deny that destructive leadership exists, arguing that (to take the classic example) Hitler did not lead the German people, he ruled and dominated them. This feels like a semantic trick to us, though. It is much more interesting to think about the possibility that leaders and leadership can be toxic or destructive.

Padilla and his colleagues develop an interesting analysis of this possibility. They suggest that destructive leadership is enabled by susceptible followers (see Lipman-Blumen's 2005 book for more on this) and a conducive environment. This model does two things: first, it spreads the responsibility for destructive leadership, so that we cannot think 'if we just change the leader then everything will be fine'. Second, it encourages us to think about the effects of leading over time – as the saying that opens this article tells us, power tends to corrupt over time. A worrying thought for leaders, as power is also rather addictive for many of us.

Being Absent, Being Present: Leadership in a 'Virtual World'

Do I really have to go to work to do leadership? Some of the people we work with seem to avoid spending time actually in the organization that employs them. Academic work is an ideal profession if you are not very keen on workplaces – certainly in the social sciences and humanities, when the majority of time is spent typing, reading, administrating, or thinking, all activities you can do at a table anywhere. Indeed, there is a fairly convincing argument made that the more time academics spend away from the workplace, the more productive they will be.

Being a virtual employee has always been possible in this line of work; most of us carry images of the lone scholar, someone like Karl Marx, toiling in the British Library behind a pile of books to write the work of genius that will change how the rest of the world thinks or how people behave. However, working from home (or on the train, or in a congenial local café, or [if we can believe mobile telecoms adverts] from a beach) has been greatly enabled by the construction of the virtual world during the last two decades. It seems almost redundant to reiterate this, but . . . this has happened through a combination of information technology hardware, software programs, and the internet/world wide web. Academics developed the internet and email to enable intercontinental research and the movement of ideas; we have now taken it further to enable teaching and research supervision to happen at a distance, and to create virtual communities of hundreds, or even thousands, of students and scholars.

But of course the virtual world is inhabited by more than academics. In Western Europe, it is difficult to imagine a work organization that does not have an internet presence or use email. Many go much further than that, encouraging the construction and maintenance of communities that never physically meet. If you have ever become frustrated by people ignoring emails, or perhaps ignored virtual requests yourself, then you are familiar with the challenges of e-leadership or virtual management. Virtual teams have become commonplace in many organizations, especially those that provide services or in which employees are not tied to high-capital machinery. The theme of this section is the leadership of such virtual teams and communities.

REVIEWING A NEW FIELD

As you know by now, Leadership Studies is a research field that is littered with reviews of research and evidence. Despite the relative recency of the idea of virtual teams and leadership, there are already people working to collate what we know and suggest what we need to know. Avolio and his colleagues (2009), in a magisterial review of a century of Leadership Studies, use the term 'e-leadership' to describe our theme in this section. At a practical level, this form of leadership involves a team of people from different departments, organizations, or countries; challenges include everything from time zones to cultures.

This area of Leadership Studies only exists separately because most of our models of leadership are founded on some form of face-to-face interaction, leaders and followers being present in the same physical space at least sporadically. Virtual leadership, then, in a minimal sense, is the science and art of providing leadership that is mediated entirely through some kind of contemporary information technology system. Key issues here include communication, clarity, developing team feeling, and effective completion of tasks. Particular attention is being paid to the development of inspirational leadership in virtual or dispersed teams (Balthazard et al., 2009; Joshi et al., 2009; Purvanova and Bono, 2009). Despite the scientific rigour of the research being conducted, there does not seem to be a lot here that is very interesting or insightful. As you can see, the key issues are remarkably similar to the research agendas driving managerialist research into non-virtual teams and leadership – how do I communicate clearly, how do I make sure people feel like they are working in a team and not alone, and how do I make sure that people do what I want them to do. Important issues, for sure, and arguably what managers and leaders are paid to do, but not radically different to the 'problems' researchers were trying to solve a hundred years ago.

Except, of course, there is what social researchers call an 'intervening variable' in all of this research. Most of the research takes the virtual part of this equation to mean 'advanced information technology'; some researchers even conduct controlled experiments on team communication and leadership behaviours, with one team all in the same room and one team's leader outside the room (Xiao et al., 2008). But there is another possibility – to think more about what being virtual means.

DIGGING INTO VIRTUAL TERRITORY

What does it mean to you? All of the authors of this book can remember the pre-virtual world, when the most complete escape from the 'real world' was the television set in the corner of the living room. If you sat really close to it you could sometimes feel like you were in another world . . . But there were few other methods of losing contact with the material world, except in science fiction.

In 2010, however, most of us in Western societies have come to accept that there are now two worlds: the one with things and people in it we can touch, and one that we experience through a screen. This is the sense in which Avolio and his colleagues refer to 'e-leadership'. The idea of 'virtual leadership' may be too ambiguous, too open to interpretation, whereas e-leadership can only really mean one thing. The 'e-' prefix has a relatively fixed collocation in everyday use, thanks to journalists and technology companies – it has become almost as clichéd as the '-gate' suffix to indicate a (usually political) scandal of some kind. To limit the research agenda in this way, however, is to assume that contemporary technologies, and computers in particular, will determine behaviour, thought, and action in fundamental ways. Despite their impact on societies, workplaces, and lives, that seems unlikely. Thinking about what this second, virtual, world is, we should also be thinking about why it is named in this way.

Curiously, the usual academic source for word definition, *Oxford English Dictionary* (OED), contains four main usages for 'virtual'. It is only in the fourth, and even more curious, in the sixth and final subsection of that, where we come across the idea of the virtual as something 'not physically existing but made by software to appear to do so from the point of view of the program or the user'. So in the research that Bruce Avolio and his colleagues review, in the majority of the research into virtual leadership and follower-ship, in the emerging idea of virtual leadership itself, we are working to a very specific notion of the virtual. What else might it involve?

Following the OED, we could think about virtual leadership in three other ways, building on the historical and contemporary usages. First, researching virtual leadership could involve exploring the 'physical virtues or powers' that enable us to exert influence. Second, acknowledging the Latin roots of 'virtual' in the idea of moral virtue, the notion of virtual leadership could be related to the ethical nature of actions – Deirdre McCloskey does this for the idea of commerce in her 2006 book *The Bourgeois Virtues*. Third, and most challenging, the idea of the virtual could be read as an invitation to think about how we construct leaders as almost complete – in the sense that virtual refers to something or someone that is almost absolute or finished. Each of these senses of virtual could of course still respond to the underlying idea of technological mediation, with the implication that those leading and being led are not present in the same physical space. The most significant implication of this, in turn, is in the area of ethics.

VIRTUAL LEADERSHIP, REAL ETHICS

So the most fundamental aspect of virtual leadership, e-leadership, virtual teams, and working in virtual realities defined by simulation and computer-mediated communication is absence. Critical analyses of globalized market capitalism are increasingly concerned with this as an ethical dynamic. In 2010, the BBC broadcast a documentary series, *Blood, Sweat & Luxuries*. The premise of the series is simple and powerful – take six British teenagers, and ask them to work at the production end of some of the things they consume. As you might expect, this involved living and working in Africa and south-east Asia, often in horrific conditions, labouring up to 12 hours a day for very little money, and with none of the workplace 'rights' that we take for granted in Western economies. Leather for shoes and coffee beans to make lattes, both produced in Ethiopia, and a Filipino component assembly plant for the everyday technology that enables e-leadership are the most striking experiences. In each location, the documentary participants are brought face to face with the people who actually do the work that enables the consumption. Their attitudes and feelings about the labour process, and the commodities themselves, change radically.

This suggests that we are willing to ignore other people's feelings, especially pain and degradation, if we can't see them. To us, that sounds extreme, yet two events linked by a research project confirm it as a hypothesis. In the early 1960s an American psychologist, Stanley Milgram, began to wonder why so many superficially 'civilized' European people had committed so many appalling atrocities during the twentieth century. Milgram (1963) became convinced that people were more willing to obey orders from figures in authority if they could not see their victims. In other words, if we are asked to inflict pain on someone, or exploit their labour, we are more willing to do so if the person is not in the same physical space. To test his idea, Milgram designed an experiment. It has since become one of the most-repeated, best-known pieces of social science research ever conducted.

Milgram placed adverts to recruit volunteers for his experiment. He told the people who came forward that they were going to help with a research project about learning; their role was to ask learners questions and administer an electric shock if the response was incorrect. Each time the learner responded wrongly, the shock increased by 15 volts. The machine for administering the shocks was clearly labelled to indicate danger levels, and a recording suggested that the learner was suffering pain and ultimately dying. Crucially, the examiners were sitting in one room with a 'scientist', a white-coated authority figure, while the learner was invisible behind a thin wall.

Milgram and his colleagues predicted that a relatively small number of people would administer dangerous levels of shock/punishment. This was not what happened. Instead, around two-thirds, 65 per cent, of the voluntary participants continued to 'punish' the learners until the machinery indicated danger and the learner fell silent, after a period of agonized screaming and warning of heart problems. These results are generally accepted to be a reliable guide as to how we behave in the presence of an authority figure, if the victim is absent from sight.

The key issue, the research question, that Milgram wanted to answer was how and why people doing apparently ordinary jobs can act contrary to conventional morality, based on observation made during the Second

World War. During the period of Nazi rule in Germany and across Europe, many ordinary people participated in the bureaucratic processes that enabled the mass murder that has come to be known as the Holocaust. There are many competing explanations of those terrible events; one of the most controversial has been developed by the Polish-born sociologist, Zygmunt Bauman. In his 1989 book, he argues that modern work organizations, particularly those with strongly bureaucratic structures and norms of behaviour (i.e. the vast majority, despite what consultants and gurus tell us), reduce our ability to make decisions based on moral analysis. In other words, a bureaucratic or 'organization man' (Whyte, 1961) mentality encourages only a focus on the task, rather than its implications for others. It is obvious but worth emphasizing that large organizations, or globalized production processes, or virtual teams, all reduce the visibility of the others that we work with and whose well-being is implicated by the decisions we make.

As Dutch consultant and academic Rene ten Bos (1997) argues, the possibility that the 'effacement of face' that is inherent to a lot of bureaucratic work can lead to profoundly immoral behaviour is a shocking idea for those of us working in or researching organizations. Many of the ideas that underpin bureaucratic organizing, such as efficiency, rationality, and goal clarity, are fundamental to how we work and are recommendations for best practice in managing or leading. If this approach to working and leading, aggrandized by the distance introduced through advanced information technology, discourages moral thinking, the implications are profound. The issue of ethics is explored in more depth in the next section.

The Social Responsibility of Business is . . . Leadership and Morality

Documentary film experienced something of a comeback as an art form in the late twentieth century. Fortunately, for teachers and students of leadership and organizations, films about business were a large part of this revival – *Roger & Me, Enron: The smartest guys in the room, Ghosts,* and numerous television documentaries all treat business, management, and leadership in depth. Perhaps the most complex film, *The Corporation,* based on Canadian academic Joel Bakan's 2004 book, focused on the notion of the organization itself (not a riveting plot at first sight, but one that proves surprisingly engaging). One of the key questions addressed is morality – asking whether corporations and the people who make them up behave ethically, or are encouraged to think in moral terms about what they do for a living. It is a fascinating question in itself, and also for the way it opens up a fault line between those who think it is a good thing to ask and those who think it is ridiculous. The eminent economist Milton Friedman makes an appearance in *The Corporation*, for example, and treats the question with puzzlement and some contempt, responding: 'The only social responsibility of business is to make profit for shareholders'. Yes, but ... well, but nothing, really. Friedman is correct, in the sense that corporations are legally obliged to maximize profit for their investors. However, people work within corporations and retain the ability to interpret this law, to allow for different approaches to making profit.

In the last two decades, and this is the issue that vexes the makers of *The Corporation* and other critical documentaries want us to think about more than anything, the morality of doing business has come under more and more scrutiny. Two research fields, business ethics, and corporate social responsibility (CSR), have emerged from the debate, and subsequently given birth to explorations of what ethical leadership might be. The question of ethics (for there is only really a question or a process of inquiry, not an answer) is the core of this section. We present the argument that ethical leadership is not an option that we can choose to take if we want to; rather, morality and ethics (or an ethic) is an inherent aspect of leading and being led (as the previous section also emphasizes). In this context, part of the social responsibility of leadership is a willingness to question the ethical status of actions, behaviours, and of leadership itself.

ETHICS: IN THE NAME OF WHAT?

As you know from this book, definitions of leadership are like noses – pretty much everyone has one. In this section, we are thinking about leading from American academic Joanne Ciulla's position:

Leadership is not a person or a position. It is a complex moral relationship between people, based on trust, obligation, commitment, emotion, and a shared vision of the good. (Ciulla, 1998: 1)

This characterization provides a useful guide to thinking about leadership in a slightly different way, outside the usual confines of whether it is a set of traits, behaviours, or goal-oriented social relationship. Instead, Ciulla would like us to orient our thinking towards the complexity of leadership as a set of social relations that are inevitably embedded in a moral universe. Despite Stanley Milgram's research findings (described above), it is a rare person indeed who is able to behave in an entirely rational, instrumental, bureaucratic way. Organizational, managerial, and leadership decisions are inevitably coloured by morality and ethical consequences.

This feels like an insight that has always been with us, yet business ethics has only really existed as a field of study or managerial action for the last twenty years or so (Parker, 2003). Of course, ethics were present in work organizations before academics and consultants began to pay attention to them; sociologist Max Weber (1930) famously explained the emergence of industrial capitalism in eighteenth-century Western Europe by arguing that a 'Protestant ethic' encouraged rational labour and organization. Similarly, Roy Jacques' wonderful history (1996) of management action and knowledge makes clear the ethical bases and implications of the discipline. But it is also clear that business ethics is now a subject in its own right, with its own academic conferences, textbooks, managerial roles, and presence on most management education programmes.

As with any field of academic inquiry and managerial action, there are controversies and disagreements as to what business ethics is (or should be). Moral philosophy, on which business ethics is founded, is an enormously complex area of thought composed of competing ways of seeing the world and humanity – from classical Greek ethics to utilitarian ethics, Marxist ethics, and virtue ethics, via feminist ethics and pragmatism. Each brings its own long history of thought and argument, starting position, and implications.

However, there is a problem with business ethics and the version of ethics that informs much leadership research. In fact, a series of problems if we believe Campbell Jones and his colleagues (2005). In their excellent little business ethics anti-textbook, they argue that the standard version of business ethics 'forecloses' or limits debate by:

- drawing on a very limited philosophical base;
- neglecting the societal contexts of management and leadership, thereby implying that there is a universal ethics of business we can all apply;
- defining only a very few organizational issues as needing ethical reflection, such as child labour or bribery;
- neglecting the core of ethical inquiry, relationships with the other; and
- staying within a conventional political economy of business that is supportive of capitalist market structures.

This means that if we go by the ethics chapter of most organizational behaviour textbooks, or the large textbooks that focus entirely on business ethics, we will find that an 'ethical' analysis of leadership actions and theories can only be conducted in specific ways. According to Jones and his colleagues, for example, the collapse of Enron, and the complicity of the auditors Arthur Andersen in that scandal, is likely to be presented as the actions of a few 'bad apples' at senior levels in the organization – a failure of leadership, in other words. This assumes that leadership as an act, and leaders as people, ought to be operating within 'normal' business rules, maximizing profit, with a little basic ethical thinking to mediate and ensure that societal norms are not challenged by ways of making profit.

This is an interesting thought, that being ethical is largely a question of common sense, something we all understand. However, journalists interviewing those involved in Enron, and in the financial services companies that are now being held responsible for the continuing recession in Anglo-Saxon economies, consistently report that those people did not and do not see their behaviours as unethical. Quite the opposite; many suggest that they were behaving *ethically* by trading derivatives and gambling on currency movements. There is little data available as yet, as academic research catches up with recent events; but we might also predict that the leaders of organizations such as Goldman Sachs, Barclays, or AIG would also describe themselves as ethical.

ETHICAL LEADERSHIP?

This leaves us, as people interested in leadership and ethics, in an odd position. Surely not everyone can be right? Something is either ethical or unethical, isn't it? People behave badly or well, do the right thing or wrong. Well, if you have ever been involved in a discussion with a small child as to why something they have done is wrong, then you know how complex apparently simple things can become. To add to this, scholars have begun to question the role that leaders occupy in organizations. Gemmill and Oakley (1992), in what has become a very influential journal paper, suggested that leadership is an 'alienating social myth'. That is, leadership may be something that deskills followers and encourages dependency. The idea that we are responsible for the leaders we have, that we make and sustain them, is central to their argument. Drawing on ideas from psychodynamics, these authors propose that, through a process of reification, the abstract notion of leadership is taken as representative of an objective reality. This leads down a cul-de-sac, at the end of which we have to argue that because we are talking and thinking about notions such as 'leader' and 'leadership' we have to believe that such things must indeed be real.

In the authors' own words, 'the leadership myth functions as a social defence whose central aim is to repress uncomfortable needs, emotions, and wishes that emerge when people attempt to work together' (Ibid.: 273), the implication being that followers learn to depend on figures in leadership roles to offer them a sense of meaning, direction, and purpose. So, 'when pain is coupled with an inordinate, widespread, and pervasive sense of helplessness, social myths about the need for great leaders and magical leadership emerge from the primarily unconscious collective feeling that it would take a miracle or messiah to alleviate or ameliorate this painful form of existence' (Ibid.: 273).

The authors were writing in response to the reappearance of an ideal of charismatic and inspirational leadership in the 1980s, which is still widely presented as an ideal within many organizations. They were concerned that 'in over-idealizing the leader, members deskill themselves from their own critical thinking, visions, inspirations, and emotions' (Ibid.: 279). Leadership, rather than empowering followers to achieve potential, engenders a sense of alienation, helplessness, and failure that leads to passivity and a childlike dependence on the leader.

Another scholar, Jay Conger (1990), expresses similar concerns but from the leader's perspective, arguing that there are three main areas in which leaders can become deluded and lose touch with reality. The first of these is strategic vision. While we know that a strong vision has been central to the apparent success of many well-known leaders, the strength of vision and personal commitment to achieving it can lead to a stubborn refusal to consider alternative and competing approaches. This conviction that the world really is – or should be – configured exactly as we see it is diagnosed by Maccoby (2000) as narcissism, common among leaders because it is one of the forces driving them to seek power, and in their ability to make the vision become regarded as reality. In this situation, the leader may fail to detect important changes in context, neglect the necessary resources required to achieve the vision, or exaggerate the needs of others involved in the organization. In effect, the leader may become partially blinded, seeking out only information that supports their vision and ignoring that which conflicts. This situation may be compounded where other people within the organization fail to challenge the leader's vision, either through fear of repercussions or overdependence and trust in the leader's judgement. Conger explains this issue:

> Others in the organization, who tend to become dependent on a visionary leader, may perpetuate the problem through their own actions. They may idealize their leader excessively and thus ignore negative aspects and exaggerate the good qualities. As a result, they may carry out their leader's orders unquestioningly – and leaders may in certain circumstances encourage such behaviour because of their needs to dominate and be admired. (Conger, 1990: 291)

Conger suggests a second way in which leaders can lose touch with reality: through their own communication and impression management techniques. It is clear that effective communication is a key leadership skill; however, it is also one that is open to abuse. In order to make a vision more appealing, a leader may be tempted to distort the information that they convey, selectively presenting only those aspects that enhance their message. As well as serving to deceive followers (either intentionally or unintentionally) it may ultimately begin to delude the presenter as well. This is particularly likely where positive responses are received from the audience, which reinforce and confirm the leader's argument.

RETURNING TO THE IDEA OF ETHICS

Perhaps this is the reason why so many of us working in complex organizations skirt around the idea of ethics. It is complex, messy, and involves a considerable degree of introspection and self-criticism, which in turn takes time and is tiring, and may lead us into very uncomfortable places. However, it is possible, perhaps even necessary. Australian academic and consultant Amanda Sinclair bases her ideas about leadership on a very clear sense of the interplay of self, behaviour, and morality:

Responsible leadership requires a deep sense of self and community – valuing diversity, ethics, the individual and the collective. It is something that involves all of us, as leaders and followers equally, binding us in a moral relationship that can be quickly undermined through neglect or indifference. Leadership should be aimed at helping to free people from oppressive structures, practices and habits encountered in societies and institutions, as well as within the shady recesses of ourselves. Good leaders liberate. Further, we can liberate leadership thinking itself from its narrow instrumental confines, so it may reconnect with ideals. (Sinclair, 2007: xv)

This is the beginning of Sinclair's wonderful book *Leadership for the Disillusioned*, an opening up of the idea of leaderly ethics that is all too rare. It opens up this area and the possibilities for everyone involved in organizations, raising the possibility that the approaches we have taken to defining and developing our leaders is narrow and damaging. The idea of a leaderly ethic or morality is embedded here, rather than separate, dependent on the individual and the context, and oriented towards a sense of what it is to live a good life which is something more than efficient production and indulgent consumption. There could not be a better place to finish this section on ethics, and to start thinking about leadership in different moral terms.

Leading into a Meaningful Future: Leadership and Spirituality

This last substantive section looks at...leadership and the meaning of life. No, really, it does. One of the most disturbing questions we can ask when we think about leading, organizing, or managing, is what the point of it all is. We can find reasons to lead or to do things in our appraisal targets, in the desire to increase profit or help our organizations survive, or to make money to 'buy more stuff' for ourselves and others. There is another question, though, relating to whether what we are doing when we lead and follow makes any sense beyond material concerns. If you ask this question, and we think most people do at some point, perhaps not in the workplace and perhaps not to colleagues, but sometime to someone somewhere – then we are inevitably involved in a conversation about the spiritual, the transcendent, and the immaterial. There are many terms for this kind of thought, all of which carry a spiritual, religious, or eschatological connotation. (Eschatological – a fine word. Not used often, perhaps because it is awkward to pronounce, but one that deserves to come into conversation more often. If something has an eschatological aspect, or if we think eschatologically, then we are thinking about its ultimate meaning or destiny. Deep waters indeed – but why not think about such things? Leadership is a serious business, we devote a lot of our time and self to work – exploration of meaning need not be confined to philosophy or theology.)

When you think about the business school context, or most organizational settings, it is not surprising that this is not a research field that is very popular. Business schools are usually defined by what they and their inhabitants can contribute to economic performance or managerial efficiency. And yet… most of the films we watch that represent experiences of work juxtapose office and industrial life with the meaning of life. Think about the 2002 film *About Schmidt*. A man retires from his job, struggles to find meaning either in his life or in the work/place he has devoted much of life to, his wife dies, and he goes on a long road trip in a camper van to try and work out what his life and work have meant. Or we could think about *The Office*, the British TV series that has been exported and remade around the world. The central character in the UK version, Tim, talks in virtually every episode about the meaning of his life and the meaninglessness of his job. As Emma Bell (2008) writes in *Reading Management and Organization in Film*, there are hundreds of examples of the exploration of meaning and work in cinema, surely reflecting the concerns of the people who watch them.

So, conversations about meaning, or eschatological discussions, might not happen very often in business schools, textbooks, or management education courses, but it is something that concerns us in everyday life and in the popular culture we consume. Fortunately, there are researchers who are willing to take up the challenge of thinking and writing about organization, leadership, and meaning as if ultimate concerns matter in this sense, and we are going to look at two key perspectives in this section. This is a developing debate and research field, and therefore a good one to finish with as it is so forward looking. The perspectives are positive organizational scholarship (including positive leadership) and spirituality at work (including spiritual leadership). First, unusually, we are going to accentuate the positive.

NEGATIVE OR POSITIVE?

During the 1990s, some people in some business schools became more critical – critical of management, leadership, and sometimes even capitalism. Researchers began to gather under a new banner, 'Critical Management Studies'. People in this movement said they were challenging some of the embedded assumptions business schools host (Fournier and Grey, 2000), especially the pressures they felt to:

- focus on efficiency and productivity;
- see management as inevitable and 'natural'; and
- be unreflexive about the research methods used to generate knowledge.

Described in this way, the Critical Management Studies movement looks eminently sensible; if business school research and education prioritizes efficiency and rationality above all else, then significant areas of work and leadership, many of them discussed in this book, will be neglected to everyone's detriment. Very few of us want to live in the kind of world depicted in the classic 1927 film *Metropolis*, where there is little or no space for emotion, humanity, or fun. Similarly, if we take the idea of management for granted, including related notions such as globalization or competitiveness, then we never think about alternatives – local commerce, for example, or cooperation.

Unfortunately, critical approaches quickly acquired a reputation for being negative – critical in the worst sense. At around the same time, US-based academics were constructing another alternative to mainstream efficiency-oriented research and education, based in part on established traditions of appreciative and cooperative inquiry developed at Case Western Reserve University (Cooperrider et al., 1999). Cooperrider and his colleagues' work provided parts of the foundation for positive organizational scholarship (also known as POS; see Cameron et al., 2003). Researchers working from a POS perspective specifically approach organizations, managers, and leaders with the assumption that virtue, wisdom, respect, honesty, and human flourishing are all part of everyday working life. Although the presence of greed, manipulation, discrimination, or abuse are all recognized as aspects of organizational behaviour and leadership, the POS movement believes that if we focus on the good, the positive, then we will be in a better position to make workplaces more humane and rewarding to be in.

As you would expect, this movement has been challenged from outside the United States. Steve Fineman (2006), a UK-based academic with a long-standing interest in emotion in organizations, argues that the positive and negative bits of working life can only be understood if we examine both; and that accentuating the positive is a culturally specific project, deeply rooted in the United States, too individualistic and optimistic for many other cultures. Notwithstanding these well thought through objections, concentrating on the positive has gathered considerable academic and practitioner followers.

In our field, Kim Cameron (2008) recently devoted a short book to looking at leadership through a positive lens. Although POS is said to be about more than competition or making profit, his book's subtitle of 'Strategies for Extraordinary Performance' suggests that we are still in the domain of encouraging people to work harder or more efficiently. This is reinforced by the book's key contribution to understanding leadership, *positive deviance*. This notion was first mooted by the underlying discipline of POS, positive psychology. The term refers to intentional behaviours that are abnormal, but in an honourable way. The POS movement does not use examples from outside the United States or from more than five to ten years ago. However, the Soviet coal miner Alexei Stakhanov would have recognized the idea of positive deviance. He became a celebrity in the 1930s when managers in his mine discovered he was producing more than ten times his quota. (Stakhanov's story has been questioned and reinterpreted, with suggestions that he was helped by workmates or attributing his amazing productivity to machinery.) Stakhanov was reputedly disliked by his colleagues as much as he was feted by his managers and government, as you can imagine – he was the ultimate rate-buster (Roy, 1952), indicating to managers that those around him were not working as hard as they possibly could – a demonstration that often leads either to renegotiation of the rate for the job or the performative norm. Either way lies work intensification.

Alongside personal performance that 'dramatically' exceeds the common run or what is expected, positive leadership should also focus on affirmation, praising other people's strengths and capabilities rather than pointing out their failings or obstacles (Buckingham, 2005). Finally, the positive leader has to concentrate on facilitating goodness and virtue, individually and organizationally. Cameron provides a series of case studies to inspire and illuminate, sometimes from organizations that have apparently been transformed into positive exemplars from previously negative and damaging settings, or sometimes workplaces that were set up with the intent of being positively different from the outset.

It is interesting that the practicalities of positive leadership fall into two categories: structured managerial systems and encouraging face-to-face contact. The latter is clearly a managerial strategy to reduce the effects of the physical distancing that Zygmunt Bauman wrote about (see previous section on ethics); if you have to look your colleague in the eye then you are less likely to do something that damages them. However, it is odd to see this humanizing principle juxtaposed alongside recommendations to introduce more managerial processes such as performance appraisal. The key message, however, emphasized throughout is that management and leadership must be done in a positive spirit, supportively and with compassion. If you do this as a leader, Cameron here and colleagues writing elsewhere argue, you will be sure to generate positively deviant performance in yourself and others.

As well as the US-specific characteristics of the POS movement that Steve Fineman identified, we can add another aspect that links us into the second part of this section. As with most management fads and fashions, POS displays many of the features of a religious or spiritual belief system. This is more than a metaphor or comparative correspondence; as Brad Jackson (2001) argues in his analysis of Stephen Covey's globally successful 'effectiveness movement', signing up to this kind of vision involves believing in a programme that affects the most fundamental aspects of the person, encouraged by the doctrine as much as the charismatic leadership that is the norm in such movements. POS and Cameron's outline of positive leadership may be seen, then, as a belief-based movement that requires faith, akin to or as a complement for other belief systems that managers and leaders follow – a kind of spiritual leadership from within the academic and consultancy communities. This is the theme of the final section, where we look at a second contemporary way of exploring the meaning of work, spiritual leadership.

FROM MATTER TO SPIRIT

The contemporary European university is in the main a strangely secular place. Although students and staff bring the usual range of religious or spiritual beliefs onto campus, this aspect of everyday life is generally ignored in the research and education that takes place. There are exceptions to this rule: theology and divinity departments are the obvious example; you can also find a sprinkling of sociologists, psychologists, and anthropologists who take religion and belief seriously. Within this context, business schools are perhaps the most fiercely secular parts of the university – after all, managing and leading are very much activities of this world, aren't they?: concerned with the material, the tangible, and the commercial, not the immaterial or metaphysical.

Two recent realizations challenge the twentieth-century idea that religion and spirituality are outside the remit of organization and Leadership Studies. First, the rise in historical analysis of management and business – Mick Rowlinson's research into Cadbury (e.g. Rowlinson, 2002) is the best example of new historical approaches. This inevitably involves telling the stories of early capitalists and industrialists, people who lived in times when (*a*) rates of religious worship were much higher than today, and (*b*) religious leaders and spiritual ideas played a much higher role in debate in the 'public square', including workplaces. If this seems rather general, then think about specific examples of business leaders who made no secret of their beliefs and sought to manifest them through management and leadership practice – the Rowntree family, the Cadbury family, Josiah Wedgwood, and William Lever in the United Kingdom alone. Rowlinson and others (see the journal *Management & Organization History* for more research of this kind) draw on and contribute to a long tradition, begun by German sociologist Max Weber (1930) and his British counterpart R. H. Tawney (1926). Both of these scholars were convinced that we have to explain economic behaviour with reference to religious beliefs, especially when we think about the roots of the market economies we all live in today. American academic Randall Collins (1997) provides an alternative to Weber and Tawney's conviction that capitalism began in the minds and through the actions of Protestants, suggesting that Buddhist monasteries were the first to display capitalist or entrepreneurial tendencies.

However, recognition and analysis of religious belief is not confined to historical accounts of organization and leadership. The largest and most prestigious community of management researchers, the US-based Academy of Management, hosts around thirty subgroups of scholars with specific interests – strategy is the largest, organizational behaviour also counts many members, you can also find smaller groups specializing in gender/diversity or the natural environment. At the end of the millennium, a small group of researchers applied to the Academy to set up a group under the title 'Management, Spirituality & Religion'. This group now counts around 600 members, among the smallest but nonetheless a healthy population.

It is difficult to characterize this group and the research or educational approaches that members are promoting. There is, however, a fundamental idea that religious or spiritual belief remains significant in everyday life and therefore workplaces.[2] Within this community, we find yet another subgroup specifically focusing on leadership and spirituality.

The ideas being explored here closely resemble the starting points of POS. Louis Fry, in a series of journal papers (e.g. Fry, 2003; Fry and Slocum, 2008; Fry and Cohen, 2009), argues that seeing leadership through a spiritual lens, in practice and theory, demands attention to: people's inner lives; people's sense of calling or vocation; and the construction of community, preferably based on altruistic love. Again echoing POS, all research and education/ development relating to spiritual leadership must also always consider ways to achieve 'performative excellence' through its implementation.

In reading this research, a basic contradiction rapidly becomes evident. Many and considerable claims are made for the introduction of spirit or soul into leadership and organizations. The depiction of spirituality and religious belief emphasizes the development of self in a non-instrumental way – in other words, the idea that following and encouraging spiritual and religious belief systems is a good in itself. A similar argument to that made by those on the more radical wing of the business ethics community – that individual or organizational performance should not be considered, or certainly not prioritized, when leaders define what is right and wrong. However, this position is continually undermined by the desire to make the ideas relevant or attractive to managers by claiming performance gains for spiritual development programmes. This is a tension that runs through many of the more developmental, humane approaches to managing and leading, but it is especially striking when scholars write about spirituality and religion.

In addition to this, as with so much leadership and management research, the ideas and research evidence are predominantly North American in tone and concerns. Sociologists of religion often note that the United States is an interesting society because of its high rates of religious engagement, particularly when compared with apparently secular Europe (although the story is more complex that this description implies – see Davie, 2007). A close examination of the research published in US journals by US-based scholars reveals interesting undercurrents. First, a suggestion that hierarchy and control should be supported by spiritual development or religious belief systems. Second, this research marginalizes the experiences of women and non-masculine believers – there is a strong sense that spiritual leadership is a return to the Protestant ethic on which the United States was founded. Third, and most significant, the version of spiritual leadership represented in mainstream accounts so far ignores 'other', non-Western spiritualities or belief systems.

Research that takes, for example, Confucian, Native American, or Maori beliefs seriously is beginning to emerge (respectively, Prince, 2005; Warner and Grint, 2006; Holmes, 2007). This provides a series of alternative perspectives that align with the ideals of Critical Management Studies, in that nature, women, or alternatives forms of organization and leadership are brought to the fore. The conventional, Anglo-Saxon, corporate forms are challenged, redefining spiritual and religious belief as ends in themselves, perhaps means to a good life, but certainly not as technologies that should be mobilized to improve organizational efficiency or stimulate positively deviant performance.

LEADERS: THE SPECIAL ONES?

This emerging debate may seem irrelevant to most of what goes on in organizations, or to figuring out the truth about leadership, especially if you live in one of the more secularized cultures of Western Europe. To end this section and the substantive part of this book, we would like to leave you with two possibilities.

First, if we accept the possibility that organizations are cultures, as most managers and consultants do today, then we should also think about the idea that belief as to the ultimate point of work, management, organization, and leadership is legitimate. If not, then we are likely to experience all of these things as somewhat lacking, to say the least. Second, following the UK's preeminent scholar of leadership, Keith Grint (2010), we should also consider the argument that leadership is made different from, for example, managing or administrating by its sacred nature. In other words, leaders are constructed as sacred beings by followers. This is not a return to Great Man theories of leadership, nor simply charismatic or transformational leadership in another form. It is more interesting than that; it raises the possibility that if we are to take leadership, leaders, and leading seriously as something distinctive, then we must accept that we have to set certain people apart from the run-of-the-mill, everyday, or profane population; that sacrifice, of leaders or followers, is an inherent aspect of this practice; and that a certain amount of silencing (of dissent or fear) is involved.

Grint's recent idea, that leadership is inherently sacred in these ways, is an interesting point on which to close. In some ways it does bring us back to where our leadership stories begin, emphasizing the individual, a certain kind of heroism, and the separation of (mainly masculine) leaders from 'others'. However, it also opens some fascinating doors, onto the possibility that perspectives on leadership should be immaterial, transcendent, and other-worldly, as well as material, immanent, and this-worldly.

Chapter Summary

As the next chapter makes clear, predicting the future is challenging for anyone. For academics and management gurus, it is especially difficult as a task or orientation, because so much of what they/we do is backward looking (and because it is so easy to get it wrong, as gurus through the ages have found). This book is as current as we could make it. However, the research that it is based on and the articles you read in peer-reviewed journals are often anything but current. From the idea at the beginning of a research project, through data collection and analysis, to writing up and then going through the long processes of peer review and eventual publication – this can take anywhere up to five years. Added to that, we tend to ask questions that focus on what has happened rather than what will or could happen.

So this chapter should be read cautiously, in the sense of having any predictive power. The issues that we are telling you are current certainly feature largely in academic and practitioner publications at the moment, but they may not reflect what leaders, managers, and led are experiencing today. In addition, as you know, management theory and practice are notorious for moving rapidly from one fashion to another, so we might be able to find five other current issues in 2015.

Notwithstanding all of this, we have come out and tried to identify some current ideas about leadership that we believe to be significant. The chapter you have just read is our assessment of the present and pointer towards future possibilities that leadership theory and practice are, should be, centrally concerned with: gender, well-being, technology, ethics, and meaning. What is striking to us looking at these topics now is how enduring they are, how potentially intractable, how awkward to do or think about, and how much a part of the human condition. This is for us the true fascination of thinking about and doing leadership, and it is the theme of the concluding chapter.

☐ NOTES

1. A practice finally made illegal by the Sex Discrimination Act in the United Kingdom in the mid-1970s.
2. Some scholars in this area insist that spirituality can be entirely separate from religion (e.g. Mitroff, 2003), others argue that they are intertwined in practice and theory (e.g. Hicks, 2003). In this section we take the position that spiritual practices and beliefs form part of the wider field of religious belief (Lynch, 2007), in the sense that all of the various traditions address similar issues of spirit, soul, or transcendence.

7 Conclusion: Where Next for Leadership Studies?

In this final chapter we draw together some of the key themes and issues discussed throughout this book and consider the implications for leadership theory, research, practice, and development. We begin, however, by considering how demands for leadership may change over the coming years.

Leadership, Society, and the Next Ten Years

Almost ten years ago two of the authors of this book, Richard and Jonathan, conducted a study of how newly appointed and aspiring strategic leaders expected leadership to change over the coming decade (see Bolden, 2004: 28). In this work we reviewed the outputs of two reflective programmes from the Windsor Leadership Trust, run between November 2001 and May 2003, in which experienced leaders from all sectors of society spent a period of four to five days reflecting on, discussing, and exploring the questions and challenges of leadership.

A total of seventeen syndicate reports were analysed, each compiled by six to eight participants – constituting the views of well over 100 middle-senior managers from a diverse cross section of organizations and occupations in the United Kingdom and beyond. The common theme of these reports was 'leadership, society and the next ten years' and, together, they revealed the following expectations about the changing nature of society, work, and leadership. Outcomes are summarised in Box 7.1.

Few would argue that these changes have not come to pass; however, there is little evidence to suggest that they are much different from what a similar group of managers would propose nowadays – an observation that holds a number of intriguing questions for the field of Leadership Studies, including:

Box 7.1 THE CHANGING NATURE OF SOCIETY, WORK AND LEADERSHIP

---

1. *The changing nature of society*: all groups gave considerable attention to changes in the society in which they operate. There was a general consensus that Western countries are undergoing an unprecedented period of change and that this appears to be accelerating. Technological advances are transforming communications and access to information; the retired population is growing while the working population is diminishing; global economies are becoming increasingly interdependent; the ethnic and religious mix is transforming; and the divide between the haves and have-nots is widening. There is an improved awareness of the social and environmental impacts of our actions; a decreasing allegiance to traditional power structures; an increasing complexity with regards to stakeholders and decision-making; a move from family groups to individualism; increasing customer (and employee) demands; and a climate of change and uncertainty.

2. *The changing nature of work*: the changes in society are impacting significantly upon the nature of work and the workforce. There is a trend towards flexible working (including part-time, working from home, and the mobile office). Decreasing job security, company loyalty, and unemployment are encouraging mid-life career changes and self-employment. Demographic changes and global trade are leading to sectoral shifts from manufacturing and production to service and leisure industries. There are an ever-increasing number of stake-holders (often with conflicting demands) and an increasing pressure to work in collaboration and to establish partnerships. Private sector organizations are becoming more powerful and influential in areas previously controlled by the public sector, such as pensions, transport, and health care.

3. *The changing face of leadership*: in this climate of change, leadership was viewed as the key to organizational success. Although the core qualities of leaders may remain constant, the manner and mix in which they are exhibited needs to become more fluid and matched to the context. Leaders need to become increasingly adaptable – making sense of uncertainty and managing complexity. The qualities of openness, empathy, integrity, and self-awareness are coming to the fore and demand a more participative leadership style, whereby leaders not only involve colleagues but listen, are responsive to feedback, and delegate responsibility. Leaders will increasingly need to 'win the right to lead', 'lead from the front', 'lead by example', and be prepared to 'share in hardship'. Developing a culture of leadership in which people can excel is being seen as increasingly important, as is the need to create and communicate a shared long-term vision.

- If we have not found answers to these challenges in the past ten years what is the likelihood that we will in the next ten?
- If these are enduring characteristics of society and the workplace does this mean that leadership will continue to have an important role in addressing them ... or do we need to look for alternative solutions?
- If we need different forms of leadership within our organizations and society, what is being done to prepare future generations for these challenges?
- In this complex and changing environment, what is the role of leadership scholarship ... to develop 'better leaders' and/or to serve as a 'critic and conscience for society'?[1]

The debates explored within this book indicate an underlying shift in thinking about leadership, not just among academics but also among practicing managers. We have moved a long way from the early trait and 'great man' theories, whereby leadership was considered the reserve of an exclusive few who were born destined to lead. There is a clear awareness that a far wider range of factors are involved – some to do with holders of leadership positions, some to do with others in the organization, and some to do with the relationship between all these and wider society. Leadership can be conceived of as a social influence process – there are things people can do to enhance specific skills and their ability to cope with situations but the processes and outcomes of leadership remain socially embedded – the result of a complex interaction between a multitude of factors. Thus, who becomes regarded as a leader, how they behave, and what they achieve are all determined as much by social and cultural factors as by any individual characteristics. Churchill, Hitler, Stalin, Gandhi, and King were all products of their time, place, and culture – or, in the words of one of the Windsor Leadership Trust groups: 'the leadership journey is a never ending one. Change is a constant. Where the journey and the constant come together true leaders flourish.'

Preparing for an Uncertain Future

In terms of how individuals, organizations, and societies may position and prepare themselves for the changes outlined above, the question becomes one of how to navigate through an uncertain, complex, and changing terrain.

Day (2000) proposes that leadership development is distinct from management development to the extent to which it involves preparing people for roles and situations beyond their current experience. Management development, he argues, equips managers with the knowledge, skills, and abilities to enhance performance on known tasks through the application of proven solutions while leadership development is defined as 'orientated towards building capacity in anticipation of unforeseen challenges' (Ibid.: 582). He continues by making a distinction between leader and leadership development, whereby leader development is about developing individuals in leadership roles, while leadership development takes a more relational view of leadership as a process involving everyone within the organization. To this extent, Day views leadership development as being fundamentally concerned with the development of collective organizational capacity.

In this way, each person is considered a leader, and leadership is conceptualised as an effect rather than a cause. Leadership is therefore an emergent property of effective systems design. Leadership development from this perspective consists of using social (i.e. relational) systems to help build commitments among members of a community of practice. (Ibid.: 583)

This distinction is useful in encouraging us to consider what it is that we wish to achieve through executive development. 'Leader development' is an investment in *human capital* to enhance intrapersonal competence for selected individuals, whereas 'leadership development' is an investment in *social capital* to develop interpersonal networks and cooperation within organizations and other social systems. According to Day, both are equally important although traditionally development programmes have tended to focus exclusively on the former. We concur and take the view that both types of development are required and should be an integral part of any development initiative.

Even when considering just 'leader development', Campbell et al. (2003) argue that the current diversity of perspectives is misleading as it suggests that, first, leadership development constitutes any understanding that develops individuals in leadership roles and second that all development activities are equally useful/effective.

Like Day, in their review, Campbell and his colleagues identify that the leadership development field is currently dominated by individualistic approaches, focused on five broad areas:

1. intrapersonal attributes (e.g. self-awareness);
2. interpersonal qualities;
3. cognitive abilities;
4. communication skills; and
5. task-specific skills.

At the intrapersonal level it could be argued that 'there is no difference between becoming an effective leader and becoming a fully integrated human being' (Bennis, 1999: 23) and thus Campbell et al. (2003: 31) conclude that 'there is little reason to label this leadership development, except in the broad sense that the developing individuals hold leadership positions'. The interpersonal level fits more closely with Day's conception of 'leadership development', viewing leadership as a social influence process and the goal of development to enhance interpersonal competence in order to obtain the trust, respect, and commitment of others (Campbell et al., 2003). The additional three categories (cognitive, communication, and task-specific skills) are a range of personal capabilities that help enhance an individual's interpersonal influence. In each case a challenge remains about how to differentiate the types of skills required by 'leaders' as opposed to 'managers' and/or 'followers' and the response remains largely dependent on your theoretical and philosophical views on the nature of leadership (e.g. if you take a distributive perspective then such a differentiation is inappropriate as who is considered the 'leader' varies over time).

Campbell and colleagues take Katz and Kahn's notion (1978) of leadership as 'incremental influence' as the foundation for their conception of leadership development. Thus, the aim of leadership development is to enhance 'interpersonal influence over and above the influence that stems from a person's positional authority or legitimate power' (Campbell et al., 2003: 39). From this perspective the most effective leadership development methods are likely to be those that develop core influencing skills including values that can serve as a 'moral compass', problem-defining and problem-solving skills, task facilitation skills, and communication and motivational skills.

In our own experience, at the Centre for Leadership Studies, of developing people for leadership positions we tend to take the view that it is important to develop all of these skills with a contextual appreciation of the cultural and organizational environment. When considering leadership, rather than management development the primary emphasis is on enabling people to think beyond the apparent restrictions of their current role and to develop the critical capabilities to move between operational and strategic modes as required – to balance an attention for detail with an understanding of the bigger picture. As one of the authors has previously argued:

All in all, leadership development within management education should develop the 'character', integrity, skills and discursive intelligence necessary for the responsible exercise of power. (Gosling, 2004)

To this extent, leadership development may well incorporate elements of more typical management and self-development programmes (including time management, project-management, delegation, self-awareness, etc.) but with the objective of creating a 'reflexive' space in which the leader/manager can critically reflect upon current practice and experience. There is no reason to consider, therefore, that leadership development should only be offered to senior managers and, indeed, there would be good reason to encourage this kind of development throughout the organization to enhance collective as well as individual capacity. The nature of the required intervention, however, is likely to vary depending on the job role and current level of experience of the participants.

Many Perspectives but no 'Right' Way of Looking at Leadership

Throughout this book we have highlighted a number of different perspectives on leadership and some of the challenges in researching and representing leadership in a balanced and integrated manner. In her book 'Rethinking

Leadership, Donna Ladkin (2010) draws on the field of phenomenology (Husserl, 1900 [2001]) to shed some light on why leadership might be quite such a difficult concept to capture and convey. To illustrate this she introduces the notion of the 'leadership cube' (Sokolowski, 2000) to demonstrate the concepts of 'sides', 'aspects', and 'identity' of a phenomenon.

> From a phenomenological perspective, an entity's identity always remains elusive. As much as we can perceive the sides which make it up, as much as we can be aware of the different aspects from which it can be viewed, as much as we can know about its internal workings, its history and its significance within human 'Lifeworlds', we can never know the totality of something which would constitute a definitive 'identity'. This is a key ontological assumption which underpins phenomenological investigations: that a 'thing's' identity will always be beyond the reach of human apprehension. In holding this position, phenomenology takes a radically different orientation to knowing from that assumed by logical positivism. (Ladkin, 2010: 24)

This insight can be used to explain the multitude of theories and definitions of leadership, in that 'each theory provides another "piece of the leadership puzzle"' (Ladkin, 2010: 32) by approaching leadership from a particular 'side' (e.g. a primary focus on 'leaders' or 'followers') and 'aspect' (e.g. a primary interest in organizational change, structures, performance, etc.). To this extent we may need to accept that, like many complex concepts, leadership is largely unknowable. Furthermore, we need to acknowledge that leadership 'is not a phenomenon which lends itself to positivistic deconstruction, measurement and logical analysis' (Ladkin, 2010: 185).

All this, however, does not mean that studying leadership is a meaningless or misguided pursuit, rather that 'methods more suited to analysing entities which are materially present will have severe limitations when applied to the investigation of leadership' (Ibid.: 185). We would never expect to produce a definitive theory of love, beauty, or humour, nor would we expect to assess or develop these as if they were a set of qualities possessed by individuals (although we may recognize that certain attributes may predispose certain people to be perceived as more loveable, beautiful, or humorous than others within certain contexts, and accept that certain skills can be learnt or developed through education and experience).[2]

Rerouting our Enquiries

In the introduction to this book we set out an argument for reframing Leadership Studies, including:

1. redressing the balance accorded to individual and collective accounts of leadership, and the relative importance attributed to leaders and followers;

2. reframing how we recognize, reward, and develop leaders; and
3. reviewing our methodologies and approaches to the study of leadership.

In the subsequent chapters we have set out a range of different perspectives, challenges, and debates that illustrate the limitations of much contemporary leadership theory and practice. Our intention in doing so has not been to 'uproot' but to 'reroute' Leadership Studies.

While this might seem a long winded way of positioning ourselves to deliver a cheap pun, the analogy is perhaps more revealing than would at first appear. The *Oxford Concise Dictionary* defines a 'root' as '...the part of a plant which attaches it to the ground or to a support, typically underground, conveying water and nourishment to the rest of the plant via numerous branches and fibres...', while a 'route' is 'a way or course taken in getting from a starting point to a destination' (http://oxforddictionaries.com, accessed 20 July 2010). A root, therefore, is concerned with attachment, sustenance, and connection, while a route is concerned with direction, movement, and accomplishment. In our view both of these are essential to any form of enquiry, but particularly to subjects such as leadership that transcend both the fields of scholarship and practice. As illustrated in this book, the roots of Leadership Studies go back for millennia and we are still discovering the wisdoms held in early writings by authors such as Plato, Aristotle, Lao Tzu, and Sun Tzu. Such writings nourish the field with the lessons of history, philosophy, aesthetics, and experience. In our search for scientific evidence and universal truths, it is easy to forget such lessons – to endeavour to reduce our calculations to 'leadership by numbers'. It would seem that in our quest for knowledge we may have lost sight of the direction in which we are headed – to generate theory for theory's sake or to seek the convenient evidence that enables us to evade some deeply inconvenient and unsettling truths about the imbalances of power, resources, recognition, status, rewards, and opportunities that permeate our organizations and societies. In this book we call for a rerouting of leadership studies in directions that are more likely to lead to equitable, effective, and engaging forms of leadership practice.

In the next four subsections we consider how this might be done and what implications it might have for leadership theory, research, practice, and development.

REROUTING LEADERSHIP THEORY

This book has given a broad overview of the field of Leadership Studies and changing perspectives and approaches to theory. In many of the traditional models outlined in Chapter 2, leadership is represented as something that resides within the leader. Later theories have presented it as something that arises through the interaction between leaders and followers and/or as a wider social process that occurs within organizations and groups. As Drath et al. (2008) highlight, though, within nearly all theories there is a common ontology whereby leadership is represented as something done by *leaders* to *followers* in pursuit of a *common goal*.

While it may well be true that this is how leadership occurs in certain situations, such a representation does not fit well with emergent, informal, and collective forms of leadership within complex and collaborative environments. Given the increasing prevalence of knowledge-based industry (in which the workers control the means of production) and the need for organizations to engage in partnerships (where hierarchical relationships are diminished), such scenarios are increasingly prevalent within organizational life and hence the need to develop theories and ways of thinking about leadership that fit these contexts.

Astley (1985: 503) proposes that: 'theories gain favour because of their conceptual appeal, their logical structure, or their psychological plausibility. Internal coherence, parsimony, formal elegance, and so on prevail over empirical accuracy in determining a theory's impact.' Dominant theories of leadership to date have been accepted to the extent that they have resonated with the experiences, perceptions, and social expectations of the times (in which it was considered appropriate to attribute 'leadership' to the actions of a 'leader'). While many of these theories are based on limited and somewhat inconclusive evidence, and are increasingly unable to account for the wide diversity of leadership forms now present within organizations and societies, they remain difficult to dislodge from the popular psyche, particularly within Western society from whence the vast majority of management and leadership literature originates.

While alternative perspectives, such as 'distributed' and 'shared' leadership, are now being developed and promoted through academic literature, in many cases they still struggle to escape the recurrent refrain of 'leaders' and 'followers' and to gain widespread recognition within organizations beyond a limited number of contexts. Furthermore, empirical evidence implies that even where more collective notions of leadership are recognized and embraced they may well mask other important organizational dynamics (such as an uneven distribution of power and rewards) so that their role is as much rhetorical (in providing a compelling account of organizing) as offering an accurate description of how leadership actually occurs (see e.g. Bolden et al., 2009).

The discursive significance of leadership, both in terms of how 'leaders' manage to influence others and of how talk of 'leadership' helps to create and maintain power relations, is a central theme in more recent theorizing (e.g. Grint, 2005a; Fairhurst, 2007). In analysing and interpreting the accounts of 'leaders' it is possible to see how, through talking about leadership, they may find a means for articulating what is meaningful and important to them and, in so doing, tend to bundle up a curious and changeable collection of perceptions, feelings, desires, expectations, experiences, and practices (Bolden and Gosling, 2008). What each of these bundles has in common is reference to the mobilization of human effort in some collective enterprise, yet, in providing their accounts, managers often reveal a number of inherent tensions and paradoxes about the role(s) in which they find themselves. Such findings illustrate the value of taking a 'dialectical' approach to the study and representation of leadership in which 'differences are not conceived as absolute' but rather 'deeply interconnected' (Fay, 1996: 224).

Take, for example, the concepts of 'leader' and 'follower'. Within much of the literature on leadership these are positioned as discrete alternatives, diametrically opposed to one another. When we reflect on our own experience of leadership, however, we can quickly see that the boundaries are fuzzier than this – that we may well be a leader *and* a follower at the same time, or perhaps neither, and the moment at which we pass from one role to the other is incredibly difficult to isolate. A dialectical approach suggests that attempting to categorize concepts in such a black-and-white manner is misleading and can be a major obstacle to understanding.

Rather than endeavouring to capture 'objective' evidence on the nature of leadership, more recent theorizing suggests a need to explore the ways in which leadership is 'socially constructed' through the interactions of multiple actors within a social context. From such a perspective the work of leaders can be considered as a form of organizing activity achieved through sensemaking (Pye, 2005) and leadership theory can offer a means for helping leaders construct and communicate a compelling narrative.

The practical contribution of organizational theory, however, need not come only from its potential for direct application but also from its role in shaping and stimulating discourses about the role and purpose of work. Spicer et al. (2009), for example, draw attention to the important role of Critical Management Studies in provoking debate about the nature and purpose of organization. They describe it as a 'profoundly performative project' (Ibid.: 537), yet one that has acquired somewhat of a reputation for negativity in its stance towards management and performance. Rather than abandoning the project, however, these authors call for 'a "critical performativity" that involves an affirmative stance, with an ethic of care, a pragmatic orientation, engagement with potentialities, and striving for a normative orientation' (Ibid.: 554).

Arguably, a similar role could be carved out for the field of Leadership Studies – not in claiming to present an objective and generalizable account of leadership practice, but in facilitating discussions about what is important and worthwhile. As Amanda Sinclair argues in her book *Leadership for the Disillusioned*: 'leadership should be aimed at helping to free people from oppressive structures, practices and habits encountered in societies and in-stitutions, as well as within the shady recesses of ourselves' (Sinclair, 2007: vx).

Leadership Studies is a field of enquiry that has much to offer contempor-ary society, yet, it is proposed, this contribution will not arise from purport-ing to offer a systematic evidence base from which leaders, managers, and policymakers can determine how to run their organizations most effectively (although some such gains may be achieved). Instead, the contribution of Leadership Studies is likely to arise from asking (and offering other people the means to ask) the challenging and potentially inconvenient questions facing society, including those very questions that may lead to the realization that 'more leadership' is not necessarily what is needed (as argued by Mintzberg, 2004a, 2009a, 2009b).

REROUTING LEADERSHIP RESEARCH

Following on from the previous points, in order to generate leadership theory, knowledge, and insights that are perceived as credible and useful to end users, as well as to wider society, consideration needs to be given to the nature and role of research. Flyvbjerg (2001, 2006) suggests that we must endeavour to 're-enchant' organizational research by making it 'matter', as outlined below.

If we want to empower and re-enchant organization research, we need to do three things. First, we must drop all pretence, however indirect, at emulating the success of the natural sciences in producing cumulative and predictive theory, for their approach simply does not work in organization research or any of the social sciences (for the full argument, see Flyvbjerg, 2001). Second, we must address problems that matter to groups in the local, national, and global communities in which we live, and we must do it in ways that matter; we must focus on issues of context, values, and power, as advocated by great social scientists from Aristotle and Machiavelli to Max Weber and Pierre Bourdieu. Finally, we must effectively and dialogically communicate the results of our research to our fellow citizens and carefully listen to their feedback. If we do this – focus on specific values and interests in the context of particular power relations – we may successfully transform organization research into an activity performed in public for organizational publics, sometimes to clarify, sometimes to intervene, sometimes to generate new perspectives, and always to serve as eyes and ears in ongoing efforts to understand the present and to deliberate about the future. We may, in short, arrive at organization research that matters. (Flyvbjerg, 2006: 370)

The personal experience of the authors of this book is that in researching a subject such as leadership insights build slowly over time, with any individual study being largely shaped by previous experience and insights and leading to new questions and challenges. While the project-based nature of much funded research and the process of presenting findings and conclusions for academic, practitioner, and policy audiences tend to result in neatly bounded arguments this is seldom how the research process is experienced by those behind the scenes. Leadership research, like all social inquiry, comprises a substantial degree of social construction yet this is seldom explicitly acknowledged in published accounts. Only through recognizing the assumptions and inevitable biases (social, cultural, philosophical, methodological, etc.) that we bring as researchers to our enquiries can we hope to gain a more realistic appreciation of the relative strengths, weaknesses, and limitations of our approach. Indeed, only through being explicit about the choices and agendas that we bring to our work may it be possible to capture an honest account of what we find. While such candour might be perceived as risky and perhaps rather self-centred, it may be exactly what is required in order to gain a deeper understanding of the underlying mechanisms of social phenomena, as illustrated in the following quote.

Revealing the logic that guides our choices in variable selection and hypothesis formulation, which often is only implicit in scholarly work, shows the reader which part of the social world we chose to explain. We can make the story of creation crisper and surface our role in that story: These are the assumptions of my story and the conditions under which my theory works, and this is what I overlooked and why. (Anderson et al., 2006: 111)

As discussed earlier in this book, dominant approaches to the study of leadership tend to be grounded in 'positivist' or 'realist' principles that endeavour to offer predictive and prescriptive advice to leaders and their organizations. While such an approach is clearly understandable, it may limit the potential for leadership research to fundamentally challenge the ways in which we think about such phenomena. If, however, we take the socially constructed nature of leadership to heart, we may come to realize that leadership research does not simply need to describe the world but can also transform it.

If viewed in this way, leadership research should not be regarded as an impartial data gathering exercise, but as an intervention in its own right. The very act of enquiring about leadership within organizations may well change, in subtle or significant ways, the aspects of individual, group, and/or organizational functioning. Interviews, questionnaires, and other social research methods do more than simply capture information – they set in motion a process of dialogue and reflection that may well change the very thing that they are designed to explore.

To this extent, we advocate taking an 'appreciative' approach to organizational research (Cooperrider and Srivastva, 1987) – not out of a desire to see the world through rose-tinted spectacles, but in an attempt to generate more positive and empowering insights. As proponents of Appreciative Inquiry suggest 'what we focus on becomes our reality'; 'reality is created in the moment, and there are multiple realities'; and 'the act of asking questions of an organization or group influences the group in some way' (Hammond, 1998). If we genuinely believe that every individual, group, organization, and/ or society have at least some positive qualities, why not focus on how to nurture and develop those rather than to assess and critique their performance against some externally imposed set of criteria? Why not take a 'worldly' approach that views differences as a rich and intricate patchwork than a universalistic approach that seeks conformance, compliance, and consistency?

If leadership research is regarded as an intervention, it also suggests that it should be considered as a collective pursuit in that it impacts upon all of those involved. Academics, research participants, practitioners, policymakers, organizations, and communities all have an important contribution to make and a vested interest in both the process and outcomes. Leadership research is not something done when shut away in a science laboratory (although there is a place for carefully designed lab-based studies), but a necessarily social pursuit. In our own work we try hard to involve participants and other stakeholders in the design, administration, and interpretation of research as they bring to bear other important voices and perspectives. In the spirit of action research we propose that 'research with human beings should be participative and democratic' (Ladkin, 2004: 536).

From what has been described above, it is probably clear that our preference is for qualitative methodologies, informed by an interpretivist epistemology, although we do value other approaches and, indeed, suggest that a degree of pluralism is essential if we are to gain a more nuanced understanding. As Joanne Ciulla argues in the conclusion to the book *The Quest for a General Theory of Leadership* (summarizing the outcomes of a five-year process of enquiry and debate between an interdisciplinary group of leading US leadership scholars):

It takes more than one scholar, discipline, or theoretical approach to understand leadership. The study of leadership forces us to tackle the universal questions about human nature and destiny. For those questions, there will probably never be a general theory. (Ciulla, 2006: 233)

The key to developing and uniting the field of Leadership Studies will be to find ways in which debates on leadership can transcend the silos and boundaries that so often prevent people from different disciplines, occupations, conceptual paradigms, and places communicating openly with one another. As Ciulla (2006) suggests, the aim of articulating an overarching theory of leadership was (for good reason) ultimately unsuccessful – there was no Holy Grail waiting to be found. Like many quests, however, making the journey is perhaps more important than arriving at the planned destination. What *The Quest for a General Theory of Leadership* uncovered the *process* of searching for a grand theory of leadership – the discussions, agreements, disagreements, brief moments of clarity, and intractable dilemmas – rather than the *product* itself. As she concludes, perhaps the main thing is just to get people talking.

REROUTING LEADERSHIP PRACTICE

The ideas discussed in this book support the idea of leadership as a shared process, widely dispersed within organizations and other social groups – both distributed across people at all levels, as well as embedded in culture, systems, and processes. Furthermore, it has been suggested that leadership takes a variety of forms that coexist alongside one another – not one 'right way' of leading but a hybrid blend of individual and shared influence (Gronn, 2008; Collinson and Collinson, 2009).

To this extent, organizations and the people within them considered responsible for 'leadership' should be encouraged to find ways in which to foster a diversity of leadership styles and approaches, and to recognize the ways in which these various 'configurations' (Gronn, 2009) complement, enhance, and/or inhibit one another. Within a school environment, for example, it has been proven that the Head Teacher plays a pivotal role in promoting change and facilitating the development of a 'distributed' approach to leadership in which teachers, classroom assistants, parents, governors, and pupils can all become actively involved, not just as 'followers' but also as 'leaders'. The question, therefore, is not one of vertical versus shared leadership, but rather how can we develop an appropriate mix for the situation and task?

A key theme within this book has been to suggest the value of a somewhat eclectic approach to leadership, in terms of nurturing a diversity of forms and perspectives rather than advocating a single generic approach. Each context is unique, as are the various actors within them, and attempts at emulating 'best practice' are unlikely to be successful. While leadership competency frameworks and associated approaches (including performance management systems and 360° appraisal), for example, may be helpful in highlighting organizational norms, values, and expectations, they cannot influence leadership behaviour directly and may, in fact, lead to unanticipated and undesired outcomes. The promotion of individualist and functionalist ways of thinking, in particular, are major risks and may diminish true collaboration and organizational citizenship behaviour (Organ, 1988).

While leadership may be widely distributed within organizations and communities, however, this does not imply that it is necessarily democratic or that power and resources are evenly dispersed (Woods and Gronn, 2009). Indeed, as Hatcher (2005: 255) suggests from work in the UK education sector, 'there is...a tension – I would say a fundamental contradiction – between distributed leadership and government-driven headteacher managerialism'. Thus, while a distributed approach to leadership may be advocated, staff experience may be one of increasing managerial control and the gradual erosion of collective bargaining. Such tensions are experienced even by senior level managers and directors; however, the crux is likely to come for those in the middle of the organization. Individuals in such roles may well find themselves having to continually navigate a series of tensions and conflicts, largely associated with issues of identity and purpose.

For such 'leaders', while there may be a number of individual and organizational practices that they can draw on in their day-to-day leadership work (Carroll et al., 2008), their primary role is to act as a hub for sensemaking – translating, communicating, and prioritizing organizational objectives in the light of the specific context in which they find themselves. Evidence from our own teaching and research is that leadership practice for such people is a largely discursive activity through which they both shape and are shaped by the social and organizational contexts in which they find themselves.

A perspective such as this would imply that a good degree of what 'leaders' do can be considered as 'identity work' (Sveningsson and Alvesson, 2003) through which they endeavour to develop and articulate a common sense of group membership and purpose for themselves and those around them. They may be considered as 'entrepreneurs of identity' (Reicher et al., 2005), who help build a sense of shared 'social identity' and craft opportunities for group members to collaborate in pursuit of joint objectives. As Ladkin (2007: 6) proposes, such work 'is essentially hermeneutic'[3] in that 'it involves the exchange of meaning and the co-creation of shared understanding'. The skills required of such people are more likely to be those of the 'critical practitioner' and/or 'reflective practitioner' than the 'management scientist' or 'competent manager' (Holman, 2000) – they need to reflect on and learn from experience rather than simply apply a standard set of practices. As Amanda Sinclair (2007) suggests: 'Leadership is a process of critical and compassionate engagement with the world [... It] is a commitment to challenging accepted wisdom, to reflecting deeply on our motives so as to avoid co-option, to being mindful of relations between our bodies and psyches, to being in the moment, and to leading with the intent of freeing – both the self and others' (Ibid.: xxiv).

Leadership, from such a perspective, requires leaders who are prepared to ask questions and involve others in determining what to do rather than seeking to provide an immediate solution or decisive action. It is a process requiring the development and application of 'social' as well as 'human' capital (Day, 2000), and is a process that depends on leaders who can apply 'practical wisdom' and 'mastery' rather than simply technical 'know-how' and 'competence' (Grint, 2007; Raelin, 2007). Within such a context, leaders can be considered as 'bricoleurs'[4] (Weick, 2001): masters at drawing on whatever is at their disposal in order to complete a particular task.

REROUTING LEADERSHIP DEVELOPMENT

From the discussion above it can be seen that the ability to reflect critically on practice is one of the key capabilities of an effective leader. Ann Cunliffe (2009) calls for the development of the 'philosopher leader' through an engagement with issues of relationality, ethics, and reflexivity. She proposes that: 'The philosopher leader thinks differently, asking: What is important? What if we think about organizations, leadership, and ethics in this way rather than that? Where will it take us?' (Ibid.: 99).

Grint (2007) makes a similar point when he calls for the development of 'practical wisdom' for leaders. Drawing on Aristotle's notions of *technē*, *epistēmē*, and *phronēsis*, he argues the latter is an essential part of leadership education, as outlined below.

Leadership is not just a technical problem requiring greater *skills* – what Aristotle referred to as *technē* – if it was we would presumably have found the appropriate training system some time ago. Nor is it just a problem of understanding, requiring greater *knowledge*, what Aristotle called *epistēmē*; again, if it was we should be less at its mercy today than we were 100 years ago, but it seems we are not. In addition, it may also require greater *wisdom* – Aristotle's *phronēsis* – through which leaders develop the wisdom to see what the good might be in the particular situation and then enact the processes that generate the good. In other words, it requires a form of action that focuses directly on fixing *the problem* itself, not a form of re-education or reskilling that fixes *the people*. (Ibid.: 242, initial emphasis)

According to Grint, *phronēsis* is concerned with elemental questions such as 'Where are we going? Is this desirable? What should be done? (and adding a concern for power that eludes Aristotle). Who gains and who loses?' (Ibid.: 237–8). He goes on to argue: '*phronēsis*, then, is not a method, and it cannot be reduced to a set of rules because it is dependent upon the situation and there is, therefore, no meta-narrative to guide the process' (Ibid.: 242). Accordingly '*phronēsis* cannot be taught in any lecture theatre but must be lived through; in fact it is rather closer to an apprenticeship or mentoring relationship in which the wisdom of the mentor is embedded in the novice over time, but only indirectly through guided practice or engagement, not directly through formal teaching (Halverson and Gomez, 2001)' (Grint, 2007: 242).

Such a conclusion supports a growing body of literature that highlights the value of coaching and mentoring for leaders and managers (e.g. Hobson, 2003; Boyatzis et al., 2006; Garvey, 2010). Such approaches, it is argued, not only benefit the recipient through the knowledge, insights, and opportunities for reflective discussion that they offer but may also bring benefits to the mentor or coach – particularly in terms of developing and strengthening their coaching and facilitation skills. In an empirical study of mentoring, Fowler and Gorman (2004) identified eight primary functions of the relationship as perceived by mentors and mentees: personal and emotional guidance; coaching; advocacy; career development facilitation; role modelling; strategies and systems advice; learning facilitation; and friendship. Additional research has demonstrated a long-term impact of mentoring on organizational commitment and company loyalty (Payne and Huffman, 2005), and the importance of coaching as a managerial skill in its own right (e.g. Hirsh et al., 2004).

With regard to more formalized leadership development interventions, the evidence demonstrates the value of experiential and reflective learning for practicing leaders and managers that directly addresses working concerns (Gosling and Mintzberg, 2004). Furthermore, reflective and experiential development opportunities such as this are important forums for identity work in which current and aspiring leaders can work through their conceptions and understandings of leadership, shedding negative and restrictive images of leadership and experimenting with alternative approaches (Bolden and Kirk, 2009). Collaborative inquiry (Palus and Horth, 2005) and action learning (Ladkin, 2005) can also be powerful tools for the development of leaders, while also developing wider social capital within their organizations.

The evidence from this book also demonstrates the inefficacy of developing leaders without considering the wider context in which they find themselves. As Joseph Raelin (2004: 131) argues, 'don't bother putting leadership into people [...] put leadership directly into the organization, where it belongs'. Leadership, management, and organizational development are integrally linked (McCauley et al., 1998) and strongly influenced by the culture and society in which they occur.

Fundamentally, however, evidence on the socially constructed nature of leadership implies that if leadership is a social process then so too is leadership development. While leadership development may empower, embolden, and enhance the capabilities of individual leaders, it also carries an important discursive function within organizations. The selection of who participates and who does not sends out important messages about who and what is valued within organizations – is leadership development regarded as a reward for those in senior roles; a recognition (and potentially self-fulfilling prophecy) of potential future leaders; or a remedial device for those failing to make the grade? The content, structure, and process of development opportunities likewise conveys a sense of what is valued – is the emphasis on personal knowledge, skills, and competencies; on developing relationships and collective engagement; and/or on questioning, challenging, and developing the organization's approach to leadership? Evidence on the impact of leadership and management development indicates that what is most important is not so much *what* is done as *how* it is done (Burgoyne et al., 2004; Bolden, 2010). Leadership development can be a powerful catalyst for change, yet may equally reinforce traditional assumptions and working practices.

Moving Forward with an Eye on the Past

So where have we got to and where are we going? These are questions that have run throughout this book and we encourage you to spend some time reflecting on these questions and their implications for you, your organization(s), and the various communities with which you are associated. Where do you act as a leader? What sort of leader would you like to be? What is stopping you from leading in other contexts? What might happen if you just gave it a go?

While most of our attention in this book has been on leadership, however, we need to beware of idealizing this over other equally important forms of engagement, such as 'followership' and 'communityship'. In an amusing yet insightful *YouTube* clip, Derek Sivers explains how 'being a first follower is an under-appreciated form of leadership' (http://sivers.org/ff, accessed 19 June 2010). This short video shows a lone 'shirtless dancing guy' in a park being joined by pretty much everyone in a period of just three minutes. The biggest lesson, according to Sivers, is that:

Leadership is over-glorified. Yes it started with the shirtless guy, and he'll get all the credit, but you saw what really happened: It was the first follower that transformed a lone nut into a leader. There is no movement without the first follower. We're told we all need to be leaders, but that would be really ineffective. The best way to make a movement, if you really care, is to courageously follow and show others how to follow. When you find a lone nut doing something great, have the guts to be the first person to stand up and join in.

So how do we make sense of this and learn to move forward in a constructive manner? Well, the main thing is to look around and be curious about what is going on. If we believe that 'leadership' is the answer and that all we have to do is to get the perfect leader or capture the definitive account of how it is done, then we are likely to be waiting a long time. If, however, we realize that leadership, and all that comes with it – including dissent, compliance, greed, generosity, hope, fear, trust, and deception – are happening around us all the time . . . always have . . . and always will . . . then we may well find ways of building on from what we already know to move forward into an uncertain and unknowable future with a sense of agency and an understanding that '*we are the people we've been waiting for*' (the title of a documentary on the future of education, directed by Daryl Goodrich). If our generation cannot find ways of dealing with climate change; the economics of an interconnected world; social exclusion; and inequality; the provision of affordable and quality health care; education to all members of society; and the other major challenges that face us, then who will?

To achieve this, however, leaders cannot act alone and nor can organizations, governments, and nation states; indeed, we are at a stage where, without doubt, 'leadership, in effect, is too important to be left to leaders' (Grint, 2005a). We need to find different ways of conceiving of leadership and leadership development that facilitate more inclusive and collective forms of engagement and of finding ways to support leaders (and followers) in coming to terms with and adapting to uncertainty and change. In all likelihood these perspectives and approaches already exist and our task is more one of rediscovery rather than invention. Take, for example, the quote by Lao Tzu in Chapter 2 'To lead people, walk beside them...', these things we know – the challenge now is to render them a realistic possibility within contemporary organizations.

Chapter Summary

In this final chapter we have reflected on the manner in which social and organizational changes place particular challenges on people who find themselves in positions where they are looked to for 'leadership'. We explore the various ways in which such people could be supported and developed, while recognizing that leadership development is integrally linked to group and organizational development. We then consider the enduring challenges of studying, developing, and practicing leadership and provide a commentary on how the field of Leadership Studies could be 're-rerouted' to generate theory and research that both 'matter' and are capable of challenging hegemonic practices and ways of thinking, in order to clear the way for the potential emergence of more ethical, inclusive, sustainable, and, ultimately, effective ways of leading and managing organizations.

□ **NOTES**

1. A term used by universities in New Zealand to refer to the principles of academic freedom as enshrined in the National Education Act of 1989 (see Bridgman, 2007).
2. In his book '*Outliers*', Malcolm Gladwell (2008) concludes that what places exceptional performers at the forefront of their field is around 10,000 hours of practice.
3. The term 'hermeneutics', when used in the social sciences, 'is concerned with the theory and method of interpretation of human action. It emphasizes the need to understand from the perspective of the social actor' (Bryman and Bell, 2007: 728).
4. A French term meaning literally 'jack of all trades'.

⬚ REFERENCES

Achua, C. F. and Lussier, R. N. (2010) *Effective Leadership*. Canada: Southwestern Cengage Learning.

Adair, J. (1973) *Action Centred Leadership*. New York: McGraw-Hill.

—— (1989) *Great Leaders*. Guildford: Talbot Adair Press.

Adarves-Yorno, I., Postmes, T., and Haslam, S. A. (2006) 'Social Identity and the Recognition of Creativity in Groups', *British Journal of Social Psychology*, 45(3), 479–97.

Adkins, L. (1992) 'Sexual Work and the Employment of Women in the Service Industries', in M. Savage and A. Witz (eds.) *Gender and Bureaucracy*, pp. 207–28. Oxford: Blackwell.

Adler, P. S. and Kwon, S. W. (2002) 'Social Capital: Prospects for a New Concept', *Academy of Management Review*, 21(1), 17–40.

Alvesson, M. (1994) 'Talking in Organizations: Managing Identity and Impressions in an Advertising Agency', *Organization Studies*, 15(4), 535–63.

—— (1996) 'Leadership Studies: From Procedure and Abstraction to Reflexivity and Situation', *The Leadership Quarterly*, 7(4), 455–85.

—— Sveningsson, S. (2003) 'The Great Disappearing Act: Difficulties in Doing "Leadership"', *The Leadership Quarterly*, 14, 359–81.

—— Willmott, H. (2002) 'Identity Regulation as Organizational Control: Producing the Appropriate Individual', *Journal of Management Studies*, 39(5), 619–44.

Anderson, D. R. (2005) *Corporate Survival: The Critical Importance of Sustainability Risk Management*. New York: iUniverse, Inc.

Anderson, P. (1999) 'Perspective: Complexity Theory and Organization Science', *Organization Science*, 10(3), 216–32.

—— Blatt, R., Christianson, M. K., Grant, A. M., Marquis, C., Neuman, E. J., Sonenshein, S., and Sutcliffe, K. M. (2006) 'Understanding Mechanisms in Organizational Research: Reflections from a Collective Journey', *Journal of Management Inquiry*, 15(2), 102–13.

Ashforth, B. E. (1998) 'Becoming: How does the Process of Identification Unfold?' in D. A. Whetten and P. C. Godfrey (eds.) *Identity in Organizations: Building Theory Through Conversations*, pp. 213–22. Thousand Oaks, CA: Sage.

—— Humphrey, R. H. (1995) 'Emotion in the Workplace: A Reappraisal', *Human Relations* 48(2), 97–125.

Astley, G. (1985) 'Administrative Science as Socially Constructed Truth', *Administrative Science Quarterly*, 30, 497–513.

Atkinson, D. (2004) 'Towards a Philosophical Basis for and Art of Management', in *Proceedings of the 2nd Art of Management and Organisation conference*, Paris, September 7–10, pp. 192–217.

Atkinson, R. (1994) *The Common Sense of Community*. London: Demos.

Avineri, S. and de-Shalit, A. (eds.) (1992) *Communitarianism and Individualism*. Oxford: OUP.

Avolio, B., Gardner, F. L, Walumbwa, W. O, Luthans, F, and May, D. R. (2004) 'Unlocking the Mask: A Look at the Process by which Authentic Leaders Impact Follower Attitudes and Behaviours', *Leadership Quarterly*, 15(6), 803–23.

—— Walumbwa, F., and Weber, T. (2009) 'Leadership: Current Theories, Research, and Future Directions', *Annual Review of Psychology*, 60, 421–49.

Badaracco, J. L. (2001) 'We Don't Need Another Hero', *Harvard Business Review*, September, 120–6.

Bain, P. and Taylor, P. (1999) '"An Assembly Line in the Head": Work and Employee Relations in the Call Centre', *Industrial Relations Journal*, 30(2), 101–17.

Bakan, J. (2004) *The Corporation: The Pathological Pursuit of Profit and Power*. London: Constable.

Balthazard, P., Waldman, D., and Warren, J. (2009) 'Predictors of the Emergence of Transformational Leadership in Virtual Teams', *The Leadership Quarterly*, 20, 651–63.

Barker, R. (1997) 'How Can We Train Leaders If We Do Not Know What Leadership Is?', *Human Relations*, 50(4), 343–62.

Barnard, C. I. (1948) *Organizations and Management*. Cambridge, MA: Harvard University Press.

Barrett, P. T., Petrides, K. V., Eysenck, S. G. B and Eysenck, H. J. (1998) 'The Eysenck Personality Questionnaire: An Examination of the Similarity of P, E, N and L across 34 Countries', *Personality and Individual Differences*, 25, 805–19.

Barrow, J. C. (1977) 'The Variables of Leadership: A Review and Conceptual Framework', *Academy of Management Review*, 2, 231–51.

Bass, B. M. (1985) *Leadership and Performance Beyond Expectations*. New York: Free Press.

—— (1990) *Bass and Stogdill's Handbook of Leadership: Theory, Research and Managerial Applications*, 3rd Edition. New York: Free Press.

—— Avolio, B. J. (1994) *Improving Organizational Effectiveness Through Transformational Leadership*. Thousand Oaks, CA: Sage Publications.

Baum, J. A. C., Greenwood, R., Jennings, P. D. (2008) 'Editorial: Up, Up and Away?', *Strategic Organization*, 6(1), 5–11.

Bauman, Z. (1989) *Modernity and the Holocaust*. Cambridge: Polity Press.

BBC News (2010) Election 2010: National Results. URL: http://news.bbc.co.uk/1/shared/election2010/results/, accessed 26 July 2010.

Bell, D. (1993) *Communitarianism and its Critics*. Oxford: Clarendon.

Bell, E. (2008) *Reading Management and Organization in Film*. Basingstoke: Palgrave Macmillan.

—— Taylor, S. (2003) 'The Elevation of Work: Pastoral Power and the New Age Work Ethic', *Organization*, 10(2), pp. 329–49.

—— —— Thorpe, R. (2002) 'A Step in the Right Direction? Investors in People and the Learning Organization', *British Journal of Management*, 13, 161–71.

Bennett, N., Wise, C., Woods, P. A., and Harvey, J. A. (2003) *Distributed Leadership*. Nottingham: National College of School Leadership.

Bennis, W. (1996) 'The Leader as Storyteller', *Harvard Business Review*, 74(1), p. 154.

—— (1999) 'The Leadership Advantage', *Leader to Leader*, 12, 18–23.

—— Nanus, B. (1985) *Leaders: The Strategies for Taking Charge*. New York: Harper and Row.

—— O'Toole, J. (2005) 'How Business Schools Lost Their Way', *Harvard Business Review*, 83(5), 96–104.

Bird, F. (1996) *The Muted Conscience: Moral Silence and the Practice of Ethics in Business*. New York: Quorum Books.

Bird, F. (1999) 'Empowerment and Justice', in J. Quinn and P. Davies (eds.) *The Ethics of Empowerment*. London: MacMillan Press.

—— (2001) 'Good Governance: A Philosophical Discussion of the Responsibilities and Practices of Organizational Governors', *Canadian Journal of Administrative Studies*, 18(4), 298–312.

—— (2004a) 'Wealth and Poverty in the Niger Delta: A Study of the Experiences of Shell in Nigeria', in Frederick Bird and Stewart Herman (eds.) *International Businesses and the Challenges of Poverty in Developing Areas*. London: Palgrave-Macmillan.

—— (2004b) 'Dilemmas of Development', in F. Bird, E. Raufflet, and J. Smucker (eds.) *International Business and the Dilemmas of Development*. London: Palgrave-Macmillan.

—— (2006a) 'Just Business Practices', in F. Bird and M. Velasquez (eds.) *Just Business Practices in a Diverse and Developing World*. London: Palgrave-Macmillan.

—— (2006b) 'Fostering Social Responsibility: The Role of Ethical Audits', in F. Bird and M. Velasquez (eds.) *Just Business Practices in a Diverse and Developing World*. London: Palgrave-Macmillan.

—— (2006c) 'Justice in International Business', in F. Bird and M. Velasquez (eds.) *Just Business Practices in a Diverse and Developing World*. London: Palgrave-Macmillan.

—— (2009) 'Why the Responsible Practice of Business Ethics Calls for a Due Regard for History', Paper submitted as part of a special issue to the *Journal of Business Ethics*.

—— Case, P. and Gosling, J. (2010) 'Management Education and the Ethical Mindset. responsibility to whom and for what?' presented to the *European Business Ethics Network*, 7–9 April 2010. Queen Mary College, London.

Blake, R. R. and Mouton, J. S. (1964) *The Managerial Grid*. Houston, TX: Gulf Publishing Co.

Bolden, R. (2004) *What is Leadership?* Exeter: Leadership South West, University of Exeter.

—— (2005) 'The True Face of Leadership', *European Business Forum*, 21, 54–7.

—— (2010) 'Leadership, Management and Organisational Development', in J. Gold, R. Thorpe and A. Mumford (eds.) *Handbook of Leadership and Management Development*, pp. 117–32. Aldershot: Gower.

—— (2011) 'Distributed leadership in organisations: a review of theory and research', *International Journal of Management Reviews*, 13(3), in press.

—— Gosling, J. (2006) 'Leadership Competencies: Time to Change the Tune?' *Leadership*, 2(2), 147–63.

—— —— (2008) 'Accomplishing Leadership: The Pitfalls and Potential of a Practice Perspective'. Paper presented at the *7th International Conference on Studying Leadership (ICSL)*, Auckland, New Zealand.

—— Kirk, P. (2009) 'African Leadership: Surfacing New Understandings through Leadership Development', *International Journal of Cross Cultural Management*, 9(1), 69–86.

—— O'Brien, A. (2009) 'Leadership in Partnerships: Evidence from an NGO-Private Sector Initiative'. Paper presented at *International Conference on Studying Leadership*. Birmingham, UK.

—— Gosling, J., Marturano, A., and Dennison, P. (2003) *A Review of Leadership Theory and Competency Frameworks*. Report for Chase Consulting and the Management Standards Centre, Centre for Leadership Studies, University of Exeter, June 2003.

—— Petrov, G., and Gosling, J. (2008a) *Developing Collective Leadership in Higher Education: Final Report*. London: Leadership Foundation for Higher Education.

—— —— —— (2008b) 'Tensions in Higher Education Leadership: Towards a Multi-level Model of Leadership Practice', *Higher Education Quarterly*, 62(4), 358–76.

—— —— —— (2009) 'Distributed Leadership in Higher Education: Rhetoric and Reality', *Educational Management, Administration and Leadership*, 37(2), 257–77.

—— Wood, M., and Gosling, J. (2006) 'Is the NHS Leadership Qualities Framework Missing the Wood for the Trees?' in A. Casebeer, A. Harrison and A. L. Mark (eds.) *Innovations in Health Care: A Reality Check*, pp. 17–29. New York: Palgrave Macmillan.

Bowlby, J. (1969) *Attachment and Loss: Vol. I. Attachment.* New York: Basic Books.

Boyatzis, R. E., Smith, M. L., and Blaize, N. (2006) 'Developing Sustainable Leaders through Coaching and Compassion', *Academy of Management Learning & Education*, 5(1), 8–24.

Brannan, M. J. and Hawkins, B. (2007) 'London Calling: Selection as Pre-emptive Strategy for Cultural Control', *Employee Relations*, 29(2), 178–91.

Bratton, J., Grint, K., and Nelson, D. L. (2005) *Organizational Leadership.* Ohio: Thomson South Western.

Brewis, J. (1996) 'The Making of the Competent Manager: Competency Development, Management Effectiveness and Foucault', *Management Learning*, 27(1), 65–86.

Bridgman, T. (2007) 'Assassins in Academia? New Zealand Academics as "Critic and Conscience of Society"', *New Zealand Sociology Volume Number*, 22(1), 126–44.

Brook, P. (1993) *There are no Secrets.* London: Methuen.

Brown, M. E. and Gioia, D. A. (2002) 'Making Things Click: Distributive Leadership in an Online Division of an Offline Organization', *The Leadership Quarterly*, 13, 397–419.

Brundrett, M. (2000) 'The Question of Competence; The Origins, Strengths and Inadequacies of a Leadership Training Paradigm', *School Leadership and Management*, 20(3), 353–69.

Bryman, A. (1992) *Charisma and Leadership in Organizations.* London: Sage.

—— Bell, E. (2007) *Business Research Methods*, 2nd Edition. Oxford: Oxford University Press.

—— Stephens, M., and a Campo, C. (1996) 'The Importance of Context: Qualitative Research and the Study of Leadership', *The Leadership Quarterly*, 7(3), 353–70.

Buckingham, M. (2005) 'What Great Managers DO', *Harvard Business Review*, 83(3), 70–9.

Burgoyne, J., Hirsh, W., and Williams, S. (2004) *The Development of Management and Leadership Capability and its Contribution to Performance: The Evidence, Prospects and the Research Need.* London: Department for Education and Skills.

Burns, J. M. (1978) *Leadership.* New York: Harper & Row.

—— (2005) 'Leadership', *Leadership*, 1(1), 11–12.

Burridge, B. (2007) 'Action-Centred Leadership in the Royal Air Force: Final Landing or New Horizon?' in J. Gosling, P. Case, and M. Witzel (eds.) *John Adair: Fundamentals of Leadership*, pp. 95–108. Basingstoke: Palgrave MacMillan.

Butler, J. (1990) *Gender Trouble: Feminism and the Subversion of Identity.* London: Routledge.

Cameron, K. (2008) *Positive Leadership: Strategies for Extraordinary Performance.* San Francisco, CA: Berrett-Keohler.

—— Dutton, J., and Quinn, R. (eds.) (2003) *Positive Organizational Scholarship: Foundations of a New Discipline.* San Francisco, CA: Berrett-Keohler.

Campbell, D., Dardis, G., and Campbell, K. (2003) 'Enhancing Incremental Influence: A Focused Approach to Leadership Development', *Journal of Leadership and Organizational Studies*, 10(1), 29–44.

Campbell, M., Baldwin, S., Johnson, S., Chapman, R., Upton, A., and Walton, F. (2001) *Skills in England: The Research Report.* London: Department for Education and Skills.

Carlyle, T. (1866) *On Heroes, Hero-Worship and the Heroic in History.* New York: John Wiley and Sons.

Carr, E. H. (2002) 'What is History?' in D. Arnold (ed.) *Reading Architectural History,* pp. 14–23. London: Penguin.

Carroll, B., Levy, L., and Richmond, D. (2008) 'Leadership as Practice: Challenging the Competency Paradigm', *Leadership,* 4(4), 363–79.

Case, P. and Gosling, J. (2009) 'Where is the Wisdom We Have Lost in Knowledge? A Stoical Perspective on Personal Knowledge Management'. Paper presented at *Sixth International Critical Management Conference,* Warwick Business School, UK, July 13–15.

—— Phillipson, G. (2004) 'Astrology, Alchemy and Retro-Organization Theory: An Astro-Genealogical critique of the Myers-Briggs Type Indicator', *Organization,* 11(4), 473–95.

Casey, C. (1995) *Work, Self and Society: After Industrialism.* London: Routledge.

—— (2002) *Critical Analysis of Organizations: Theory, Practice and Revitalization.* London: Sage.

Cattell, H. E. P. and Mead, A. D. (2008) 'The 16 Personality Factor Questionnaire (16PF)', in G. J. Boyle, G. Matthews, and D. H. Saklofske (eds.) *The Sage Handbook of Personality Theory and Assessment,* Vol. 2, pp. 135–59. London: Sage.

Centre for Leadership Studies (2010) *Mission, Vision and Values.* University of Exeter Business School, URL: http://centres.exeter.ac.uk/cls/about/mission.php

Chatwin, B. (1998) *The Songlines.* London: Vintage.

Chomsky, N. and Foucault, M. (2006) *The Chomsky-Foucault Debate: On Human Nature.* New York: New Press.

Ciulla, J. (1998) *Ethics: The Heart of Leadership.* Westport, CT: Praeger.

—— (1999) 'The Importance of Leadership in Shaping Business Values', *Long Range Planning,* 32(2), 166–72.

—— (2002) 'Trust and the Future of Leadership', in N. E. Bowie (ed.) *The Blackwell Guide to Business Ethics,* pp. 334–51. Oxford: Blackwell.

—— (2004) *Ethics: The Heart of Leadership,* 2nd Edition. London: Praeger.

—— (2005) 'The State of Leadership Ethics and the Work that Lies Before Us', *Business Ethics: A European Review,* 14(4), 323–35.

—— (2006) 'What We Learned Along the Way: A Commentary', in G. R. Goethals and G. L. J. Sorenson (eds.) *The Quest for a General Theory of Leadership,* pp. 221–33. Cheltenham: Edward Elgar.

Clarke, M., Butcher, D., and Bailey, C. (2004) 'Strategically Aligned Leadership Development', in J. Storey (ed.) *Leadership In Organizations: Current Issues and Key Trends,* pp. 271–92. Oxon: Routledge.

Cohn, N. (1970) *The Pursuit of the Millennium: Revolutionary Millenarians and Mystical Anarchists of the Middle Ages.* Oxford: Oxford University Press.

Collins, R. (1997) 'An Asian Route to Capitalism: Religious Economy and the Origins of Self-Transforming Growth in Japan', *American Sociological Review,* 62, 843–65.

Collinson, D. (2005) 'Dialectics of Leadership', *Human Relations,* 58(11), 1419–42.

—— Collinson, M. (2009) 'Blended Leadership': Employee Perspectives on Effective Leadership in the UK Further Education Sector', *Leadership,* 5(3), 365–80.

Collinson, D. L. (2003) 'Identities and Insecurities: Selves at Work', *Organization,* 10(3), 527–47.

Colville, I. (2008) 'On the (be)coming and Going of Organizational Change: Prospect and Retrospect in Sensemaking', in S. Clegg and C. Cooper (eds.) *Handbook of Macro-Organizational Behaviour*. London: Sage.

Conger, J. A. (1990) 'The Dark Side of Leadership', *Organizational Dynamics*, 19, 44–5.

—— (1998) 'Qualitative Research as the Cornerstone Methodology for Understanding Leadership', *The Leadership Quarterly*, 9(1), 107–21.

—— Kanungo, R, N. (1987) 'Towards a Behavioural Theory of Charismatic Leadership in Organizational Settings', *Academy of Management Review*, 12(4), 637–47.

Conger, J. M. and Kanungo, R. N. (1998) *Charismatic Leadership in Organizations*. Thousand Oaks, CA: Sage.

Cooper, B. R. and Baker, J. N. (1995) 'Fair Play or Foul? A Survey of Occupational Test Practices in the UK', *Personnel Review*, 24(3), 3–18.

Cooper, R. K. and Sawaf, M. (1998) *Executive EQ: Emotional Intelligence in Leadership and Organizations*. New York: Berkeley Publishing Group.

Cooperrider, D. L. and Srivastva, S. (1987) 'Appreciative Inquiry in Everyday Organizational Life', in R. Woodxman and W. Passmore (eds.) *Research in Organizational Change and Development*, Vol. 1, pp. 129–69. Westview, CT: JAI Press Inc.

—— Sorensen, P., Whitney, D., and Yaeger, T. (eds.) (1999) *Appreciative Inquiry: Rethinking Human Organization Toward a Positive Theory of Change*. Champaign, IL: Stipes Publishing.

Covey, S., Merrill, A. R., and Merrill, R. R. (1994) *First Things First: To Live, to Love, to Learn, to Leave a Legacy*. New York: Simon and Schuster.

Cunliffe, A. L. (2009) 'The Philosopher Leader: On Relationalism, Ethics and Reflexivity— A Critical Perspective to Teaching Leadership', *Management Learning*, 40(1), 87–101.

Czarniawska-Joerges, B. (1998) *A Narrative Approach to Organization Studies*. London: Sage.

Daly, H. and Cobb, J. (1990) *For the Common Good*. London: Beacon Press.

Damasio, A. R. (1994) *Descartes' Error*. New York: G.P. Putnam's Sons.

Dansereau, F. J., Graen, G., and Haga, W. J. (1975) 'A Vertical Dyad Linkage Approach to Leadership within Formal Organizations: A Longitudinal Investigation of the Role Making Process', *Organizational Behavior and Human Performance*, 13, 46–78.

Davie, G. (2007) *The Sociology of Religion*. London: Sage.

Day, C., Sammons, P., Hopkins, D., Harris, A., Leithwood, K., Gu, Q., Penlington, C., Mehta, P., and Kington, A. (2007) *The Impact of School Leadership on Pupil Outcomes: Interim Report*. Nottingham: National College for School Leadership.

Day, D. V. (2000) 'Leadership Development: A Review in Context', *The Leadership Quarterly*, 11(4), 581–613.

de Rond, M. (2003) *Strategic Alliances as Social Facts: Business, Biotechnology, and Intellectual History*. Cambridge: Cambridge University Press.

Deal, T. E. and Kennedy, A. A. (1982) *Corporate Cultures: The Rites and Rituals of Corporate Life*. Reading, MA: Addison Wesley.

Deloitte and Touche (2003) 'Human Capital Survey', *Personnel Today*, January.

Denning, S. (2001) *The Springboard: How Story-telling Ignites Action in Knowledge-Era Organizations*. Boston, MA: Butterworth-Heineman.

DeNora, T. (2000) *Music in Everyday Life*. Cambridge: Cambridge University Press.

—— (2003) *After Adorno: Rethinking Music Sociology*. Cambridge: Cambridge University Press.

DfEE (2000) *Labour Market and Skills Trends 2000*. London: Department for Education and Employment.

DfES (2002) *Government Response to the Report of the Council for Excellence in Management and Leadership*. Nottingham: Department for Education and Skills.

DoH (2000) *The NHS Plan*. London: Department of Health.

Dotlich, D. and Cairo, P. (2003) *Why CEOs Fail*. San Francisco, CA: Jossey Bass.

Drath, W. (2001) *The Deep Blue Sea: Rethinking the Source of Leadership*. San Francisco, CA: Jossey Bass.

—— McCauley, C. D., Palus, C. J., Van Velsor, E., O'Connor, P. M. G., and McGuire, J. B. (2008) 'Direction, Alignment, Commitment: Toward a More Integrative Ontology of Leadership', *The Leadership Quarterly*, 19(6), 635–53.

Dulewicz, V. and Higgs, M. (1999) 'Can Emotional Intelligence by Developed and Measured?', *Leadership and Organization Development Journal*, 20(5), 242–53.

Eagly, A. and Carli, L. (2003) 'The Female Leadership Advantage: An Evaluation of the Evidence', *The Leadership Quarterly*, 14, 807–34.

Elkington, J. (1998) *Cannibals with Forks: The Triple Bottom Line of 21st Century Business*. Stony Creek, CT: New Society Publishers.

Elloy, D. (2005) 'The Influence of Superleader Behaviors on Organization Commitment, Job Satisfaction and Organization Self-Esteem in a Self-Managed Work Team', *Leadership and Organizational Development*, 26(2), 120–7.

Engels, F. (1987) *The Condition of the Working Class in England*. New York: Penguin.

Ensley, M. D., Hmieleski, K. M., and Pearce, C. L. (2006) 'The Importance of Vertical and Shared Leadership within New Venture Top Management Teams: Implications for the Performance of Startups', *The Leadership Quarterly*, 17, 217–31.

Etzioni, A. (1993) *The Spirit of Community*. New York: Crown.

Eysenck, H. J. and Eysenck, S. B. G. (1975) *Manual of the Eysenck Personality Questionnaire*. Sevenoaks, Kent: Hodder and Stoughton.

Ezzamel, M., Willmott, H., and Worthington, F. (2001) 'Power, Control and Resistance in the Factory that Time Forgot', *Journal of Management Studies*, 38(8), 1053–79.

Fairhurst, G. T. (2007) *Discursive Leadership: In Conversation with Leadership Psychology*. London: Sage.

—— (2009) 'Considering Context in Discursive Leadership Research', *Human Relations*, 62(11), 1607–33.

—— Sarr, R. A. (1996) *The Art of Framing: Managing the Language of Leadership*, 1st Edition. San Francisco, CA: Jossey-Bass.

Fay, B. (1996) *Contemporary Philosophy of Social Science: A Multicultural Approach*. Oxford: Blackwell.

Fayol, H. (1949) *General and Industrial Management*. London: Pitman.

Fiedler, F. E. (1964) 'A Contingency Model of Leadership Effectiveness', in L. Berkowitz (ed.) *Advances in Experimental Social Psychology*. New York: Academic Press.

—— (1967) *A Theory of Leadership Effectiveness*. New York: McGraw-Hill.

Fineman, S. (2006) 'On Being Positive: Concerns and Counterpoints', *Academy of Management Review*, 31, 270–91.

Fleishman, E. A. (1953) 'The Description of Supervisory Behavior', *Personnel Psychology*, 37, 1–6.

—— Harris, E. F. (1962) 'Patterns of Leadership Behavior Related to Employee Grievances and Turnover', *Personnel Psychology*, 15, 43–56.

Fletcher, J. (2002) 'The Greatly Exaggerated Demise of Heroic Leadership: Gender, Power, and the Myth of the Female Advantage', *CGO Insights*, 13, 1–4.

Flyvbjerg, B. (2001) *Making Social Science Matter: Why Social Inquiry Fails and How it can Succeed Again*. Cambridge: Cambridge University Press.

—— (2006) 'Making Organization Research Matter: Power, Values, and Phronesis', in C. H. Stewart R. Clegg, Thomas B. Lawrence, and Walter R. Nord (ed.) *The Sage Handbook of Organization Studies*, 2nd Edition, pp. 370–87. Thousand Oaks, CA: Sage.

Follett, M. P. (2003 [1942]) *Dynamic Administration: The Collected Papers of Mary Parker Follett*. London: Routledge.

Forrester, J. W. (1961) *Industrial Dynamics*. Cambridge, MA: MIT Press.

Foucault, M. (1979) *Discipline and Punish: The Birth of the Prison* (trans. Alan Sheridan). New York: Vintage Books.

—— (1980) *Power/Knowledge: Selected Interviews and Other Writings, 1972–1977*. London: Harvester Press Ltd.

—— (2002) *The Order of Things: An Archaeology of the Human Sciences* (trans. Tavistock Publications/Routledge). Abingdon, Oxon: Routledge.

Fournier, V. and Grey, C. (2000) 'At the Critical Moment: Conditions and Prospects for Critical Management Studies', *Human Relations*, 53, 7–32.

Fowler, J. and Gorman, J. (2004) 'Mentoring Functions: A Contemporary View of the Perceptions of Mentees and Mentors', *British Journal of Management*, 16(1), 51–7.

Fraser, C. (1978) 'Small Groups: Structure and Leadership', in H. Tajfel and C. Fraser (eds.) *Introducing Social Psychology*, pp. 176–200. Harmondsworth: Penguin Books.

Freeman, R. E. (1984) *Strategic Management: A Stakeholder Approach*. London: Pitman Publishers.

—— (2004) 'Ethical Leadership and Creating Value for Stakeholders', in R. A. Peterson and O. C. Ferrell (eds.) *Business Ethics*. London: M.E. Sharpe.

French, J., Jnr and Raven, B. H. (1959) 'The Bases of Social Power', in D Cartwright (ed.) *Studies of Social Power*, pp. 150–67. Ann Arbor, MI: Institute for Social research.

French, R. (2001) 'Negative Capability: Managing the Confusing Uncertainties of Change', *Journal of Organizational Change Management*, 14(5), 480–92.

Friedman, M. (1970) 'The Social Responsibility of Business is to Make Profit', *New York Times Magazine*, 13 September.

Frost, P. (2003) *Toxic Emotions at Work: How Compassionate Managers Handle Pain and Conflict*. Boston, MA: Harvard Business School Press.

—— Robinson, S. (1999) 'The Toxic Handler: Organizational Hero—And Casualty', *Harvard Business Review*, July–August, 96–106.

Fry, L. (2003) 'Toward a Theory of Spiritual Leadership', *The Leadership Quarterly*, 14, 693–727.

—— Cohen, M. (2009) 'Spiritual Leadership as a Paradigm for Organizational Transformation and Recovery from Extended Work Hours Cultures', *Journal of Business Ethics*, 84, 265–78.

—— Slocum, J. (2008) 'Maximising the Triple Bottom Line Through Spiritual Leadership', *Organizational Dynamics*, 37, 86–96.

Fulmer, R. M. (1997) 'The Evolving Paradigm of Leadership Development', *Organizational Dynamics*, 25(4), 59–73.

Gallos, J. (2008) 'Leading from the Toxic Trenches: The Winding Road to Healthier Organizations and to Healthy Everyday Leaders', *Journal of Management Inquiry*, 17: 354–67.

Gardner, H. and Laskin, E. (1996) *Leading Minds: An Anatomy of Leadership*. New York: Basic Books.

Gardner, J. W. (1990) *On Leadership*. New York: Free Press.

Garvey, B. (2010) 'Mentoring for Leaders and Managers', in J. Gold, R. Thorpe, and A. Mumford (eds.) *Gower Handbook of Leadership and Management Development*, pp. 423–39. Farnham: Gower.

Geertz, C. (1999) 'Thick Description: Toward an Interpretive Theory of Culture', in A. Bryman and R. Burgess (eds.) *Qualitative Research Volume III*, pp. 346–68. London: Sage.

Gemmill, G. and Oakley, J. (1992) 'Leadership: An Alienating Social Myth?', *Human Relations*, 45(2), 113–29.

George, J. M. (1995) 'Leader Positive Mood and Group Performance: The Case of Customer Service', *Journal of Applied Social Psychology*, 25, 778–94.

—— (2000) 'Emotions and Leadership: The Role of Emotional Intelligence', *Human Relations*, 53(8), 1027–55.

George, W. (2003) *Authentic Leadership: Rediscovering the Secrets to Creating Lasting Value*. San Francisco, CA: Jossey Bass.

Gergen, K. J. (1999a) 'Agency: Social Construction and Relational Action', *Theory and Psychology*, 9(1), 113–15.

—— (1999b) *An Invitation to Social Construction*. London: Sage.

Ghoshal, S. (2005) 'Bad Management Theories are Destroying Good Management Practices', *Academy of Management Learning and Education*, 4(1), 75–91.

Gibson, J. J. (1966) *The Senses Considered as Perceptual Systems*. Boston: Houghton Mifflin.

—— (1977) 'The Theory of Affordances', in R. E. Shaw and J. Bransford (eds.) *Perceiving, Acting, and Knowing*, pp. 67–82. Hillsdale, NJ: Lawrence Erlbaum.

—— (1979) *The Ecological Approach to Visual Perception*. Boston, MA: Houghton Mifflin.

Giddens, A. (1990) *The Consequences of Modernity*. Cambridge: Polity.

Gill, J. and Johnson, P. (2010) *Research Methods for Managers*, 4th Edition. London: Sage.

Gill, R. (2006) *Theory and Practice of Leadership*. London: Sage.

Gilligan, C. (1982) *In a Different Voice: Psychological Theory and Women's Development*. Cambridge, MA: Harvard University Press.

Gladwell, M. (2008) *Outliers: The Story of Success*. New York: Little, Brown and Company.

Glisson, C. and Durrick, M. (1988) 'Predictions of Job Satisfaction and Organizational Commitment in Human Service Organizations', *Administrative Science Quarterly*, 37, 161–81.

Goethals, G. R. and Sorenson, G. L. J. (2006) *The Quest for a General Theory of Leadership*. Cheltenham: Edward Elgar.

Goldberg, L. R. (1990) 'An Alternative "Description of Personality": The Big Five Factor Structure', *Journal of Personality and Social Psychology*, 59(6), 1216–29.

Goldman, A. (2008) 'Company on the Couch: Unveiling Toxic Behavior in Dysfunctional Organizations', *Journal of Management Inquiry*, 17, 226–38.

Goldstein, J. and Hazy, J. K. (2006) 'Editorial Introduction to the Special Issue: From Complexity to Leadership and Back to Complexity', *Emergence: Complexity and Organization*, 8(4), v–vii.

Goleman, D. (1995) *Emotional Intelligence*. New York: Bantam Books.

—— (1998) 'What Makes a Leader?' *Harvard Business Review*, 76(6), 93–103.

—— Boyatzis, R., and McKee, A. (2002) *Primal Leadership: Realizing the Power of Emotional Intelligence*. Boston: Harvard Business School Press.

Gosling, J. (1996) 'The Business of Community', in S. Kraemer and J. Roberts (eds.) *The Politics of Attachment*, (138–51) London: Free Association Books.

—— (2004) 'Leadership Development in Management Education', *Business Leadership Review*, 1 (1), URL: http://www.mbaworld.com/blr.

—— (2008) 'Leading Continuity in Times of Change', in J. Jupp (ed.) *Air Force Leadership: Changing Culture*. Shrivenham: RAF Leadership Centre.

—— (2009) 'Foreword', in L. Mitchell (ed.) *Cyrus the Great and the Obedience of the Willing*, pp. 4–7. University of Exeter: Centre for Leadership Studies, Extended Essay Series.

—— Mintzberg, H. (2003) 'The Five Minds of a Manager', *Harvard Business Review*, 81(11), 54–63.

—— —— (2004) 'The Education of Practicing Managers', *Sloan Management Review*, 45(4), 19–22.

Grace, M. (2003) 'The Origins of Leadership: The Etymology of Leadership'. Paper presented at *Annual Conference of the International Leadership Association*, Guadalajara, Mexico.

Graeff, C. L. (1983) 'The Situational Leadership Theory: A Critical View', *Academy of Management Review*, 8, 285–91.

Graen, G. and Cashman, J. F. (1975) 'A Role Making Model of Leadership in Formal Organizations: A Developmental Approach', in J. G. Hunt and L. L. Larson (eds.) *Leadership Frontiers*. Kent, OH: Kent State University Press.

—— Uhl-Bien, M. (1995) 'Relationship-based Approach to Leadership: Development of Leader-Member Exchange (LMX) Theory of Leadership over 25 years: Applying a Multi-level, Multi-domain Perspective', *Leadership Quarterly*, 6(2), 219–47.

Gray, D. E. (2009) *Doing Research in the Real World*, 2nd Edition. London: Sage.

Greenleaf, R. K. (1977) *Servant Leadership: A Journey into the Nature of Legitimate Power and Greatness*. New York: Paulist Press.

—— (2004) 'Who is the Servant-Leader?' in L. C. Spears and M. Lawrence (eds.) *Practicing Servant-Leadership: Succeeding Through Trust, Bravery, and Forgiveness*. San Francisco, CA: Jossey Bass.

Grey, C. (2009) *A Very Short, Fairly Interesting and Reasonably Cheap Book About Studying Organizations*, 2nd Edition. London: Sage.

Grint, K. (1997) *Leadership: Classical, Contemporary, and Critical Approaches*. Oxford: Oxford University Press.

—— (2001) *The Arts of Leadership*. Oxford: Oxford University Press.

—— (2004) 'Actor Network Theory', in G. R. Goethals, G. J. Sorenson, and J. M. Burns (eds.) *Encyclopedia of Leadership*. Thousand Oaks, CA: Sage Publications Inc.

—— (2005a) *Leadership: Limits and Possibilities*. Basingstoke: Palgrave Macmillan.

—— (2005b) 'Problems, Problems, Problems: The Social Construction Of "Leadership"', *Human Relations*, 58(11), 1467–94.

—— (2007) 'Learning to Lead: Can Aristotle Help us find the Road to Wisdom?', *Leadership*, 3(2), 231–46.

Grint, K. (2010) 'The Sacred in Leadership: Separation, Sacrifice, and Silence', *Organization Studies*, 31, 89–107.

Grint, K., and Holt, C. (2011) 'Leadership Questions: If "Total Place" and "Big Society" and local leadership as the answers, what are the questions?' *Leadership*, 7(1), 85–98.

Gronn, P. (1999) 'Substituting for Leadership: The Neglected Role of the Leadership Couple', *Leadership Quarterly*, 10(1), 41–62.

—— (2002) 'Distributed Leadership as a Unit of Analysis', *The Leadership Quarterly*, 13(4), 423–51.

—— (2003) 'Leadership: Who Needs It?' *School Leadership & Management*, 23(3), 267–90.

—— (2008) 'Hybrid Leadership', in K. Leithwood, B. Mascall, and T. Strauss (eds.) *Distributed Leadership According to the Evidence*, pp. 17–40. Mahwah, NJ: Erlbaum.

—— (2009) 'Leadership Configurations', *Leadership*, 5(3), 381–94.

Guthey, E., Clark, T., and Jackson, B. (2009) *Demystifying Business Celebrity*. Abingdon: Routledge.

Halpin, A. and Winer, B. (1957) 'A Factorial Study of the Leader Behavior Descriptions', in R. Stogdill and A. Coons (eds.) *Leader Behavior: Its Description and Measurement*. Columbus, OH: Bureau of Business Research, Ohio State University.

Halverson, R. and Gomez, L. (2001) 'Phronesis and Design: How Practical Wisdom is Disclosed through Collaborative Design'. Paper presented at the 2001 *American Educational Research Association Annual Meeting*, Seattle, WA.

Hambrick, D. (1994) '1993 Presidential Address: What if the Academy Actually Mattered?', *Academy of Management Review*, 19(1), 632–6.

—— (2005) 'Venturing Outside the Monastery', *Academy of Management Journal*, 48(6), 961–3.

—— (2007) 'The Field of Management's Devotion to Theory: Too Much of a Good Thing?', *Academy of Management Journal*, 50(6), 1346–52.

Hammersley, M. (1992) *What's Wrong With Ethnography?* London: Routledge.

Hammond, S. A. (1998) *The Thin Book of Appreciative Inquiry*. Plano, TX: Thin Book Publishing Co.

Hancock, P. and Tyler, M. (2001) *Work, Postmodernism and Organization: A Critical Introduction*. London: Sage.

Handy, C. (1994) *The Empty Raincoat*. London: Hutchinson.

—— (1995) *Beyond Certainty*. London: Random House.

Harris, J. R. and Sutton, C. D. (1995) 'Unravelling the Ethical Decision-making Process: Clues from an Empirical Study Comparing Fortune 1000 Executives and MBA Students', *Journal of Business Ethics*, 14, 805–17.

Harrison, J. K. and Clough, M. W. (2006) 'Characteristics of "State of the Art" Leaders: Productive Narcissism Versus Emotional Intelligence and Level 5 Capabilities', *The Social Science Journal*, 43, 287–92.

Haslam, S. A. (2004) *Psychology in Organizations: The Social Identity Approach*, 2nd Edition. London: Sage Publications.

—— Ryan, M. (2008) 'The Road to the Glass Cliff: Differences in the Perceived Suitability of Men and Women for Leadership Positions in Succeeding and Failing Organizations', *The Leadership Quarterly*, 19, 530–46.

—— Reicher, S. D., and Platow, M. J. (2010) *The New Psychology of Leadership: Identity, Influence and Power*. Basingstoke: Routledge.

Hatch, M. J. and Schultz, M. (2003) 'Bringing the Corporation into Corporate Branding', *European Journal of Marketing*, 37(7/8), 1041–64.

Hatcher, R. (2005) 'The Distribution of Leadership and Power in Schools', *British Journal of Sociology of Education*, 26(2), 253–67.

Hawkins, B. (2008) 'Double Agents: Organizational Culture, Gender and Resistance', *Sociology*, 42(3), 418–35.

Heenan, D. and Bennis, W. (1999) *Co-Leaders: The Power of Great Partnerships*. Hoboken, NJ: Wiley.

Hemphill, J. K. and Coons, A. E. (1957) 'Development of the Leader Behavior Description Questionnaire', in R. M. Stogdill and A. E. Coons (eds.) *Leader Behavior: Its Description and Measurement*, pp. 6–38. Columbus, OH: Bureau of Business Research, Ohio State University.

Hersey, P. and Blanchard, K. (1969) 'Life-cycle Theory of Leadership', *Training and Development Journal*, 2, 26–34.

—— —— (1977) *Management of Organizational Behaviour*. Englewood Cliffs, NJ: Prentice-Hall.

—— —— (1988) *Management of Organizational Behavior: Utilizing Human Resources*. Englewood Cliffs, NJ: Prentice-Hall.

—— —— (1993) *Management of Organizational Behaviour: Utilizing Human Resources*, 6th Edition. Englewood Cliffs, NJ: Prentice-Hall.

HESA (2008) 'Student Tables by Subject of Study 1996/7 and 2006/7'. Higher Education Statistics Agency, UK.

Hicks, D. (2003) *Religion and the Workplace: Pluralism, Spirituality, leadership*. New York: Cambridge University Press.

Hirsh, W., Silverman, M., Tamkin, P., and Jackson, C. (2004) *Managers as Developers of Others*. Brighton: Institute of Employment Studies.

Hobson, A. (2003) *Mentoring and Coaching for New Leaders*. Nottingham: National College for School Leadership.

Hochschild, A. (1983) *The Managed Heart: Commercialization of Human Feeling*. Berkeley, CA: University of California Press.

Hofstede, G. (1980) *Culture's Consequences*. London: Sage Publications.

Hogg, M. A. (2001) 'A Social Identity Theory of Leadership', *Personality and Social Psychology Review*, 5(3), 184–200.

Holman, D. (2000) 'Contemporary Models of Management Education in the UK', *Management Learning*, 31(2), 197–217.

—— Hall, L. (1996) 'Competence in Management Development: Rites And Wrongs', *British Journal of Management*, 7, 191–202.

Holmes, J. (2007) 'Humour and the Construction of Maori Leadership at Work', *Leadership*, 3, 5–27.

Honey, P. and Mumford, A. (1982) *The Manual of Learning Styles*. Maidenhead: Honey Press.

Horne, M, and Stedman Jones, D. (2001) *Leadership: A Challenge for All?* London: Chartered Management Institute.

Hosking, D. M. (1988) 'Organising, Leadership and Skillful Process', *Journal of Management Studies*, 25, 147–66.

House, R. J., Hanges, P. J., Javidan, M., Dorfman, P. W., and Gupta, V. (2004) *Culture, Leadership, and Organizations: The GLOBE Study of 62 Societies*. London: Sage Publications.

Husserl, E. (1900 [2001]) *Logical Investigations Vol. 1 (N. Findlay trans)*. London: Routledge.

Hutcheson, F. (1969 [1738]) *An Inquiry into the Original of our Ideas of Beauty and Virtue*. Farnborough: Gregg International.

Jackall, R. (1988) *Moral Mazes*. Oxford: Oxford University Press.

Jackson, B. (2001) *Management Gurus and Management Fashions*. London: Routledge.

—— Parry, K. (2008) *A Very Short, Fairly Interesting and Reasonably Cheap Book about Studying Leadership*. London: Sage Publications.

Jacobs, M. (1995) 'Thoughts on Community'. Presented during the *MPhil in Critical Management*, Lancaster University, UK.

Jacques, R. (1996) *Manufacturing the Employee: Management Knowledge from the 19th to the 21st Centuries*. London: Sage Publications.

Jarzabkowski, P. (2004) 'Strategy as Practice: Recursiveness, Adaptation, and Practices-In-Use', *Organization Studies*, 25(4), 529–60.

Jepson, D. and Edwards, G. (2009) 'Is Leadership an Aspirational Identity? Reflections on Discourse and Practice'. Paper presented at the *British Academy of Management Conference*, Brighton, UK.

Jones, C., Parker, M., and ten Bos, R. (2005) *For Business Ethics*. Abingdon: Routledge.

Jones, S. and Gosling, J. (2005) *Nelson's Way: Leadership Lessons from the Great Commander*. London: Nicholas Brealey.

Joshi, A., Lazarova, M., and Liao, H. (2009) 'Getting Everyone on Board: The Role of Inspirational Leadership in Geographically Dispersed Teams', *Organization Science*, 20, 240–52.

Jowell, T. (2004) *Government and the Value of Culture*. London: DCMS. URL: http://www.culture.gov.uk/images/publications/valueofculture.pdf, accessed 24 August 2008).

Judge, T. A. and Bono, J. E. (2000) 'Five-Factor Model of Personality and Transformational Leadership', *Journal of Applied Psychology*, 85(5), 751–65.

Jung, C. (1923) *Psychological Types*. New York: Harcourt Brace.

Katz, D. and Kahn, R. (1978) *The Social Psychology of Organizations*. New York: Wiley.

Kellerman, B. (2004a) *Bad Leadership: What It Is, How It Happens, Why it Matters*. Boston, MA: Harvard Business School Press.

—— (2004b) 'Leadership: Warts and All', *Harvard Business Review*, January, 40–5.

—— (2008) *Followership*. Boston, MA: Harvard Business School Publishing.

Kelly, S. (2008) 'Leadership: A Categorical Mistake?', *Human Relations*, 61(6), 763–82.

Kempster, S. and Stewart, J. (2010) 'Becoming a Leader: A Co-produced Autoethnographic Exploration of Situated Learning of Leadership Practice', *Management Learning*, 41(2), 205–19.

Kerr, S. and Jermier, J. M. (1978) 'Substitutes for Leadership: Their Meaning and Measurement', *Organizational Behavior and Human Performance*, 22, 375–419.

Kirkpatrick, S. A. and Locke, E. A. (1991) 'Leadership: Do Traits Matter?', *The Executive*, 5, 48–60.

Klein, K. J., Ziegert, J. C., Knight, A. P., and Xiao, Y. (2006) 'Dynamic Delegation: Shared, Hierarchical, and Deindividualized Leadership in Extreme Action Teams', *Administrative Science Quarterly*, 51, 590–621.

Knights, D. and Willmott, H. (1999) *Management Lives: Power and Identity in Work Organizations*. London: Sage.

Kotter, J. P. (1990) 'What Leaders Really Do', *Harvard Business Review*, May–June, 103–11.

—— (1995) 'Leading Change: Why Transformation Efforts Fail', *Harvard Business Review*, March/April, 59–67.

Kouzes, J. M., and Posner, B. Z. (2002) *The Leadership Challenge*. San Francisco, CA: Jossey-Bass.

Ladkin, D. (2004) 'Action Research', in C. Searle, G. Gobo, J. F. Gubrium, and D. Silverman (eds.) *Qualitative Research Practice*, pp. 536–48. London: Sage.

—— (2005) 'The Use and Abuse of Psychometrics in Leader Development', in R. Bolden (ed.) *What is Leadership Development? Purpose and Practice*, pp. 35–7. Exeter: Leadership South West, University of Exeter.

—— (2006a) 'When Deontology and Utilitarianism Aren't Enough: How Heidegger's Notion of "Dwelling" Might Help Organisational Leaders Resolve Ethical Issues', *Journal of Business Ethics*, 56: 87–98.

—— (2006b) 'The Enchantment of the Charismatic Leader: Charisma Reconsidered as Aesthetic Encounter', *Leadership*, 2(2): 165–80.

—— (2006c) 'Leading Beautifully: How Mastery, Congruence and Form Contribute to Inspirational Leadership Performance', *Leadership Quarterly*, 19: 31–41.

—— (2007) 'Leading from the Middle: Operational Leadership as Hermenutic Practice'. Paper presented at *6th International Studying Leadership Conference*, University of Warwick.

—— (2010) *Rethinking Leadership: A New Look at Old Leadership Questions*. Cheltenham: Edward Elgar.

Ladkin, R. (2005) 'Action Learning in Leadership Development', in R. Bolden (ed.) *What is Leadership Development? Purpose & Practice*, pp. 27–30. Exeter: Leadership South West, University of Exeter.

Latour, B. (1993) *We Have Never Been Modern*. London: Prentice-Hall.

Lawrence, T. E. (1935) *Seven Pillars of Wisdom*. London: Penguin.

—— (1997) *Seven Pillars of Wisdom*. Ware, Herts: Wordsworth Editions Limited.

Leithwood, K., Day, C., Sammons, P., Harris, A., and Hopkins, D. (2006) *Seven Strong Claims About Successful School Leadership*. Nottingham: National College for School Leadership.

Lester, S. (1994) 'Management Standards: A Critical Approach', *Competency*, 2(1), 28–31.

Levy, D. L., Alvesson, M., and Willmott, H. (2003) 'Critical Approaches to Strategic Management', in M. Alvesson and H. Willmott (eds.) *Studying Management Critically*, pp. 92–110. London: Sage.

Lewin, K. (1947) 'Group Decision and Social Change', in T. N. Newcombe and E. L. Hartley (eds.) *Readings in Social Psychology*. Troy: Mo: Holt, Reinehart and Winston.

—— Lippitt, R., and White, R. (1939) 'Patterns of Aggressive Behavior in Experimentally Created "Social Climates"', *Journal of Social Psychology*, 10, 271–99.

Lichtenstein, B. B. and Plowman, D. A. (2009) 'The Leadership of Emergence: A Complex Systems Leadership Theory of Emergence at Successive Organizational Levels', *The Leadership Quarterly*, 20, 617–30.

Lipman-Blumen, J. (2005) *The Allure of Toxic Leaders*. New York: Oxford University Press Inc.

Lord, R. G. and Maher, K. J. (1991) *Leadership and Information Processing: Linking Perceptions and Performance*. Boston: Unwin-Everyman.

Lorenz, E. (1972) 'Does the Flap of a Butterfly's Wings in Brazil set off a Tornado in Texas?' Paper presented at the *139th meeting of the American Association for the Advancement of Science*, Washington DC, 29 December.

Lukes, S. (2005) *Power: A Radical View*. Hampshire: Palgrave Macmillan.

Luthans, F. and Avolio, B. J. (2003) 'Authentic Leadership: A Positive Developmental Approach', in K. S. Cameron, J. E. Dutton, and R. E Quinn (eds.) *Positive Organizational Scholarship*, pp. 241–61. San Francisco, CA: Barrett-Koehler.

Lynch, G. (2007) *The New Spirituality: An Introduction to Progressive Belief in the Twenty-First Century*. London: I.B. Tauris.

Maak, T. (2007) 'Responsible Leadership, Stakeholder Engagement, and the Emergence of Social Capital', *Journal of Business Ethics*, 74, 329–43.

—— Pless, N. M (eds.) (2006a) *Responsible Leadership*. Abingdon: Routledge.

—— —— (2006b) 'Responsible Leadership in a Stakeholder Society—A Relational Perspective', *Journal of Business Ethics*, 66, 99–115.

—— —— (2006c) 'Responsible Leadership: A Relational Approach', in T. Maak and N. M. Pless (eds.) *Responsible Leadership*. Abingdon: Routledge.

Mabey, C. and Ramirez, M. (2004) *Developing Managers: A European Perspective*. London: Chartered Management Institute.

Macartney, T. (2007) *Finding Earth, Finding Soul*. Higher Ashton: Mona Books.

Maccoby, M. (2000) 'Narcissistic Leaders: The Incredible Pros, the Inevitable Cons', *Harvard Business Review*, 78(1), 69–77.

—— (2003) *The Productive Narcissist: The Promise and Peril of Visionary Leadership*. New York: Broadway Books.

MacLeod, J. (1995) *Community Organizing: A Practical and Theological Appraisal*. London: Christian Action.

Mann, R. D. (1959) 'A Review of the Relationship between Personality and Performance in Small Groups', *Psychological Bulletin*, 56, 241–70.

Manz, C. C. and Sims, H. P. (1980) 'Self-management as a Substitute for Leadership: A Social Learning Theory Perspective', *Academy of Management Review*, 5, 361–7.

—— —— (1991) 'Superleadership: Beyond the Myth of Heroic Leadership', *Organizational Dynamics*, Spring, 18–35.

Marshall, J. (1984) *Women Managers: Travellers in a Male World*. London: John Wiley.

—— (1995) *Women Managers Moving on: Exploring Career and Life Choices*. London: Thomson.

Marturano, A., Gosling, J., and Wood, M. (2010) 'Leadership and Language Games', *Philosophy of Management*, 9(1), 59–84.

Mayer, J. D. and Salovey, P. (1997) 'What is Emotional Intelligence?' in P. Salovey and D. Sluyter (eds.). *Emotional Development and Emotional Intelligence: Implications for Educators*, pp. 3–31. New York: Basic Books.

Mayo, E. (1960) *The Human Problems of an Industrial Civilization*. Boston: Harvard Business School Press.

McCabe, D. (2000) 'The Team Dream: The Meaning and Experience of Teamworking for Employees in an Automobile Manufacturing Company', in S. Procter and F. Mueller (eds.) *Teamworking*, pp. 203–21. Basingstoke: Macmillan.

McCauley, C. D., Moxley, R. S., and Van Velsor., E (eds.) (1998) *The Centre for Creative Leadership Handbook of Leadership Development*. San Francisco, CA: Jossey Bass.

McCloskey, D. (2006) *The Bourgeois Virtues: Ethics for an Age of Commerce*. Chicago: Chicago University Press.

McDowell, L. (1997) *Capital Culture: Gender at Work in the City*. Oxford: Blackwell.

McGregor, D. (1960) *The Human Side of Enterprise*. New York: McGraw-Hill.

McIntosch, M., Woodock, S., and G. Kell (eds.) (2004) *Learning to Talk: Corporate Citizenship and the Development of the UN Global Compact*. Sheffield: Greenleaf Publishing.

Meindl, J. R., Ehrlich, S. B., and Dukerich, J. M. (1985) 'The Romance of Leadership', *Administrative Science Quarterly*, 30(1), 78–102.

Milgram, S. (1963) 'A Behavioral Study of Obedience', *Journal of Abnormal and Social Psychology*, 67, 371–8.

Mintzberg, H. (1973) *The Nature of Managerial Work*. New York: Harper and Row.

—— (1975) 'The Manager's Job: Folklore and Fact', *Harvard Business Review*, July–August, 49–61.

—— (1987) 'Five P's for Strategy', *California Management Review*, 30, 11–24.

—— (1998) 'Covert Leadership: Notes on Managing Professionals', *Harvard Business Review*, Nov–Dec, 140–7.

—— (1999) 'Managing Quietly', *Leader to Leader*, 12 (November), 24–30.

—— (2004a) 'Enough Leadership', *Harvard Business Review*, 82(11), 22.

—— (2004b) *Managers not MBAs*. San Francisco, CA: Berrett-Koehler Publishers Inc.

—— (2006) 'The Leadership Debate with Henry Mintzberg: Community-ship is the Answer', *FT.com*, URL: http://tinyurl.com/aaxcoz, accessed 07 January 2010.

—— (2009a) *Managing*. London: FT Prentice-Hall.

—— (2009b) 'Rebuilding Companies as Communities', *Harvard Business Review*, 87(7/8), 140–3.

—— Gosling, J. (2002) 'Management Education beyond Borders', *Academy of Management Learning and Education*, 1(1), 64–76.

—— Waters, J. A. (1982) 'Tracking Strategy in an Entrepreneurial Firm', *Academy of Management Journal*, 25(3), 465–99.

—— —— (1985) 'Of Strategies, Deliberate and Emergent', *Strategic Management Journal*, 6(3), 257–72.

Mitchell, L. (2009) *Cyrus the Great and the Obedience of the Willing*. Centre for Leadership Studies, Extended Essay Series, University of Exeter.

Mitroff, I. (2003) 'Do not Promote Religion under the Guise of Spirituality', *Organization*, 10, 375–82.

Morgan, G. (1986) *Images of Organization*. London: Sage Publications.

Mowday, R. T., Porter, L. W., and R. M. Steers (1982) *Employee-Organizational Linkages: The Psychology of Commitment, Absenteeism, and Turnover*. New York: Academic Press.

Mulhall, S. and Swift, A. (1992) *Liberals and Communitarians*. Oxford: Blackwell.

Mumby, D. K. (1987) 'The Political Function of Narrative in Organizations', *Communication*, 54(2), 113–27.

Myers, I. B. and McCaulley, M. H. (1985) *Manual: A Guide to the Development and Use of the Myers-Briggs Type Indicator*. Palo Alto, CA: Consulting Psychologists Press.

Ng, K. Y., van Dyne, L., and Ang, S. (2009) 'From Experience to Experiential Learning: Cultural Intelligence as a Learning Capability for Global Leader Development', *Academy of Management Learning & Education*, 8, 511–26.

NHS (2002) *NHS Leadership Qualities Framework*. London: NHS Leadership Centre.

—— (2003) *NHS Leadership Qualities Framework: Full Technical Research Paper*. London: NHS Leadership Centre.

Northouse, P. G. (2004) *Leadership: Theory and Practice*, 3rd Edition. London: Sage.

—— (2007) *Leadership: Theory and Practice*, 4th Edition. London: Sage.

Organ, D. W. (1988) *Organizational Citizenship Behavior: The Good Soldier Syndrome*. Lexington, Massachusetts/Toronto DC: Heath and Company.

Osborn, R. N., Hunt, J. G., and Jauch, L. R. (2002) 'Towards a contextual Theory of Leadership' *The Leadership Quarterly*, 17(6), 797–837.

Ospina, S. and Sorenson, G. L. J. (2006) 'A Constructionist Lens on Leadership: Charting New Territory', in G. R. Goethals and G. L. J. Sorenson (eds.) *The Quest for a General Theory of Leadership*, pp. 188–204. Cheltenham: Edward Elgar.

O'Toole, J., Galbraith, J., and Lawler, E. (2003) 'When Two (or more) Heads are Better than One: The Promise and Pitfalls of Shared Leadership', in C. L. Pearce and J. Conger (eds.) *Shared Leadership: Reframing the Hows and Whys of Leadership*, pp. 250–67. London: Sage.

Padilla, A., Hogan, R., and Kaiser, R. (2007) 'The Toxic Triangle: Destructive Leaders, Susceptible Followers, and Conducive Environments', *The Leadership Quarterly*, 18, 176–94.

Pahl, R. (1996) 'Friendly Society', in Kramer and Roberts (eds.) *The Politics of Attachment*. London: Free Association Books.

Palazhchenko, P. (2009) *There's More to Leadership Than you Think*. URL: http://rbth.ru/articles/2009/04/29/290409_leadership.html, accessed 22 July 2010.

Palus, C. J. and Horth, D. M. (2005) 'Leading Creatively: The Art of Making Sense', *Ivey Business Journal*, September/October.

Parker, M. (2002) *Against Management: Organization in the Age of Managerialism*. Cambridge: Polity Press.

—— (ed.) (2003) *Ethics and Organization*. London: Sage.

—— (2004) 'Becoming Manager or, the Werewolf Looks Anxiously in the Mirror, Checking for Unusual Facial Hair', *Management Learning*, 35, 45–59.

Parker, P. and Ogilvie, D. (1996) 'Gender, Culture and Leadership: Toward a Culturally Distinct Model of African-American Women Executives' Leadership Strategies', *The Leadership Quarterly*, 7, 189–214.

Parry, K. W. and Bryman, A. (2006) 'Leadership in Organizations', in S. Clegg, C. Hardy, and W. Nord (eds.) *Handbook of Organization Studies*, pp. 447–68. London: Sage.

Payne, S. and Huffman, A. (2005) 'A Longitudinal Examination of the Influence of Mentoring on Organizational Commitment and Turnover', *Academy of Management Journal*, 48(1), 158–68.

Pearce, C. and Conger, J. A. (2003a) *Shared Leadership: Reframing the Hows and Whys of Leadership*. London: Sage.

—— —— (2003b) 'All Those Years Ago: The Historical Underpinnings of Shared Leadership', in C. L. Pearce and J. A. Conger (eds.) *Shared Leadership: Reframing the Hows and Whys of Leadership*, pp. 1–18. Thousand Oaks, CA: Sage Publications.

—— Sims, H. P. J. (2002) 'Vertical versus Shared Leadership as Predictors of the Effectiveness of Change Management Teams: An Examination of Aversive, Directive, Transactional, Transformational, and Empowering Leader Behaviors', *Group Dynamics: Theory, Research, and Practice*, 6(2), 172–97.

—— Conger, J. A., and Locke, E. A. (2008) 'Shared Leadership Theory', *The Leadership Quarterly*, 19, 622–8.

Pedler, M., Burgoyne, J., and Boydell, T. (2004) *A Manager's Guide to Leadership*. Berkshire: McGraw-Hill.

Perren, L. and Burgoyne, J. (2001) *Management and Leadership Abilities: An Analysis of Texts, Testimony and Practice.* London: Council for Excellence in Management and Leadership.

Pescosolido, A. T. (2002) 'Emergent Leaders as Managers of Group Emotion', *The Leadership Quarterly,* 13, 583–99.

Peters, T. J. and Waterman, R. H. (1982) *In Search of Excellence: Lessons from America's Best-Run Companies.* New York: Harper and Row.

Pettigrew, A. M. (1997) 'The Double Hurdles for Management Research', in T. Clarke (ed.) *Advancement in Organizational Behaviour: Essays in Honour of D.S. Pugh,* pp. 277–96. London: Dartmouth Press.

Pfeffer, J. (2007) 'A Modest Proposal: How We Might Change the Process and Product of Managerial Research', *Academy of Management Journal,* 50(6), 1334–45.

—— Fong, C. T. (2002) 'The End of Business Schools? Less Success than Meets the Eye', *Academy of Management, Learning and Education,* 1(1), 78–96.

Pondy, L. R. (1978) 'Leadership as a Language Game', in M. McCall and M. Lombardo (eds.) *Leadership: Where Else Do We Go?* pp. 87–99. Durham, NC: Duke University Press.

Porter, L. W. and McLaughlin, G. B. (2006) 'Leadership and the Organizational Context: Like the Weather?', *The Leadership Quarterly,* 17, 559–76.

Porter, M. E. (1985) *Competitive Advantage.* New York: Free Press.

—— Ketels, C. H. M. (2003) *UK Competitiveness: Moving to the Next Stage.* Great Britain: Department of Trade and Industry.

Prahalad, C. K. and Hamel, G. (1990) 'The Core Competence of the Organization', *Harvard Business Review,* May/June, 79–91.

Prince, L. (2005) 'Eating the Menu rather than the Dinner: Tao and Leadership', *Leadership,* 1(1), 105–26.

Purvanova, R. and Bono, J. (2009) 'Transformational Leadership in Context: Face-To-Face and Virtual Teams', *The Leadership Quarterly,* 20, 343–57.

Pye, A. (2005) 'Leadership and Organizing: Sensemaking in Action', *Leadership,* 1(1), 31–50.

Quirke, B. (2008) *Making the Connections: Using Internal Communication to turn Strategy into Action.* London: Ashgate.

Raelin, J. (2004) 'Don't Bother Putting Leadership into People', *Academy of Management Executive,* 18, 131–5.

Raelin, J. A. (2003) *Creating Leaderful Organizations: How to Bring out Leadership in Everyone.* New York: Berrett-Koehler.

—— (2007) 'Toward and Epistemology of Practice', *Academy of Management Learning and Education,* 6(4), 495–519.

Ray, L. (1996) *The Economisation of Culture and the Culturalisaton of Economy.* Paper to the Centre for the Study of Cultural Values, Lancaster University, UK, May 22.

Ray, T., Clegg, S., and Gordon, R. (2004) 'A New Look at Dispersed Leadership: Power, Knowledge and Context', in J. Storey (Ed.) *Leadership in Organziations: Current Issues and Key Trends,* pp. 319–36. Oxon: Routledge.

Reicher, S., Haslam, S. A., and Hopkins, N. (2005) 'Social identity and the Dynamics of Leadership: Leaders and Followers and Collaborative Agents in the Transformation of Social Reality', *The Leadership Quarterly,* 16, 547–68.

Ricoeur, P. (1992) *Oneself as Another* (trans. K. Blamey). Chicago: University of Chicago Press.

Rioch, M. (1979) 'The A.K. Rice Group Relations Conferences as a Reflection of Society' in W. G. Lawrence (ed.) *Exploring Individual and Organizational Boundaries: A Tavistock Open Systems Approach*. Chichester: Wiley.

Rittell, H. and Webber, M. (1973) 'Dilemmas in a General Theory of Planning', *Policy Sciences*, 4, 155–69.

Ritzer, G. (1996) *The McDonaldization of Society*. Thousand Oaks, CA: Pine Forge.

Robinson, V. M. J. (2001) 'Embedding Leadership in Task Performance', in K. Wong and C. W. Evers (eds.) *Leadership for Quality Schooling*, pp. 90–102. London: Routledge/Falmer.

Rosen, M. (1985) 'Breakfast at Spiro's: Dramaturgy and Dominance', *Journal of Management*, 11(2), 31–48.

Rost, J. (1991) *Leadership for the Twenty-First Century*. Westport, CT: Praeger.

—— (2008) 'Leadership Definition', in A. Marturano and J. Gosling (eds.) *Leadership, The Key Concepts*, pp. 94–9. Abingdon: Routledge.

Rowlinson, M. (2002) 'Cadbury World', *Labor History Review*, 67, 101–19.

Roy, D. (1952) 'Quota Restriction and Goldbricking in a Machine Shop', *The American Journal of Sociology*, 57, 427–42.

Rubery, J., Carroll, C., Cooke, F. L., Grugulis, I., and Earnshaw, J. (2004) 'Human Resource Management and the Permeable Organization: The Case of the Multi-client Call Centre', *Journal of Management Studies*, 41(7), 1199–222.

Ryan, M. and Haslam, S. A. (2005) 'The Glass Cliff: Evidence that Women are Over-represented in Precarious Leadership Positions', *British Journal of Management*, 16, 81–90.

Rynes, S. L. (2007) 'Afterword: To the Next 50 years', *Academy of Management Journal*, 50(6), 1379–83.

Salaman, G. (2004) 'Competences of Managers, Competences of Leaders', in J. Storey (ed.) *Leadership in Organizations: Current Issues and Key Trends*, pp. 58–78. London: Routledge.

Salovey, P. and Mayer, J. D. (1990) 'Emotional Intelligence', *Imagination, Cognition and Personality*, 9(3), 185–121.

Schein, E. H. (1992) *Organizational Culture and Leadership*. San Francisco, CA: Jossey-Bass.

Schroeder, J. (2008) 'Aesthetic Leadership', in A. Marturano, and J.Gosling (eds.) *Leadership: Key Concepts*. London: Routledge.

Schyns, B. and Meindl, J. (2005) *Implicit Leadership Theories*. Greenwich, CT: Information Age Publishing.

Seibert, S. E. and Kraimer, M. L. (2001) 'The Five-Factor Model of Personality and Career Success', *Journal of Vocational Behaviour*, 58(1), 1–21.

Senge, P. (1990) *The Fifth Discipline: The Art and Practice of the Learning Organization*. New York: Doubleday.

Senge, P. M., Roberts, C., Ross, R. B., Smith, B. J., and Kleiner, A. (1994) *The Fifth Discipline Fieldbook: Strategies and Tools for Building a Learning Organization*. London: Nicholas Brealey.

Sewell, G. and Wilkinson, B. (1992) '"Someone to Watch over me": Surveillance, Discipline and the Just-in-Time Labour Process', *Sociology*, 26(2), 271–89.

Shaw, M. (1976) *Group Dynamics*, 2nd Edition. New York: McGraw-Hill.

Sinclair, A. (2007) *Leadership for the Disillusioned: Moving beyond Myths and Heroes to Leading that Liberates*. Crows Nest, Australia: Allen and Unwin.

Smircich, L. (1983) 'Concepts of Culture and Organizational Analysis', *Administrative Science Quarterly*, 28, 339–58.

Sokolowski, R. (2000) *Introduction to Phenomenology*. Cambridge: Cambridge University Press.

Sorenson, G. and Hickman, G. R. (2002) 'Invisible Leadership: Acting on Behalf of a Common Purpose', in C. Cherrey and L. R. Matusak (eds.) *Building Leadership Bridges*, pp. 7–24. College Park: James MacGregor Burns Academy of Leadership.

Sparrowe, R. T. (2005) 'Authentic Leadership and the Narrative Self', *Leadership Quarterly*, 16, 419–39.

Spicer, A., Alvesson, M. and Karreman, D. (2009) 'Critical Performativity: The Unfinished Business of Critical Management Studies', *Human Relations*, 62(4), 537–60.

Spillane, J. (2004) *Distributed Leadership: What's All the Hoopla?* Institute for Policy Research, Northwestern University.

—— (2006) *Distributed Leadership*. San Francisco, CA: Jossey-Bass.

Stacey, R. D., Griffin, D., and Shaw, P. (2000) *Complexity and Management: Fad or Radical Challenge to Systems Thinking*. London: Routledge.

Sternberg, R. J. (1985) *Beyond IQ: A Triarchic Theory of Human Intelligence*. New York: University of Cambridge Press.

Stogdill, R. M. (1974) *Handbook of Leadership: A Survey of Theory and Research*. New York: Free Press.

Storey, J. (2004) 'Signs of Change: "Damned Rascals' and Beyond", in J. Storey (ed.) *Leadership in Organizations: Current Issues and Key Trends*, pp. 3–10. London: Routledge.

Strangleman, T. and Roberts, I. (1999) 'Looking Through the Window of Opportunity: The Cultural Cleansing of Workplace Identity', *Sociology*, 33(1), 47–67.

Sun Tzu (2009) *The Art of War* (trans. Lionel Giles). El Paso, TX: El Paso Norte Press.

Sutherland, I. and Gosling, J. (2010) 'Cultural Leadership: The Power of Culture from Affordances to Dwelling', *Journal of Arts Management, Law and Society*, 40(1), 6–26.

Sveningsson, S. and Alvesson, M. (2003) 'Managing Managerial Identities: Organizational Fragmentation, Discourse and Identity Struggle', *Human Relations*, 56(10), 1163–93.

—— Larsson, M. (2006) 'Fantasies of Leadership: Identity Work', *Leadership*, 2(2), 203–24.

Tajfel, H. (1974) 'Social Identity and Intergroup Behaviour', *Social Science Information*, 13(2), 65–93.

—— Turner, J. C. (1979) 'An Integrative Theory of Intergroup Conflict', in W. G. Austin and S. Worchel (eds.) *The Social Psychology of Intergroup Relations*, pp. 33–47. Monterey, CA: Brooks/Cole.

Tawney, R. (1926) *Religion and the Rise of Capitalism*. New York: Harcourt Brace.

Taylor, F. W. (1911) *The Principles of Scientific Management*. New York: Harper and Row.

ten Bos, R. (1997) 'Essai: Business Ethics and Bauman Ethics', *Organization Studies*, 18, 997–1014.

Terry, D. J. and O'Brien, A. T. (2001) 'Status, Legitimacy and Ingroup Bias in the Context of an Organizational Merger', *Group Processes and Intergroup Relations*, 4(3), 271–89.

Thornborrow, T. and Brown, A. D. (2009) 'Being Regimented: Aspiration, Discourse and Identity in the British Parachute Regiment', *Organization Studies*, 30(4), 335–76.

Thorndike, R. L. and Stein, S. (1937) 'An Evaluation of the Attempts to Measure Social Intelligence', *Psychological Bulletin*, 34(5), 275–85.

Tönnies, F. (2001 [1887]) *Community and Civil Society* (ed. Jose Harris). Cambridge: Cambridge University Press.

Townley, B. (1994) *Reframing Human Resource Management: Power, Ethics and the Subject at Work*. Thousand Oaks, CA: Sage.

Turnbull James, K. and Collins, J. (2008) 'New Perspectives on Leadership: How Practical is a Good Theory?' in K. Turnbull James and J. Collins (eds.) *Leadership Perspectives: Knowledge into Action*, pp. 1–12. Basingstoke: Palgrave Macmillan.

Turnbull, S. (1996) *Self Managed Teams: Filling the Empty Shrine? Meaning and Control in a Telephone Bank*, MPhil in Critical Management, Lancaster University, UK.

Turner, J. C. (1985) 'Social Categorization and the Self Concept: A Social Cognitive Theory of Group Behaviour', in E. J. Lawler (ed.) *Advances in Group Processes*, Vol. 2, pp. 77–122. Greenwich, CT: JAI Press.

Uhl-Bien, M. (2006) 'Relational Leadership Theory: Exploring the Social Processes of Leadership and Organizing', *The Leadership Quarterly*, 17, 654–76.

—— Marion, R., and McKelvey, B. (2007) 'Complexity Leadership Theory: Shifting Leadership from the Industrial Age to the Knowledge Era', *The Leadership Quarterly*, 18(4), 298–318.

Ulrich, D. and Smallwood, N. (2007) 'Building a Leadership Brand', *Harvard Business Review*, July–August, 93–100.

Unilever (1996) *Annual Report to Shareholders*. London: Unilever.

van Knippenberg, D. and Hogg, M. A. (2003) 'A Social Identity Model of Leadership Effectiveness in Organizations', in B. M. Staw and R. M. Kramer (eds.) *Research in Organizational Behaviour*, Vol. 25, pp. 243–95. New York: Elsevier.

Villiers, P. and Gosling, J. (forthcoming) *Leadership and Literature*. Axminster: Triarchy Press.

Waldman, D. A. and Galvin, B. M. (2008) 'Alternative Perspectives of Responsible Leadership', *Organizational Dynamics*, 37(4), 327–41.

Ward, A. (1963) *John Keats: The Making of a Poet*. London: Secker and Warburg.

Warner, L. and Grint, K. (2006) 'American Indian Ways of Leading and Knowing', *Leadership*, 2(2), 225–44.

Wasielewski, P. L. (1985) 'The Emotional Basis of Charisma', *Symbolic Interaction*, 8(2), 207–22.

Watson, T. J. (2000) 'Making Sense of Managerial Work and Organizational Research Processes with Caroline and Terry', *Organization*, 7(3), 489–510.

Webb, K. (2004) *Voluntary Codes: Private Governance, Public Interest, and Innovation*. Ottawa: Carleton University Press.

—— (2005) 'The ISO 26000 Social Responsibility Guidance Standard—Progress So Far', Depot Legal—Bibliotheque Nationale du Quebec.

Weber, M. (1930) *The Protestant Ethic and the Spirit of Capitalism*. London: George Allen & Unwin.

—— (1978) *Economy and Society: An Outline of Interpretive Sociology*. Berkeley: University of California Press.

Weick, K. E. (1995) *Sensemaking in Organizations*. Thousands Oaks, CA: Sage.

—— (2001) *Making Sense of the Organization*. Oxford: Blackwell.

—— Sutcliffe, K. M., and Obstfeld, D. (2005) 'Organizing and the Process of Sensemaking', *Organization Science*, 16(4), 409–21.

Wenger, E. (1998) *Communities in Practice: Learning, Meaning and Identity.* Cambridge: Cambridge University Press.

Wheatley, M. (1994) *Leadership and the New Science: Discovering Order in a Chaotic World.* San Francisco, CA: Berrett-Koehler.

—— (2006) *Finding our Way: Leadership for an Uncertain Time.* Presentation to Centre for Leadership Studies, Exeter University, UK, 11 December.

Whiteman, G. (2004) 'Forestry, Gold Mining, and Amerindians: The Troubling Example of Samling in Guyana', in F. Bird and S. Herman (eds.) *International Businesses and the Challenges of Poverty in Developing Areas.* London: Palgrave-Macmillan.

Whittington, R. (2006) 'Completing the Practice Turn in Strategy', *Organization Studies,* 27(5), 613–34.

Willmot, H. (1993) 'Strength is Ignorance, Slavery is Freedom: Managing Culture in Modern Organizations' *Journal of Management Studies,* 30(4): 515–52.

Whyte, W. (1961) *The Organization Man.* Harmondsworth: Penguin.

Wood, M. (2002) 'Nomad Leadership and the Corporate War Machine'. Paper presented at the *International Conference on Studying Leadership,* Said Business School, University of Oxford.

—— (2005) 'The Fallacy of Misplaced Leadership', *Journal of Management Studies,* 42(6), 1101–21.

—— Ladkin, D. (2008) 'The Event's the Thing: Brief Encounters with the Leaderful Moment', in K. Turnbull James and J. Collins (eds.) *Leadership Perspectives: Knowledge Into Action.* Houndmills: Palgrave Macmillan.

Woods, P. A. and Gronn, P. (2009) 'Nurturing Democracy: The Contribution of Distributed Leadership to a Democratic Organizational Landscape', *Educational Management Administration and Leadership,* 37(4), 430–51.

Xiao, Y., Seagull, F., Mackenzie, C., Klein, K., and Ziegert, J. (2008) 'Adaptation of Team Communication Patterns. Exploring the Effects of Leadership at a Distance: Task Urgency, and Shared Team Experience', in S. Weisband (ed.) *Leadership at a Distance: Research in Technologically-Supported Work.* New York: Erlbaum.

Young, S. (2003) *Moral Capitalism: Reconciling Private Interest with Public Good.* San Francisco, CA: Berrett-Kohler Inc.

Yukl, G. (1999) 'An Evaluation of Conceptual Weaknesses in Transformational and Charismatic Leadership Theories', *The Leadership Quarterly,* 10(2), 285–305.

—— (2006) *Leadership in Organizations,* 6th Edition. Upper Saddle River, NJ: Pearson Prentice-Hall.

Zaccharo, S. J. and Banks, D. J. (2001) 'Leadership, Vision and Organizational Effectiveness', in S. J. Zaccaro and R. J. Klimoski (eds.) *The Nature of Organizational Leadership: Understanding the Performance Imperatives Confronting Today's Leaders.* San Francisco, CA: Jossey Bass.

Zaleznik, A. (1977) 'Managers and Leaders: Are They Different?' *Harvard Business Review,* May–June, 67–78.

Zuckerman, M. (1998) 'Psychobiological Theories of Personality', in D. F. Barone, M. Hersen, and V. B. Van Hasselt (eds.) *Advanced Personality,* pp. 123–54. New York: Springer.

▢ INDEX